The Toss of a Coin

An autobiography of a railway career

By DAVID MAIDMENT

Best wishes,
David Maidment

Published in the United Kingdom by PublishNation

Copyright © David Maidment 2014

The right of David Maidment to be identified as the author of this work had been asserted by him in accordance with the Copyright, Designs and Patents Act 1988. All rights reserved. No part of this publication may be reproduced or transmitted in any form or by any means, electronic or mechanical, including photocopy, recording or any information storage and retrieval system, without the prior written permission of the publisher, nor by way of trade or otherwise shall it be lent, re-sold, hired out or otherwise circulated without the publisher's prior consent in any form of binding or cover other than that in which it is published and without a similar condition including this condition being imposed on the subsequent purchaser.

Cover picture:
David Maidment in the cab of a TGV en route from Paris to Lyons, July 1986

ISBN: 978-1-291-75499-5

All royalties from this book will be donated to the Railway Children charity (reg. no. 1058991) (www.railwaychildren.org.uk)

Previous Books:

Novels
Religious historical fiction
The Child Madonna, Melrose Books, 2009
The Missing Madonna, PublishNation, 2012

Railway fiction
Lives on the Line, Max Books, 2013

Non-Fiction
The Other Railway Children, PublishNation, 2012
Nobody ever listened to me, PublishNation, 2012

THE TOSS OF A COIN
An autobiography of a railway career
by David Maidment

'The Divisional Manager drew a half crown from his pocket, tossed it, my colleague called correctly and chose Ebbw Vale because he'd heard of it. I became Stationmaster Aberbeeg, the Operating job, by default. This event influenced the rest of my railway career…'

Acknowledgements

To Rodney Meadows who opened my eyes to the possibilities, to Bob Hilton for the toss of the coin, to Gerry Orbell who encouraged me to do things differently, to Alan Englert who opened new doors, to Jim O'Brien who took a risk on me, to Jim Urquhart and David Rayner who backed me, to Frank Paterson who stimulated me to write it all down, and above all to Stan Judd, my friend, who won the toss, chose Ebbw Vale and whose career intertwined with mine from training days to the Railway Children charity.

To my wife, Pat, who put up with years of being a 'railway widow' and to the small girl on Bombay Churchgate railway station who was the inspiration for my other career in the 'Railway Children'.

All photos in the book taken by the author except where captioned otherwise.

CONTENTS

	Page
Preface	viii

Chapter 1
Why did I become a railwayman? — 1

Chapter 2
Joining the railways (1956 – 1960) — 17

Chapter 3
Management training –
Western Region's London Division
(1961 – 1962) — 31

Chapter 4
Training in South Wales (1962 - 1963) — 45

Chapter 5
Headquarters and Plymouth Division
(1963 – 1964) — 55

Chapter 6
Stationmaster, Aberbeeg (1964 – 1965) — 65

Chapter 7
Area Management, Bridgend (1965 – 1967) — 88

Chapter 8
Cardiff Divisional Office (1968 – 1971) — 107

Chapter 9
222 Marylebone Road (1972 – 1974) — 115

Chapter 10
Management Services, WR and BRB (1974 – 1982) — 119

Chapter 11
Regional Operating Manager, Crewe (1982 – 1986) — 130

Chapter 12
Reliability Management (1986 – 1988) — 162

Chapter 13
Clapham Junction (1988 – 1989) — 175

Chapter 14
Safety Management (1990 – 1996) — 183

Chapter 15
International railway safety consultant
(1992 – 2001) — 206

Chapter 16
The Railway Children (1995 – 2013) — 224

Chapter 17
Making sense of it all — 251

Glossary of Railway Terms & Other Acronyms — 256

Index — 260

PREFACE

This book is a variation on a theme – another book is being published by 'Pen & Sword' recounting in much more detail my experiences as an enthusiast from being a toddler taken to see steam trains from Esher Common to my time as a Traffic Apprentice in the early 1960s via a boyhood as a trainspotter and ardent student of Cecil J Allen's articles on 'Locomotive Practice and Performance' in the monthly magazine, 'Trains Illustrated'. This book, however, is intended for those interested more generally in railways and for those for whom the rapid change of Britain's railways between the 1950s and the end of the century is of historical significance. It might be of interest and some amusement to some of my colleagues who shared similar experiences in the time of metamorphosis from a nationalised bureaucracy of the 1950s to the current renewal as railways reclaim their national transportation role having passed through some traumatic times in the transformation.

It's a personal account of what it was like inside the industry - from joining the railways when I decided to turn my hobby into my career, when it was still very acceptable to be an enthusiast and hold a management position, through the Beeching era, through the railway's rediscovery of its role in the 1980s to the convulsions of privatisation. And then, a second career as a railway safety consultant and a third, founding and leading the railway's favourite charity, 'Railway Children'.

The genesis of the book grew from ten hours of interviews I shared with Frank Paterson, former General Manager of the Eastern Region and subsequently Chairman of the Friends of the National Railway Museum, who asked me for material as part of a project that the NRM was undertaking with funding from the National Lottery - an oral history compiled by railwaymen and women from all spheres of duty within the UK railway industry. Hours of tapes can be accessed through the NRM's search engine and some excerpts are selected from time to time for the Museum's website under the heading of 'Railway Voices'.

Looking back over seventy years of interest and fifty years in careers associated with the railway, I realise how lucky I've been and the debt of gratitude I owe to many. In particular I think of my

Dad who stimulated my interest in the first place by taking me to see the engine whenever - as a very young child - I travelled. My Aunt Enid, who brought me a new railway book every time she visited. My friend Cedric Utley, with whom I used to go trainspotting in London as a 12 year old. My colleague Stan Judd, who was a fellow Traffic Apprentice and with whom I shared a baptism of fire in a Welsh Valley and whose career has subsequently been entwined from time to time with mine. Gerry Orbell, Frank Paterson and the late Leslie Lloyd who backed me when I was a fledgling Train Planner and Operator in South Wales, Alan Englert who gave me opportunities in new fields and Jim O'Brien who took a risk by appointing me as the London Midland's Regional Operating Manager in 1982. David Rayner who encouraged me to develop new ways of managing safety on the railways in the 1990s and Andrew Smith who enabled me to utilise my knowledge and experience on the wider map and which led ultimately to the change in direction towards my third career as the Founder and Chairman of the charity, Railway Children. To the small child on Bombay Churchgate station who was the catalyst for that act and lastly, but by no means least, to my family and my wife Pat, who over the years must many times have felt herself a 'railway widow'. To all these and many more too innumerable to mention, a big thank you. It's only now when I look back and write it all down that I realise just how fortunate I have been.

David Maidment
February 2014

Chapter 1
Why did I become a railwayman?

It was not a family tradition. I can't really explain my passion for trains, which began at a very early age. Perhaps I associated trains with meeting my father when he was so often absent during the war years. My only other railway connection was my Great Uncle George, husband of my paternal grandmother's sister. She, Aunt Kate, had been one of Queen Mary's maids in the Brunswick Tower at Windsor Castle with my grandmother, and after her marriage to George, an engine driver, had moved to Guildford. Uncle George had worked Guildford top link turns on the Waterloo - Portsmouth direct line during the 1920s with his 'own' engine, Drummond D15 4-4-0, No.466, but had retired through ill health in 1929. (He eventually died of old age aged 98 in the 1970s!). In the late 1940s when I was nine or ten, I'd visited them for the day, and my Uncle, as a treat, took me down to Guildford engine shed, and put me on the footplate of the shed pilot, 0-4-0 saddletank, *Ironside*. My main memory is of being in the diminutive cab as we hauled a dead locomotive onto the turntable and burning my shins on the open fire as I only wore short trousers.

This did not put me off. My maternal grandmother once told me that a distant relative of hers had been a driver on the 'broad gauge' at Gloucester in the 1860s, so the story went, but I never traced the truth of this rumour.

Neither of these somewhat tenuous links with the railway industry was a conscious remembrance when, as a two year old, I'm told I used to bully my mother into pushing me the two and a half miles from our home in East Molesey to the open land to the north of the Southern main line at Esher to see the trains go by - you couldn't do that easily now as the growth of trees and shrubs would obscure the view. Apparently the electric trains at Hampton Court would not do; only the 'King Arthurs' and 'Lord Nelsons' winging their wartime loads to the South Coast, Salisbury Plain and the West Country would satisfy my infant demands. Perhaps there is something in 'reincarnation' after all – that distant relative at Gloucester may have had more in common with me than I had supposed...

My father quickly ascertained that I could be entertained by toys and books of trains and whilst in the army, used to send me letters adorned with a simple line drawing of a train at the top corner. My earliest memory of all is of standing at the bottom of steps to the platform of Shrewsbury station (we had been evacuated to Shropshire for a while in 1941) waiting for my father to book his soldier's warrant ticket and being lifted to the top just in time to see the tail light of the London express disappearing along the platform. I can remember the frustration of not being allowed to look out of the window on the next train (two hours later) because it was dark and the blackout. I was 3 years old. I think it was in the Welsh border country at that time that my father was involved with the building - or relaying – of part of the former Shropshire & Montgomery Railway for the storage of foodstuffs imported through Liverpool Docks off the transatlantic convoys. He used to tell us tales of the diminutive steam engine, 'Gazelle' which was apparently employed in the line's reconstruction and of its propensity to derail – a mishap easily corrected because of its midget size.

I learned later, much later, that my father, like many men in the nineteen thirties, was a conscientious objector because of his religious beliefs. It must have been a cause of great argument and mutual distress, for my grandfather was a sergeant in the Royal Artillery Regiment and fought in the First World War. Politically too they were poles apart though their relationship in the years I knew them revealed no split or tension to me. My father volunteered for ambulance work on the front line, but was sent as a private to the Non-Combatant Corps (NCC) and spent several months initially as a fire-watcher on Liverpool Docks during the air raids there. Subsequently he with a motley collection of colleagues with similar religious beliefs was used to construct various essential wartime building works. A few years ago he told me that had he known then what he knew later, he would have seen fighting Hitler's evil as a religious duty. At the time I did not know what he did or where he was, but sometimes he came home on leave and we used to see him off again at the station. He always took me to see the engine. He told me that he remembered 'Queen Guinevere' once, I suspect on the way to his camp on Salisbury

Plain. We would get into the train before departure time to say farewell and I would panic because I thought the train would take us with him, and we would have to get out lest my mother was embarrassed by my piercing screams. I didn't understand train timetables yet.

After the war, and once he had been demobbed, we set off for our first seaside holiday in 1946 on the 'Brighton Belle'. In exasperation at a small boy's boredom and tiresome cries of 'When are we going to get there?' he somewhat foolishly replied, 'Well, why don't you collect engine numbers like other boys?' So I did. I still wonder how much he regretted that chance remark.

A favourite maiden aunt who lived in Brighton soon cottoned on to my interest and every time we met she enhanced her reputation by producing a new 1/6d Ian Allan booklet in the series 'My Best Railway Photographs' - my first was of the Great Western by Maurice Earley and the second, a book of Southern photos by O.J.Morris. I have to admit that my loyalty was for the Great Western (the imprint of all those photos in Maurice Earley's book did their job only too well) and although my career developed on the Western Region from 1960 onwards, I lived until 1962 on the Southern and so its trains were the familiar ones.

In the autumn of 1949 I started at Surbiton County Grammar School and travelled daily by train from Hampton Court. The school sat beside the Southern Region's south west main line, just on the Waterloo side of Surbiton station, high above the embankment there. A few of us collected each morning in a small clearing above the line (you can't do it now - the undergrowth is too thick and the school is gone) to see the action before the school whistle blew at 9 o' clock. We watched the 8.30am Waterloo - Bournemouth with its Nine Elms 'Merchant Navy' or 'West Country' sidle beneath the high road bridge, braking for the Surbiton stop. And simultaneously and almost noiselessly apart from the distant whistle as it approached the Up Main platform at speed would come a malachite green 'Lord Nelson'. We soon lost interest in this because within weeks we've 'copped' the whole class!

The evening, whilst waiting for the 4.25 home on Surbiton station, was even more interesting. School finished at 4pm sharp and although I couldn't get the 4.5, I was at the station at least by 4.10 in time to see the Up 'Atlantic Coast Express' roar through with its Exmouth Junction 'Merchant Navy' and almost simultaneously see the 3.54pm Waterloo - Basingstoke come bucketing down the track working hard with one of its collection of Nine Elms veterans - old Drummond T14 'Paddleboxes' - which would leave a fog of pungent brown smoke hanging under the wide platform overbridge. After a couple of down line electrics taking some of my friends to Oxshott and Esher respectively, the ACE would be followed by the Eastleigh Van Train - mixed ECS and parcels with the possibility of almost anything at the front end. Although booked for an Eastleigh based 'King Arthur', it was obviously used for running in ex-works locos. I remember seeing just once the unfamiliar vision of a 'Schools' which surprised us all and caused extraordinary scenes of merriment among the crowd of small boy witnesses - after all, few of us at that stage could afford a trip to Charing Cross from our meagre pocket money.

Finally, just before my own electric slunk round the corner from under the high bridge below the school, the Clapham Junction Milk Empties, a train on which Bulleid's West Country *Torrington* performed for months, would charge through the station amid the clatter of its six wheelers, followed by the pungent smell of Kentish coal. And all the time an ancient Drummond L11 4-4-0 would be slithering up and down the adjacent coal yard (now a car park). On one memorable occasion it was, of all things, the malachite green royal T9, 30119. Looking back now, I realise that in those two years I never failed to see those four steam services between 4.5 and 4.25pm and the sheer consistency of the Southern Region's punctuality could be taken for granted. One of my schoolmasters at Charterhouse lived near Worplesdon, his garden backing onto the Woking - Guildford mainline and he told me a few years ago that his party trick was to take visitors to see the hourly fast Pompey electrics crossing each other at the end of his garden - and it never failed!

It would have been around this time that I discovered the monthly Ian Allan magazine, *Trains Illustrated*. My first purchase was No.10, although since then I've managed to pick up a couple of the earliest editions. I used to long for the time of the month when the new magazine would arrive and pore over it until the next one appeared. I can remember those early editions and the photos much better than those in more recent magazines. It was the regular article by Cecil J. Allen on locomotive practice and performance that inspired me in particular and led later to my own interest in recording locomotive performance although I compiled no serious logs until about 1956.

And the anticipated thrill of making trips each school holiday with a friend to London, where we spent the day trainspotting at Paddington, Euston, Kings Cross and Liverpool Street – Waterloo, Charing Cross and Victoria's engines were too familiar and Marylebone and Fenchurch Street were too small to be bothered with – St Pancras might justify a quick peek en route to Kings Cross.

Then, in 1951, I managed to win a Surrey County Council assisted place at Charterhouse public school and, initially, thought my enthusiasm might have to be dampened as my local barber advised me to keep my interest quiet as only cars or planes were deemed suitable to provide credibility among my future peers. I was deeply apprehensive about this new venture, although it provided some relief from bullying at the Grammar school, as I'd been a bit of a 'teacher's pet' being acclaimed only too frequently and embarrassingly as the first son of an 'Old Boy' to attend there.

There was not much to see of interest on the local railway at Godalming. My school had a unique rule. To cross a railway line was out of bounds. That stopped unauthorised trips into the local towns of Godalming or Guildford but allowed plenty of latitude on the northwest and southwest sides of the school. I had an old bike given me by my grandfather (1936 Raleigh vintage) and between 1951 and 1956 frequently cycled the five or six miles to Wanborough (which meant a stiff climb over the Hog's Back), as two trains on the Reading - Redhill 'Rattler', as it was known, would pass near Wanborough station half an hour or so after our lunch finished. The westbound train would come first, huffing and puffing its three 'birdcage' carriages, normally behind a Guildford or Redhill Wainwright 'D' 4-4-0, or even an occasional 'C' goods 0-6-0. Memory reveres the ancient old 'D' struggling to lift its period formation out of the station amid a cloud of black smoke and leaking steam - a stark contrast to the burnished locomotive 737 in S.E & C.R livery in the National Railway Museum.

As a 14 year old, I had inherited the Chair of the Charterhouse Railway Society, after a period of disinterest from older pupils. I had the help of a few 13 year olds - Martin Probyn as Secretary, James Evans, later like myself a BR senior officer also, as Treasurer and the new boys, Philip Balkwill (who later became a master at the school and died of cancer tragically young a few years ago) and his friend, Conrad Natzio.

We were highly energetic, boosted the membership to over 300 (!) by putting on regular film shows using the marvellous BT films you can now see at the National Rail Museum (remember 'Train Time' and that obese Western Region Operating Manager ensconced behind a desk festooned with the largest number of telephones I have ever seen in one place?). We charged 3d a show or gave free admission to the four shows a year if you joined the Railway Club (annual subscription 6d) and as entertainment in those pre TV days was at a premium, we had a lot of takers. I vaguely remember that 'London to Brighton in 4 Minutes' had a regular showing by popular demand and a brief sighting of a train on an adjoining track and the possibility of a race (which failed miserably to materialise) was enough to get hordes of schoolboys jumping up and down in their seats yelling on the driver! We also achieved a great coup in our early years by getting our little exhibition on 'Societies Day' opened by the Chairman of the British Transport Commission, Sir Brian Robertson. He happened to be an Old Carthusian and a colleague of Jim Evans' parents' friend, Sir John Elliot, then at London Transport.

By 1955 I'd become a bit more ambitious with my primitive Kodak camera and started cycling to various locations nearby. That year we had fixed a visit to Rugby Locomotive Testing Plant for our Society's Day outing, caught the 'Royal Scot' from Euston and were abandoned by our master at Rugby where he announced he was off to see his aunt. We duly went round the shed and then were met by an angry boss of the Testing Plant who'd been watching us wandering unsupervised all over the shed and wanted to know who was in charge. When I admitted to this, we got a safety lecture and the master who was supposedly in charge of us must have got a rocket, as he was replaced thereafter by the musical William Llewellyn (founder and conductor of the 'Linden Singers'), a true enthusiast who really took an interest and inspired us.

Another fond memory of Railway Society activities related to the model railway layout of a retired surgeon named Romanis, another 'Old Carthusian' who lived just half a mile from the school in Hurtmore. In the summer term, half a dozen of us would be invited every Sunday afternoon to operate his magnificent 'gauge 1' layout - a system with 25 locos modelled on the late pre-grouping period, with three signalling block posts and a 60 or 90 minute timetable we had to operate with precise punctuality. At the end of the session, if we had operated the layout to his satisfaction, we would round off the visit with a glass of cider in his beautiful mansion.

However, I'd always assumed you had to be an engineer to progress in railway management and as my skills were more in the humanities, my greatest potential relevant exposure was a four week Easter holiday course at the Sorbonne in Paris where I and a like-minded colleague learned most of our French on the Gare du Nord and the Gare de l'Est. I drifted into the Modern Languages Sixth Form because at that stage of my life I was best at German, mainly because of the influence of an excellent German teacher – Dr Gerstenberg, a Jewish refugee from Nazi Germany where he'd been a distinguished headmaster. A career as a school teacher myself was looking increasingly likely as I could think of nothing else and I began to sit for the various Oxford college scholarship examinations anticipating that my hobby would remain just that. I spent hours watching the workings on freezing Oxford station instead of revising for the imminent exams and interviews.

I left school in December 1956 and spent a few months in a holiday job at Old Oak Common locomotive depot in North West London, whilst awaiting the university term to start at the end of September 1957. I'd not succeeded in my efforts to become an Oxford scholar - the competition was very tough, and whilst I'd chosen to pursue Modern Languages as these were my best school subjects, I was stronger on the literature aspects than the basic language. I eventually obtained a place at University College London in the small German Language Department, and quickly established that I'd need to live at home as hostel places at UCL were limited to 171 beds for over 3,000 students and most were having to find lodgings in bedsits all over the capital, many with daily travelling longer than I had from my parents' home in Woking. In fact I welcomed this for two reasons - I'd been at boarding school for over five years and it was good to re-establish close relationships with my own family again. Secondly, I was obliged to purchase an annual season ticket, funded by Surrey County Council in lieu of a grant for London accommodation, which my memory suggests was just £33. This meant that I could both study and enjoy my hobby as I chose to travel by steam train to and from London each day, one of the few occasions when I have excelled at multi-tasking!

One might question my choice of faculty as languages and European literature do not seem an obvious route for a railway management career which was already featuring in my mind, following some further research on opportunities on the railway which had established that there were possibilities for arts graduates. In my second year I had to select a specialist subject for research and deeper study, occupying some expected 4-6 hours per week for the final two years, and one might well doubt my sanity when I finished up as one of only two students in the whole of London University selecting 'stylistic analysis of mediaeval German epic poetry'.

In fact the choice happened - like so much in my life - by apparent chance. I had started on nineteenth century German drama - not that much more relevant I suppose - but the course was crowded and the professor less than charismatic. A friend pleaded with me to join him as he, the lone student selecting such an esoteric course, found himself facing a professor and a senior tutor for a couple of long afternoons every week, which he found too much of a strain, even though it was held in the professor's flat and accompanied by the occasional glass of wine or sherry! So I made the switch and for about three weeks floundered in near panic as I found the subject initially incomprehensible, even though we started learning the techniques with more modern literature. Suddenly something clicked, I received back an analysis of a Goethe poem with a row of double-ticks in the margin (the professor's highest accolade) and the fog in my brain seemed to lift.

At that time managers undertaking the railway industry 'milk-round' of universities seemed to be looking for evidence of an ability to assimilate learning quickly, apply logic and exhibit some creativity. They did not appear to give much weight to the relevance of the course to the knowledge required in the industry. That could be learned during three years' training. Of course, the types of people required by the UK railway industry in 1960 were very varied - for as well as engineers, BR was looking for managers in train operations, marketing and selling, publicity, communications, architecture, finance, law, hotels, shipping...

Anyway, I discovered with hindsight that my course was not quite as irrelevant as I thought. It taught me to see patterns in thought, to read quickly and identify the important bits, to apply logic and find evidence - all fairly useful skills in BR's bureaucracy.

And we had a lot of fun in the process. Most of the mediaeval texts were from the Arthurian romances, but the French epics of Chrétien de Troyes, translated and further developed by several German poets such as Hartmann von Aue, Wolfram von Eschenbach and Walther von der Vogelweide, were bawdy and irreverent and were themed round something that was highly relevant to BR in the 1960s - the role of the outsider in bringing about change to a closed society. All the Arthurian heroes were outsiders or challenged the system. Sir Launcelot of course conspired with the King's wife, Guinevere. Sir Erec (in mediaeval English and Norman French, Harry son of King Lake - Harry le fils Lac) married and took his young bride to bed for six months until tongues wagged, then strode off into the dangerous forest in a blind rage using his wife to direct and tend him until he was severely wounded; was nursed back to health by his long-suffering wife, when his eyes were 'opened', a significant symbol. Or the story I love of brave Sir Ivan (Uweine) whose pet lion used to join in jousts if they went on too long and all the knights would cry 'foul' as it broke all the courtly rules. But when they made a sortie to rescue a damsel in distress at some giant's castle outside the court, all said to Ivan, 'You will bring your lion with you, won't you!' Of course, Arthur's famous table was round, symbol of church or school or whatever closed society took your fancy (BR?) and yet all the adventures took place outside it, never in Arthur's castle itself. I hear you identifying the errant BR knights now...

In the meantime, however, exposure to a British Rail 'Short Works' course, as recounted in the next chapter, had opened my eyes to other opportunities. And so it seemed possible that I could turn my hobby into a career and get paid for what I liked doing. Now I look back on a 36 year career for British Rail, a further period of consultancy work on railway safety that took me all over the globe, fifteen years of leading the industry's niche charity, 'Railway Children' and an assessed two million miles of travelling by train. And I reflect just how lucky I have been to have had the opportunity to do something fulfilling in an industry, which has fascinated me from my pushchair outings to the latest opportunities coming my way to ride the GW 175 anniversary vintage trains conducting raffles for the street children supported by the Railway Children charity – and the final and astonishing honour (in the Summer of 2013) of having a locomotive bearing my own name!

Guildford's shed pilot, 30458 Ironside at Eastleigh in the 1950s: photo MLS Collection

The author, aged 12 months

The author's mother and father, Jack and Audrey Maidment, newly married in 1937, members of the East Molesey Methodist Church Tennis Club

My first Ian Allan ABC trainspotting books

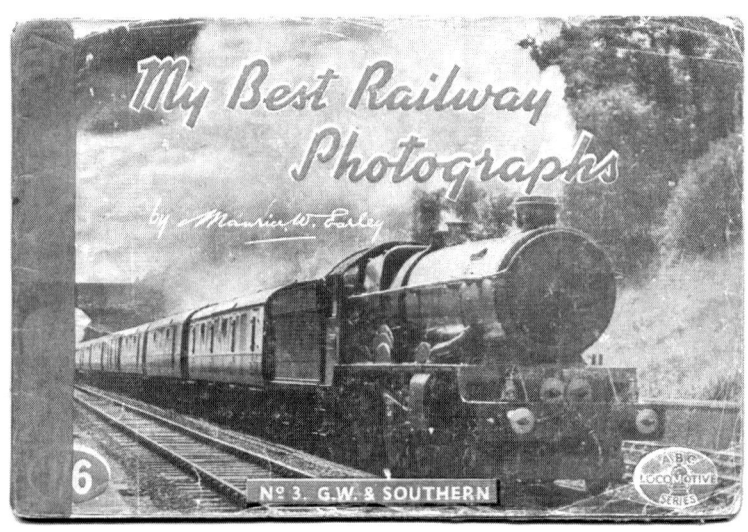

The well-thumbed cover of the first book presented to the author by Aunt Enid in 1947

'King Arthur' 30455 *Sir Launcelot* passes beneath the site of Surbiton County Grammar School with a Basingstoke – Waterloo semi-fast train, 1957.

Cover of one of the early copies of 'Trains Illustrated' from September 1950

Trainspotters at the end of platform 13 at Euston sandwiched between the Summer Saturday 'Welshman' and its relief, 18.8.51

Wainwright 'D' 31586 near Ash Junction with the 2.23pm Guildford – Reading, 25.6.55

Chapter 2: 1956 - 1960
Joining the railways

In 2000 I was involved at the Old Oak Common Open Weekend in the naming of EWS AC electric locomotive, 90031 *The Railway Children Partnership,* and in support of that event, was present during the two days with a stand and display about the international street children charity after which the locomotive was named. Coincidentally, that stand was on the ground floor of the old train crew accommodation - where 42 years previously, immediately above on the first floor, I had spent several weeks, just before the building's completion, copying out new train crew rosters in isolation as the Chief Clerk feared I might be subject to some animosity (as I was apparently doing some clerk out of overtime he had been expecting in order to complete the same task!) As a result I found myself unsupervised with a grandstand view of all the mainline locomotives going on and off shed – 'Kings', 'Castles', 'Britannias', '4700s', the lot! So my banishment was hardly an ordeal.

    How did I arrive at this happy situation? Back in the summer of 1956 I'd enrolled in what was termed 'a short works course' with British Railways - a scheme to show Sixth Formers career opportunities. I'd always believed that I'd need an engineering degree to turn my hobby into paid work, but this course seemed to advertise other potential opportunities. I was instructed to make my way on a Sunday evening to a hotel in Bath and duly caught the 4.15pm from Paddington behind one of the Western Region's derided Britannias, *Lightning,* which did not live up to its name enduring a lot of slow line running because of engineering work. Seven fellow students joined me there and we spent the week under the tutelage of the Bristol District Assistant Operating Superintendent, Rodney Meadows, a former Traffic Apprentice, who was to show us the opportunities such a scheme offered. The week was a joy for train enthusiasts - and most of us were - although I gathered later that I was the only one of the eight that actually joined BR. We had a tour of Bristol Docks in a brakevan, spent an afternoon at Severn Tunnel Junction marshalling Yard, visited a new signalbox at Bathampton and had a most fruitful day at Swindon Works where we were permitted to view *Lode Star* and a row of stored 'Dean Goods' and 'Dukedogs' in the Works 'Stock Shed'. I kept in touch with Rodney Meadows who became the agent through whom I got the opportunity to work at Old Oak Common.

Having nothing better to do in my 'half gap year' between school and college during the first half of 1957, I applied, with a reference from Rodney, to the London Divisional Office of the Western Region for temporary employment, knowing by then that I wished to pursue a railway career. During my first summer vacation from London University in 1958 I repeated the experience, but the summer vacation of 1959 was spent brushing up my German at Munich University and discovering the delights of Bavarian compound pacifics on the Munich - Lindau - Lake Constance route to Geneva and Zurich and learning most of my new German vocabulary at the Hauptbahnhof which was being rebuilt after the ravages of the Second World War.

Old Oak was always short staffed during the holiday periods, so for most of the time there I was employed in various clerical jobs, which involved spending time in different sections of the shed. Initially I spent a few (rather boring) weeks doling out thick green engine lubrication oil to drivers and just enjoying the atmosphere of the depot. At that time Old Oak Common's allocation included 170 steam locomotives - about half of the 'Kings' and 43 'Castles' amongst others - and 20 diesel shunters. Every morning, as I walked down the long slope from Old Oak Common Lane into the depot, I was greeted by the sight of at least two of the large Churchward 2-8-0s simmering at stop blocks by the carriage shed after arrival on overnight fast freights. In fact, one particular siding there was known to all as the '47 hundred road'. I would then cut through the side entrance of the shed, across one of the four electric turntables, glancing at the 'Kings' and 'Castles' on display, searching for a rare visitor. I would need to be careful at this point because the turntable, being fully covered in and electrically operated, would often start off with little warning and at quite a lick.

On my first day I was given a tour of the shed, which included a trip in the cab of 5074 *Hampden* being prepared for the 'Torbay Express' down to the coaling plant and shed exit signal. The depot was a very cosmopolitan place and although work seemed to be allocated on apparently racist lines there seemed to me to be only good natured banter between the various groups - perhaps I was just a little naïve at the time. The shed labourers working the coaling plant and emptying the ashes from smokeboxes and dropping fires near the coaling plant were all Irish. The cleaners employed in the shed itself were all of West Indian origin and a gang would be seen cheerfully smothering an engine with oil until it gleamed and if it was still there after the gang had gone round one of the roundhouses cleaning the other locomotives, it would get another dose. We had many Welsh firemen and I learned that they had come on promotion to get their foot onto the driver's promotional ladder, as there was little hope of becoming a driver in the Welsh valley depots before one was in the mid 50s.

The stores where I was initially employed joined on to the 'Factory' where facilities existed for the repair of several steam locomotives, which usually included two or three undergoing the three monthly valves and piston renewals and a couple of hot box repairs involving lifting the engine from the bogie which seemed the location of most problems. When a locomotive had been repaired here, it was despatched under the eyes of Billy Gibbs, the Maintenance Foreman, for a high speed trip round the Ealing - Greenford triangle to see that all was well. As well as driver and fireman, Billy Gibbs and a fitter from the Factory, it was practice to allow one of the apprentices to make the trip. I got a turn too and my loco was 6024 *King Edward I* after a bogie hot box repair. I remember sitting on the tender toolbox, head above the cab roof (any railway inspectors please shut your eyes - although I did wear a pair of motor cycle goggles) as we accelerated hard from Old Oak West after a signal check, although we only got up to around 65mph before we had to slow for Greenford, instead of the 80 hoped for to test the bearing. A sedate run on the branch, pauses to feel the offending bearing, and then another burst of speed back from West Ealing to Acton, saw all successfully concluded and 6024 was on the 'Limited' the next day.

By this time I was getting used to the smell of the place. Although it can't be true, I remember the shed always baking in a heat wave and everywhere was bathed in a peculiar pungent odour of hot oil, sulphur and a faint whiff of stale urine, which seemed especially strong around the dead locos awaiting repair outside the Factory. Once I was working on clerical rather than stores duties I used to wear a white shirt (why?) and my poor mother had a dreadful time trying to get them clean after one day's wear in that atmosphere.

By early spring 1957 I had graduated to the Central Office at Old Oak, so named because it was located exactly in the centre of the engine shed, the bullseye between the four turntables that made up the main depot. But it was central in another way, because it was from here that all the maintenance work of the shed's allocation was organised. The clerk that was in charge of engine histories was on longterm sick leave and Billy Gibbs put me to work covering his post. This was a delight, because my role involved recording the oil and coal consumption of each locomotive from dockets issued by the stores or coaling plant, compiling mileage records from the loco rosters operated for Old Oak's engines, and preparing routine maintenance plans (boiler washouts and valves and piston exams) as well as shopping proposals for Swindon Works Heavy and Intermediate repairs.

Whilst the location of this Central Office was ideal in one sense, it was literally hard on other senses. The noise around meant that phone calls were a strain and at the end of the day a sore throat and headache were quite common. One day a locomotive failed before going off shed after the fireman had prepared a big fire for its duty, and it stood inside the shed on one of the roads adjoining our offices blowing off steam furiously for what seemed like hours. On another occasion a Britannia's whistle got stuck and the loud chime lost its attraction somewhat quickly until it petered out ages afterwards into a feeble cracked note.

Around this time one of the shed's regulars was *City of Truro* which for several weeks came up to town on a commuter train and returned home on either the 5.20 or 6.20pm Paddington - Reading (I can't remember which). I travelled on it one day to the first stop - West Drayton - with its eight non-corridor coaches, in a fine drizzle - a most unsuitable duty, as the driver had great difficulty in controlling the slipping of the large driving wheels. I did record that we just managed to touch 60 mph before the stop and we only lost about a minute on schedule, but it must have been hard going thereafter as the train was then all stations to Reading. At the end of this stint, 3440 returned to Didcot and was used on the Didcot-Newbury-Winchester service, a much more suitable assignment.

My presence at Old Oak did cause some consternation. Clerical work was jealously guarded and local staff did all in their power to ensure no excuse for staff cuts could be made. As well as the embarrassment of doing a clerk out of his overtime copying out the 1958 winter rosters, I completed my day's duties in the Mechanical Foreman's office around 11am on most days. This flummoxed the other clerks and I was told to take an early and long lunch break in the Old Oak hostel canteen and, as they knew I was interested, spend the afternoon with a different fitter each week. I remember vividly spending one week with Joe Parrott (then 72 years of age) who was the ATC fitter, going out to North Acton, to knock out the ATC shoes of GW locos coming from the Midlands and travelling to the South Coast on Summer Saturdays. Another week was spent with the boilersmith (who was only 67!) enduring the usual ritual of being sent into the firebox of a loco whose fire had only just been dropped. On one occasion I came across one rather rotund Traffic Apprentice who had actually got stuck in the firehole door after such an initiation and we all had to haul him out to his severe loss of face.

My first attempt at carrying out any maintenance work myself was a total disaster. I was told to remove the clack box of one of the depot's many pannier tanks and I found the nuts so worn that I managed to break two substantial monkey spanners and dismantle half the engine before I prised off the offending part. However, I can't have been completely useless as the locomotive concerned, 5764, survives to this day on the Severn Valley Railway!

The following year I spent more time acting as the Running Foreman's Assistant in the main office block (before my banishment to the new train crew depot). I was actually in charge of booking the engines out to their jobs as well as receiving other depot messages about incoming locos turning round at Ranelagh Bridge. Although I tried to manipulate some turns, in fact my scope for choice was very limited. We had the practice of keeping the best locos on the same turns for weeks (as opposed to the Eastern Region method of allocating specific engines to regular crews). The distances involved on the Region - to Bristol, Cardiff, Gloucester, Worcester and Wolverhampton - all meant that the loco and crew could do 'out and back' easily in the day and the loco be serviced and ready for the same turn next day. Only on the West of England route to Plymouth or through to Swansea were engines not turned back immediately and many crews on those turns at that time worked 'double-home', ie they lodged overnight on a two day diagram.

The top link engines got best Welsh coal - Oakdale or Markham - whilst the second link engines went to the other side of the coaling stage and got briquettes or worse. I could choose which 'Castle' to banish to act as Ranelagh Bridge standby - one of my predecessors, I was told, had regularly despatched the old rebuilt 'Star' 4037 *The South Wales Borderers* when it was at Old Oak (around 1956) to stand there in the knowledge that it looked superb with its huge polished nameplate, but such was its reputation for rough riding that no foreign crew would think of taking it unless their steed was a total failure!

Whilst at Old Oak I was given the opportunity for my first 'official' footplate ride by a very generous and sympathetic shedmaster, Ray Sims. He had obtained a pass for me to ride the 11.5am Paddington – Gloucester and return diagram and allocated one of Old Oak's best Castles, 7001 *Sir James Milne,* on the turn for my initiation, knowing that I would have a very comfortable journey in which to learn the art of firing which he guessed would be offered to me. After Swindon my rite of passage began in earnest as I was handed the shovel and expected to keep steam up as we climbed to Sapperton Tunnel, a feat accomplished although I have to say not all the coal found its way into the firebox at the first attempt. I had expected to have a clean up and eat my sandwiches during the Gloucester break, but Inspector George Price who was my mentor on that occasion had other ideas and took me round Gloucester cathedral – the sight of two boilersuited men, one still filthy from the enforced exercise, must have seemed a little odd to the other tourists and pilgrims!

A couple of months later, Ray Sims hinted that I might like to apply for a second pass and I duly received one for a return trip to Wolverhampton on the 9 o' clock Paddington. I joined 6015 *King Richard III* (the first King fitted with a double chimney) on the turntable at Old Oak and went up with it to Paddington where we awaited the Inspector. Departure time came and there was no sign of the Inspector, the train crew said 'Not to worry' - they were happier without - so off we went. A good punctual run ensued, but I was left to my own devices at Wolverhampton. As I was wondering what to do - I still had a return footplate pass, but no particular train was specified - I saw 5032 *Usk Castle* backing on to an Up express. I introduced myself to Driver Bert Griffiths and Fireman Forrester of Stafford Road and was made most welcome. Until Banbury we were hampered by a presence of a horse-box marshalled behind the engine, restricting us to 60mph (why was this permitted?) but after Banbury we went to town and whirled our 13 coach load to 84 mph after Ardley and through Gerrards Cross. When I got back to Old Oak I found that everyone was searching for me - the Inspector had turned up at Paddington for the 9.10 and had waited for me. I was deemed to be in trouble until they examined my pass, which was clearly made out for the 9 o'clock and not the slower 9.10!

It wasn't always undiluted pleasure. Emboldened by this I applied to the Southern and was granted a footplate pass for the 9am Waterloo as far as Salisbury. Unrebuilt West Country 34026 *Yes Tor* backed on in good time, but for the first and only time in my experience I was made less than welcome by the footplate crew. The driver (Cross by name and cross by nature) complained bitterly that he didn't want a passenger and I made to dismount, but was stopped by the Inspector. However, the driver was an absolute misery and kept muttering under his breath all the way, until after Andover, the Inspector suddenly asked me what my highest speed on the footplate had been, and when I said 84, he persuaded the driver to let 34026 run down Porton bank until we touched 87. I think the Inspector was sorry for me and I had a lingering hope he might, to compensate, take me back to Waterloo on the footplate of the Up 'Atlantic Coast Express', with which I returned to the capital, but no such luck.

At the time, as an enthusiast 'in heaven', the impressions of the locomotives were uppermost. In later years, it was the interaction with the people I met there that stood me in good stead in my railway management career - Ray Sims, Norman Willis, the Chief Clerk, Billy Gibbs, the fitters who humoured me, the character who realised after a few hours that I did not swear and apologised profusely that he called a spade a spade (he didn't - he called it an f****** expletive deleted spade; when he was telling me what to do I almost had to stand, notebook in hand, extracting the odd word that meant something from the string of obscenities preceding and succeeding it).

Following college vacations spent at Old Oak Common in 1957 and 1958, I graduated from London University in 1960 with my degree in Modern Languages (with my aforesaid special skill in interpreting twelfth century German poetry) and began to seek a career on the railway. I had anticipated an interruption through an obligation to undertake my deferred two years' National Service in the armed forces, but during my Finals I had received a letter informing me of the abolition of this requirement. I framed the letter and hung it in my bedroom and began to seek employment.

However, by the time I had left college in June 1960 I had missed that year's intake into the Traffic Apprenticeship scheme and therefore, with the help of contacts made earlier, joined the Western Region London Division's Passenger Train Office as a 'Class 4 clerk' - the junior grade. Perhaps as an omen of things to come, I was made redundant within two weeks of my induction, and filled the post of an 'Office Junior' without any apparent change in my pay or role - which was sorting Guards' Journals, a document prepared for each journey indicating the locomotive number, train formation, number of passengers and time gained and lost by the engine, signal checks, speed restrictions, station overtime etc. Part of my job was to refer any significant signal delays to the District Signalling Inspector for explanation - an activity that was not well received by experienced time served Inspectors from the hands of enthusiastic young new entrants to the service!

After three months I regained my status as a class 4 clerk, being put in charge of the production of the 'Daily Manuscript Notice' - a document that was compiled, roneo'd and distributed each day to stations and depots in the Division, indicating last minute changes to the timetable, the schedule for specials and relief trains and formation strengthening to accommodate surges in traffic and special parties - a need I would identify through scrutiny of train loadings from the Guards' Journal records and the details of bookings from the Party Section. The culture of the day can best be illustrated by one incident I remember vividly - I was summoned before an angry General Manager (Keith Grand) one day to explain why, during his morning promenade along Paddington's platform 1, he had seen the chocolate and cream formation of the Cornish Riviera despoiled by one maroon coach at the back. Apparently I should have required Old Oak depot, in my Notice, to attach a suitably liveried vehicle or leave the train short-formed! When I rang his secretary to arrange for my interview in which I was to be dressed down, his secretary suggested I should come in the early afternoon. When I duly arrived, quaking at the prospect, she told me to go back to work as he was never fit enough in the early afternoon to see anyone after his usual alcoholic lunch, she would tell him that I'd fulfilled the appointment and that I'd hear no more about it. I didn't.

During the spring I duly applied for the Traffic Apprenticeship scheme and as a staff entrant, took the exam and passed the interview ready to start in the autumn of 1961. However, in the interim, after nine months or so in my first clerical job, I applied for promotion to a Class 3 post in the Freight Train Office where I was in charge of special and out-of-gauge loads, a subject on which I knew virtually nothing, but apparently I was the only serious applicant for the post, so I was appointed. My boss was astounded, he told me that it had taken him 25 years to get his first promotion from Class 5 clerk (a grade long abolished) to a Class 4! Although my new office was next door to the Passenger Train Office, the culture was as different as could be. The regime in the Passenger Office was to work and play hard - that is when we had a lot to do, we knuckled down, took short lunch breaks and worked till everything was done without claiming overtime. When things were slack, we took longer breaks and went home when everything was finished for the day. There was a lot of interplay and banter between staff and a lot of laughter - some of a black nature when we were under pressure.

In the Freight Office everyone watched the clock and tried to look occupied, whether the work existed or not. Throughout the day silence reigned, you could hear the occasional rustle of papers. The phones rarely rang - in the Passenger Office they never seemed to be silent. At one minute to five o'clock everyone would rise, put on their overcoats and at five o'clock precisely the room would be empty. One day I had a bout of hay fever or some allergy for which I was prescribed some anti-histamine tablets with a warning that they could make me drowsy. I duly turned up to work and within half an hour my head was down and I fell into a deep sleep. I woke at midday - and no-one noticed, or if they did, said nothing. I had a desk in the corner of the room so I was not too conspicuous, but even so… I was not happy in this atmosphere and it was with some relief that I commenced my management training less than three months after promotion to this section.

The author on the footplate of 6024, during a pause to feel the bearings on the Greenford – Ealing branch, 29.7.57

'City of Truro' on shed at Old Oak Common between its commuter train duties, 18.5.57

The Severn Valley restored pannier tank 5764 at Highley, 2009

7001 *Sir James Milne* at Swindon just before the author's initiation into the art of firing began, 19.6.57

Driver Bert Griffiths and Fireman Forrester of Stafford Road on arrival at Paddington after the author's footplate trip, 21.8.57

The last 'Cornish Riviera Express' to be rostered for steam power, with 6004 *King George III*, 11.6.58

Chapter 3: 1961 - 1962
Management training
Western Region's London Division

In September 1961 I was appointed as one of six Western Region Traffic Apprentices (known in later years as Management Trainees). I had an unfair advantage in the selection process. Normally around 20 young men (there was little encouragement for potential women managers in those days) would be selected throughout BR by examination and interview - but after negotiation with the clerical Trade Union, TSSA, it had been agreed that 50% should come from the ranks of railway staff and not be recruited directly from university. Because of my year's service, I counted as a staff entrant and therefore the railways got the bonus of an additional graduate entrant! At that time, the scheme consisted of 3 years' training, the first year being basic training in railway operating activities at ground level. Managers in those days had a belief that it would be useful for managers of the future to have an understanding of what their staff were meant to do (and did do!).

I commenced the Western Region Traffic Apprenticeship scheme after a final interview with Assistant General Manager, George Bowles, was sent to the Headquarters Staff Officer in charge of trainees to be allocated to a Division for year 1 training and to receive my initial programme. The London Division was my first year's location, and the immediate programme was six weeks at Maidenhead passenger station, six weeks at Slough Goods, four weeks at South Lambeth, a larger Goods Depot, four weeks at a medium sized station, Oxford, four weeks at a large station, Reading, and six weeks at a locomotive depot, Old Oak Common. After that I was to go to Margam Yard in South Wales as the London Division was not considered to have a large enough yard for training purposes - Acton apparently did not count.

As Reading seemed to be the focal point of the programme and daily commuting from Woking seemed impracticable (my own transport was still the 1936 built cycle), I took lodgings with an elderly widow in a terraced house five minutes' walk from

Reading station. So I was sent for my first six weeks' basic training to Maidenhead station to learn the roles of booking clerk, parcels clerk, how to wield a shunting pole in the small goods yard and to watch activity in the signalbox. My first dose of real responsibility came during such a spell when the signalman, closeted in the loo, shouted instructions to me to clear signals for the Down 'Cornish Riviera' (again - this train was becoming my nemesis). I accepted the train, pulled off the semaphores, watched the 'Warship' roar past with some trepidation and remembered to give train out of section and replace the pegs before my mentor emerged from his cubby hole.

My six week stint at Slough Goods started on 13th November and lasted until the Christmas holiday. I would spend a somewhat tedious day looking at freight charge calculations, cartage returns and wagon demurrage. I can remember little else, which shows how ineffective that part of the training was. What I did learn was that a large part of my training might consist of what we nicknamed 'sitting next to Nellie' - ie obeying an instruction to go and sit next to a clerk and watch what he or she did. This was one rung higher than the other frequent training technique which management trainees were subjected to - reading files.

After a Christmas spent in North Germany (in temperatures of -20 degrees C) as best man to a college friend who was getting married to a girl who'd escaped from East Germany, I came back to a month's training at South Lambeth Goods Depot where I learned a lot (mainly how not to conduct industrial relations) but commuted from my home at Woking as that was easier, spending such free time as I had on evening railway jaunts with my 'priv' tickets to Banbury, Peterborough, Swindon and Rugby. At that time South Lambeth was a hotbed of militant trade unionism and I witnessed an incident, which thankfully I never saw again in my railway career. In the middle of the meeting during a particularly angry exchange, the Chief Clerk, a hefty man with a walking impediment requiring him to carry a stick, and the LDC Secretary got up and began a fight, the Chief Clerk wielding his walking stick to some effect. All this time the Goods Agent, theoretically in charge, just laid his head on the table and buried it in his arms and made no attempt to intervene. No-one walked out - I got the impression that this was not the first such occurrence.

I spent another instructive few days with the only two clerks in the cartage section. Both men were far too intelligent for the job they had - one had been a Polish RAF pilot, the other the manager of a steelworks in Dhurgapur in India. Both men finished their tasks by 11am, and then spent their time regaling me with the sins of management and staff at the depot and running rings round everyone else fabricating elaborate and fictitious cartage returns and other paperwork, making the entire job farcical. Neither had any respect for the job but unfortunately due to racial prejudice prevalent at the time, neither could get jobs that were appropriate for their skills and experience.

I resumed my Reading lodgings on 26th February as a base from which to perform my training at Oxford - with unwary strangers I can impress by referring to my Oxford days! It was really a repeat of my Maidenhead days although on a slightly larger scale - I really don't think I learned an awful lot more except by meeting different people and seeing their personalities in action. At the time my main interest was catching the 5.30pm Oxford back to my Reading digs each night via Paddington. This train was the 'Oxford Flyer' requiring 'Cheltenham Flyer' or 'Bristolian' style running from Didcot to Paddington if it was to keep time and I enjoyed practising my train timing skills and egging on the drivers to beat the previous efforts. One trip made the 63 miles in just over 53 minutes, a start to stop average of 71 mph with a 'Castle' and six coaches and one Old Oak driver was rumoured to have done it in 51 minutes (74 mph) but unfortunately I was on the wrong shift that day. I worked out that I could get home to Reading nearly as quickly by catching this train and the 7.5pm Paddington - Cheltenham as if I'd waited for the 4.5pm Hereford, it was much more fun and no cost as I had a Divisional free pass throughout my London Division training! At both Oxford and Reading, where I moved next to observe a large passenger station operation, I had to mix day shifts with some evening and night shifts, mainly to observe the parcels working at both the platform and cartage bays - parcels and GPO traffic was still important in the early sixties.

In the spring of 1962 I was allocated to Old Oak Common for my depot and footplate training - the highlight of most Traffic Apprentices' three-year stint. The intention was to ensure management trainees had an understanding of operations from a driver's perspective and the normal arrangement was the provision of a Divisional footplate pass for three weeks of the depot training. As I had been at Old Oak during my college years and Ray Sims, the Shedmaster, knew of my interest in locomotive matters, he handed me a driver's all stations route learning footplate pass (covering Paddington - Penzance, Fishguard, Chester and all stations between) on my first day, only to be returned on my last. My official pass had got 'lost' somewhere between the Superintendent's Office in Paddington and Old Oak Common in the railway internal postal system!

I had been surprised to be sent to Old Oak for this part of my training for two reasons. Normally one avoided locations where one had previously worked and also Old Oak had been known to ask Head Office not to send trainees there, as there was a certain amount of hostility towards future bosses in that somewhat militant location. Traffic Apprentices had to be sensitive to the feelings of many ordinary railwaymen and women who sometimes resented the 'fast track' promotion that would follow our training and not all Traffic Apprentices were the most tactful of individuals. In this case, apparently, because I had worked at Old Oak previously and had got on well with most staff (apart from the guy whose overtime I had usurped in 1958!), I was warmly accepted as 'one of them' and received full co-operation.

While my early training at Old Oak involved experience of rostering, trade union negotiations, maintenance planning, driver route learning and training practices etc., I sought opportunities to use my privileged footplate pass facility. On the first Saturday lunchtime (one worked to noon on Saturdays then) I made my way to Paddington and showed my pass to the crew of 7031 *Cromwell's Castle*, newly transferred from Laira to Worcester and working the 1.15pm Paddington - Hereford. We had a very comfortable and punctual trip to Oxford where I alighted, the gleaming locomotive and Worcester crew well on top of the job. After a quick sandwich, a Worcester double chimney Castle, 7013 *Bristol Castle* (which had exchanged number and name with the royal engine 4082 *Windsor Castle* in 1952 as the latter was in no fit state to work King George VI's funeral train) rolled into Oxford on time and I joined the crew. We had a very straightforward run, economical on coal and water, with sustained running in the mid 70s and an early arrival. 7013 was not quite as smooth running as 7031, but it was 26 years older!

During those first few weeks while my training was constrained to the depot environment, I increasingly utilised my pass for evening trips to Reading, Swindon or Oxford. By mid May 1962, it was my turn for the three rostered weeks of formal footplate training in which I was required to sample both steam and diesel, freight and passenger, local and mainline work. One of my first days was to be spent on shunting and empty carriage working (the Old Oak - Paddington 'in and outs') with condenser pannier 9709.

Because of my supposed firing prowess (had my successful showing with 'Castles' on the road got onto the Old Oak grapevine?) I was entrusted with looking after the fire of 9709 while the fireman was despatched to the office to collect the wages of driver and fireman, taking the little brass discs that acted as proof of identity. We were marshalled ahead of a long train of parcels vehicles to form the 2.34pm Paddington - Plymouth Parcels from platform 1A, awaiting the road to leave Old Oak carriage sidings. The fireman had been gone for some time and the driver had engrossed me in a long discourse on a number of topics, including, I believe, the correct way to prune raspberries, when we got the road to leave. The fireman was still nowhere to be seen, so the driver said 'you'll do' and went to open the regulator. I decided it was time to put coal on the fire and opened the firehole door and to my horror, found that the fire had gone out! To my surprise the driver was not unduly fazed and helped me find some timber and firelighters to relight the fire. Meanwhile we went, using what steam remained, at least as far as the bottom of the flyover at North Pole. 80lbs of steam frankly was not adequate to lift 14 large parcel vehicles up the gradient of the flyover, so we gesticulated to the driver of a 'Castle' waiting to follow us light engine and he gave us an almighty shove up to the top, whereafter I just raised enough steam to keep the brakes off until our arrival in platform 1A. I never heard anything more about it, and the driver did not even tell the fireman when he returned with their wages on our eventual arrival back at the depot.

I had worked pretty long hours to make full use of my pass while undergoing depot training, but once my scheduled footplate programme came round, I could not squeeze enough hours into the day to do all I wanted. No-one sought to challenge my 14-15 hour turns of duty and only once did I appear to suffer when I nearly fell asleep while trying to fire a 'King' on the first Up

Wolverhampton, after an all night shift on a Paddington - Hockley fast freight. In order to maximise my day, and avoid the anxious entreaties of my uncomprehending landlady, I lodged for three weeks with the jovial stationmaster of Twyford, Bob Poynter, a former Traffic Apprentice in his first substantive post which covered the Henley branch as well as the mainline. Many of the commuter trains were formed with former GWR rolling stock with the T-shaped door handles that had to be turned and Bob was much exercised by station overtime while doors were shut and handles operated - he learned from bitter experience that you don't blow whistles to hurry commuters off the Henley branch! Most mornings I would travel up to Paddington in the cab of a Castle or Hall on a commuter service, and go back to Old Oak shed on the light engine.

My programme required me to travel on a variety of train types and one of the stipulated journeys was meant to be on a steam hauled stopping service. This seemed a little unnecessary from a training point of view, as by 1962 most local services were DMUs (which I dutifully covered from Banbury to Paddington) but I decided to fulfil my remit by turning up for a Saturday Paddington - Oxford train (calling at all stations after Reading) whose DMU was replaced one day a week by engine and coaches. After an uneventful run from Paddington as far as Reading, the driver turned to me and offered me his seat and the controls.

So here I was, in charge of 5986 *Arbury Hall* and 8 (fairly empty) non-corridor coaches. We set off on the Down Relief line in brisk style and I was bowling merrily along at about 60 mph when Tilehurst station came into view. As a novice I had been expecting some tuition, but the driver said nothing and my somewhat late and increasingly severe brake application saw us sailing through the long platform with only the rear coach making it! I held my breath watching to see how many doors opened off the platform, but no-one stirred and off we went. I repeated the performance at Pangbourne, but managed to get three coaches in the platform, a distinct improvement. Still the driver seemed totally unperturbed, so I requested guidance for Goring, and he pointed out a white cottage, which he used as a marker for braking. Third time lucky - a perfect stop! By now I was becoming overconfident and was finding a sedate 60 mph limit on the Relief Line unexciting, so in accelerating from Cholsey I moved the regulator into second port position. 5986 responded by almost leaping into the air and produced a lovely roar from the chimney and this was the only time the driver took any interest in my activity and laid a restraining hand on my shoulder.

At Didcot for some reason we changed engines and I continued to Oxford very sedately with a new crew. On this Saturday I decided to return to London on the 'Oxford Flyer', the 5.30pm Oxford, booked non-stop in exactly the hour - this was one of the fastest schedules still worked by steam in 1962. Oxford shed covered the turn on a Saturday and they turned out one of their own Modified Halls, 7911 *Lady Margaret Hall* and I rode this to Paddington. The engine was on top of the job, running in the low 80s, and we reached Paddington in exactly 59 minutes and 55 seconds, but I learned a major lesson en route. We had a tender full of ovoids (coal dust cemented in ovoid shape which produced a lot of dust and had an irritant chemical if you got it in the eye). The fireman had been busy with the hose throughout the journey, attempting to control the dust, but as we shot under the station overbridge at Southall at 80 mph, the swirling coal dust got in my eyes. I had bought myself a pair of motor-cycle goggles to wear as protection, but had allowed myself to be laughed into not wearing them by a succession of macho train crews. A visit to the First Aid Room at Paddington was not successful in removing all the dust and I was sent to the Casualty Department of the adjacent St Mary's Hospital, where I spent a very painful four hours awaiting attention. Thereafter I ignored the teasing and put my own safety first - I wore my goggles. This was a lesson in safety culture that I remembered in later years when I led the change in safety management after the Clapham accident.

The Western Region diesel hydraulics were just being introduced about this time and I had already travelled in the cab of brand new Hymek D7025 on an Up South Wales express. The 'Warships' were now fairly common, but were still causing the fitters some problems, and while I was at Old Oak, drawings arrived from Germany - but unfortunately the explanations were in German. Knowing that I was a graduate in German, the Shedmaster asked me if I would translate the sheaf of documents. Unfortunately, as I was no engineer, I didn't know the English for half the engine parts described! During my stay, the first two 2,700 hp 'Westerns' appeared and I arranged to come in specially on a

Saturday to travel down to Plymouth on D1001 on the Cornish Riviera. Unfortunately it failed the previous evening on the Up run, and when I arrived at the platform end at Paddington, I found North British built D851. It kept time without trouble, but the North British engines in particular were prone to the production of unpleasant fumes from badly fitted pipes and by the time we reached Exeter I was suffering from a filthy headache.

Seeing a 'Hall' waiting to back onto the Kingswear three coach portion of our train was too tempting, so I opted to breathe the ozone along the Dawlish wall. After a pleasant couple of unhurried hours in Kingswear, we returned to Exeter with a portion of the 1.50pm Penzance, only to find another fume-filled North British Warship, D855. But this was reality, one of the purposes of my training was to experience life as the train crews found it and cab design and conditions were important, as I found later in my operating posts when dealing with Trade Union complaints over health and safety, or looking at the causes of SPADs (signals passed at danger).

At this time the Paddington - Wolverhampton service had been augmented to replace Euston services curtailed during electrification, and most of the Laira Kings had been transferred to Old Oak or Stafford Road for the Northern Road. One of the extra services was an 8.20am Paddington - Birmingham, scheduled for two hours and ten minutes with one stop and named 'The Inter City'. This was very attractive to me as a day out, and I had runs with 'Kings' on this train and on a 9.0am Paddington MO train that was non-stop. Surprisingly two had major problems, although for different locomotive reasons. On the first, I rode 6016 *King Edward V*. The tender was filled with an appalling load of coal dust and we struggled for steam throughout. I spent at least half the journey knee deep in the stuff mining the odd lump of genuine coal and flinging it forward to the perspiring fireman. We somehow kept time, but it was a struggle and I doubt if we'd have made it without the two of us working flat out to make steam.

On the second occasion we had 6000 itself, and a good lot of Welsh coal, but as we accelerated up to Seer Green the steam pressure dropped ominously quickly. As soon as we shut off for the High Wycombe curves, the steam pressure rose again, and we progressed in fits and starts, working hard uphill and drifting downhill while we recovered breath. We roared over Hatton summit at 53 mph and sailed into Snow Hill on time, but again it had been touch and go. We later learned that superheater tubes in the smokebox were leaking. 6000 did not in any case have a very good reputation for steaming and it was discovered at some point that the double blast pipes were slightly out of alignment.

Just before my time at Old Oak came to an end, I had one last trip up the GW Birmingham route behind 6022 *King Edward III*. This was a Stafford Road engine and we had a Wolverhampton crew who were on a punctuality bonus scheme. Unfortunately, although going well, we failed to pick up any water from the nearly empty troughs just south of Banbury and tried to take water during the Princes Risborough scheduled stop. The fireman climbed onto the tender to put the bag in the tank and I was sent to turn on the hydrant. Nothing came. I fiddled with the handle trying all positions in case I had got it wrong (everyone assumed you knew everything without instruction and as a young trainee, I was sometimes too embarrassed to admit my ignorance) so we abandoned the attempt and set off with great gusto to get time in hand as we would have to make a special stop at High Wycombe for water. Here I was again sent to operate the water column hydrant and managed somehow to get the handle off the valve seat so that it just revolved without connection. The driver saw the mess I was in, and immediately assumed I had made the same mistake at Princes Risborough, so I became the target of a few well aimed epithets as he saw his bonus disappearing. With the water column restored to action, we topped up as far as was necessary, and then set off for Paddington, the driver taking his frustration and pent up rage out on the locomotive. I have no idea what speed we reached - I just huddled in the fireman's corner and tried to will myself to disappear! We arrived seven minutes late and I made myself scarce.

One week during this time I heard a rumour about a high speed test to Wolverhampton and back. The 'Kings' were living on borrowed time and it was anticipated that there would be sufficient 'Western' diesels for the winter timetable on the Birmingham line. The Civil Engineer was a little nervous about the state of the track for sustained higher speed running and to be sure he wanted a test with the 'Whitewash Car' - the vehicle that would evaluate track condition at speed and let splashes of whitewash fall on track which did not come up to standard. We had two 'Castles' in store in the Paint Shop, 4098 and 7030, and I noticed activity around the latter and the rumours were confirmed when I was told 7030 *Cranbrook Castle* was being prepared for the test run - the diesel availability was not good enough to spare a 'Warship' for the special. I asked Ray Sims for permission to travel on the locomotive but he refused on the grounds that there would be an additional fireman and an Inspector in the cab. Someone overheard my request and suggested I just turn up at Paddington and ask the Civil Engineer in charge if I could travel in the train.

I did as suggested and was given permission surprisingly easily and made my way to the front BSK (Brake Second Corridor) in splendid isolation - the engineering party were all in the test vehicle and the rest of the train was empty. We left Paddington at 10.25, fifteen minutes behind the 'Blue Pullman', and with five minute stops booked at High Wycombe and Leamington to ensure the Pullman did not delay us, we were scheduled to reach Wolverhampton in just over two hours. However, in the event even this margin was insufficient and we caught the Pullman up in the Black Country, arriving in consequence a few minutes late. Highlights on the Down journey were 96 mph at Haddenham and acceleration to 70 at Warwick, with 66 mph approaching Hatton summit before braking for the curve at the top of the bank.

This was small beer compared with the return journey, which, after Leamington, became extremely lively. I made it 105 mph below Bicester, although I only claimed 103 mph subsequently when I tested my average speeds with maxima claimed, and after the High Wycombe stop, we again touched 103 at Denham and 97 at Greenford. The latter fireworks got both driver and Inspector into hot water as it was claimed that we would never have stopped had Old Oak West Junction signals been against us. Incidentally, I gathered from an engineering test point of view that the exercise was very limited in value as the riding south of Banbury on the return journey was so rough that the whitewash obliterated almost every mile of track as well as the rear windows of the test car, breaking the hearts of a number of p.way gangers in the process.

The following day, 16th May 1962, (my birthday) 7030 was on the 'Oxford Flyer' turn and I decided to use my footplate pass to see what high speed on 7030 was like. We got to Paddington in 56 minutes, with a top speed of 90 mph near Maidenhead, but the driver was dubious when I told him about the previous day's exploits. He was not disbelieving that 7030 could reach those speeds, but thought the driver and inspector foolhardy as the engine rolled quite pronouncedly at 90 mph. It was not rough but was enough for the 'Oxford Flyer' driver to ease off once that speed was reached. The best bit – sitting in the fireman's tip up seat on the left hand side, leaning out of the cab window as we roared through the middle road at Reading in the mid 80s, whistle howling – what a sight we must have made for the crowds waiting the next Up express!

On the whole, former Great Western engines rode extremely well, but I was quite keen to experience a really rough locomotive to see just how bad it could be for the crew. I had been on a Hall (4917) which rode like a bicycle with a flat tyre, but that was irritating rather than rough. One of Old Oak's older double chimney Castles, 5008, had been a star, but was getting run down as it neared its shopping date and as it was rostered to an evening commuter train I decided to go with it to Reading. The first alarm was when I leant against the cab side and found that it moved under my weight (a few days later 5008 was removed from a South Wales milk train because the crew complained of a dangerous cab - many rivets were found to be missing). Steam pressure on getting the right away was only 180lbs and the fireman was trying manfully to clean the fire. However, once under way, 5008 proved herself to be very strong, steam pressure recovered and good timekeeping was made. The engine was rough but not uncomfortably so. She rolled and pitched in a sort of corkscrew motion, but if you learned to move with it, it was quite predictable and rather fun.

However, I did at last find a real shocker - but it was not a GW engine. On one of my very long days I decided to do 'the triangle' - ie Paddington - Bristol - Shrewsbury via the North & West and back up the Birmingham mainline. I picked up the 7.55am Paddington at Reading to Newport, went over to Bristol on a DMU, and joined the 7.5am Penzance - Manchester with an ex works Hall to Pontypool Road. The special attraction was that this train was rostered for a Crewe 'Royal Scot' from Pontypool Road through to Manchester. Sure enough, at Pontypool Road, a grubby 46166 *London Rifle Brigade* was waiting, complete with Salop crew (ex LMS driver and GW fireman).

The first impression was the comfort and roominess of the cab after the Western engines, but this was soon undermined by its behaviour in motion. Although our running was 'gentle' to put it mildly, the locomotive riding was erratic and unpredictable and over 50 mph was decidedly rough. The schedule was very easy, the train on time and the load only moderate (9 coaches), so little exertion was called for and our maximum speed on the way to Shrewsbury was 66 mph at Tram Inn and 65 mph on the descent from Church Stretton at Dorrington. At these modest speeds, the riding became very uncomfortable with a jerky side 'waggle' that caused me to hang on and not relax my grip for fear of being thrown across the cab. The firing technique was very different to the GW engines - large lumps of coal were manhandled through the firehole door until the box was full, then rest was taken while it burned through, whereas Western engines almost invariably were fired little and often. 46166 was taken very easily up the banks - in fact the fireman confided in me that he thought his mate took it too easily - but we arrived in Shrewsbury on time without discovering what the 'Scot' could really do, if pushed.

At the other end of the spectrum for ride was a run up from Swansea on 5056 *Earl of Powis*, a couple of months out of Swindon after overhaul and in its prime. I'd joined the Cardiff crew on 7036 *Taunton Castle* on the 7.55 am Paddington from Reading, which ran very energetically and was early at every calling point. I'd prearranged with Driver Ward of Old Oak that I'd return with him on the 11.10 Milford Haven from Swansea - a double home job, as he would have gone down to Swansea the previous night with 5056 on the 6.55pm Paddington - Fishguard. Despite a load of 11 coaches, 420 tons gross, the return journey could not have been made to seem easier. The only alarm was the drop in steam pressure as we climbed through Landore and Llansamlet to the summit at Skewen, but on arrival at Neath Fireman Thomas found the smokebox door had not been sufficiently tightened and was drawing air, and after his attention we had no further problems. Arrival at Swindon was a full five minutes early and running in the upper 60s was sufficient to get us into Paddington equally ahead of time, with the locomotive running very quietly and riding like a Pullman coach.

As I made my way back to Twyford station house for the night we passed the next Up South Wales express (the 12.5pm Neyland) running equally early behind my favourite Castle, 4087, an engine I remembered from my extreme youth, and I found myself wishing I had waited a further hour in Swansea although this would have meant disappointing my Old Oak crew who seemed genuinely pleased to have someone on board who took an interest in their work. In fact, one of the lessons I learned during my footplate spell was the fact that management were often not aware of the attitudes and concerns of footplate staff as they so rarely saw them undertaking their normal duties. Drivers told me, all too often, that they only ever saw management when they were 'on the carpet' for some disciplinary misdemeanour. I remembered this when I became Chief Operating Manager of the LMR in 1982, and sought wherever possible to ride with train crews when I had to travel round the Region to get to meetings or conduct other business.

In fact, I was later censored for being too uncritical of my time at Old Oak by the senior management whose job it was to evaluate the reports I had to write after each period of training. I was, as a 'bright young thing', expected to produce reports full of criticism of the way things were done and come up with lots of new ideas and suggestions which the local management would be encouraged to implement or explain why not - a practice which did not endear Traffic Apprentices to many of the local managers. By this time, the Traffic Apprentices' mentor at Paddington, Assistant General Manager, George Bowles (an avuncular figure reputed to be a scoutmaster, who actually encouraged trainees to be interested in railways) had been replaced by the Stanley Raymond/Lance Ibbotson era to 'de-great westernise' the Region and bring about a more appropriate management culture.

At the end of this particular period of my training I'm sure my supervisory managers felt that I had been the 'enthusiast' rather than management trainee and had spent too much of my time at Old Oak sampling obsolete steam trains rather than the new traction. (But it was management that sent me to an 'all steam' depot, with little diesel work.) In due course, though, I had plenty of opportunity living with new traction as it flooded the Western Region over the next couple of years. In retrospect, because of my intense interest in all that was going on, I realised just how much I had picked up of value that stayed with me throughout my working life. Supremely, the lesson was one of sensitivity to people, their interests and concerns, and a respect for the knowledge and experience of many who would not count themselves as managers but whose opinions and views were well worth the effort of canvassing through both formal and informal contacts. I look back at my training in the old London Division of BR's Western Region with great affection and gratitude to the managers and men who gave me the opportunities, enabled me to develop my potential and allowed me to have a lot of fun in the process.

Chapter 4: 1962 - 1963
Training in South Wales

On the 4th June 1962 I caught the 7.55am from Paddington to Swansea to report to the District Operating Superintendent, Jack Brennan, on arrival at 12.30pm. The interview was eccentric to put it mildly. Having greeted me and told me gruffly that I was not to expect to be able to turn up at midday every Monday, he fell asleep in the middle of a question. I was completely thrown, did not know whether to wake him up, creep out or sit it out. He suddenly woke, shook himself and finished the question. I later found out that he had contracted 'sleeping sickness' in the jungle during the war and my experience was common - but no-one had thought to warn me!

I spent the next week at Margam Yard in the Hump Tower Control Panel in one of the most glorious June weeks ever - one night shift was so light that the sun had hardly disappeared before dawn was already breaking. There was an evening local back from Port Talbot station (we had to use a transit van for shuttles from the yard to the station) I caught that week obviously intended mainly for steelworkers from the Steel Company of Wales Port Talbot plant.

I risked Jack Brennan's wrath the following Monday as I was told that the following week would be the last rostered for steam before the Hymeks took over. In view of the weather the previous week I had brought beachwear, swimming trunks and summer shirts in my hand luggage and it poured with rain for the rest of the summer. I was in lodgings with a Mrs Beynon a good ten-minute walk along the main Walter Road towards Sketty and I got soaked so many times that by week three I had invested in my first umbrella. The digs were again bed and breakfast only and a fellow trainee and I ventured out most evenings, as we had no wish to be regaled by Mrs Beynon's extreme right wing views. She opined that Winston Churchill was a 'pinky' (my colleague was a young Conservative and was tempted to argue) but I made the mistake of admitting voting Liberal, which was totally off her political spectrum, and I needed to make myself scarce! On the few dry evenings John and I would go down to a little pitch and putt golf course between the Mumbles Road and the Swansea Victoria

Central Wales line dividing the course from Swansea Bay, but most other evenings we made our way to High Street station and caught the 1.55 or 3.55 Paddington on its West Wales leg and diverted to a Carmarthen pub for a pint, although the locals often reverted to the Welsh language when they saw two foreigners coming. The comparison between Swansea and Cardiff was strange - the enmity between the two cities was palpable, the Welsh of Swansea seemed to have a feeling of inferiority and I was constantly asked if I didn't prefer Swansea to Cardiff. The latter was much more cosmopolitan and easy-going; it least in 1962 it was. Not sure about now.

One day, as part of my authorised training, I explored the colliery workings fanning out from Margam up the Llynfi Valley to Cwmdu colliery in the brakevan behind a train of unfitted mineral wagons hauled by a Churchward 2-8-0T. Our load of 39 mineral wagons was reduced to 25 at Duffryn Yard as no banker was available and we held a minimum of 17 mph up the 1 in 41 to Bryn Tunnel just short of Maesteg. We returned to Margam with 19 loaded coal wagons, having taken four and a half hours for the 40 mile round trip excluding time at Cwmdu dropping off the empties and collecting our loaded train.

Shortly afterwards Jack Brennan decided that I'd better make myself useful and asked me to help his Assistant, Grant Woodruff, a former Traffic Apprentice himself, who'd been given the task of reducing the costs of running Margam Yard. Grant explained a number of concerns in the way that the yard was operating and asked me to trace the activities of a number of diesel shunters (08s) that ran trips around the area over 24 hours. I spent a week following their activities and coloured in the regular movements of each trip engine on an enlarged yard track diagram. It looked very pretty, a somewhat complex schematic that bore some relationship to Beck's London Underground diagrammatic map. I was assured by Grant that it was useful and that it had enabled rationalisation of the trip workings to be developed and a locomotive saved in consequence. I had a nagging feeling, however, that Margam was really in the wrong place. Later studies I undertook in 1968 after I'd become Divisional Train Planning Officer, confirmed my gut feeling. It was too far west - a modern marshalling yard in the Marshfield area between Cardiff and Newport could have avoided the need for Margam and replaced Severn Tunnel Junction. I was given to understand, however, that the decision to build Margam had been swayed by a generous contribution from the Steel Company of Wales Port Talbot plant which had 15 transfer sidings at Margam for the reception of coal and ore for their activities.

I had to go to London for a training interview with the new Assistant General Manager (Lance Ibbotson) and got a shock at his reaction to my answer to the first question he asked me: 'Had I visited the new diesel depot at Landore yet?' I'd only been in South Wales a couple of weeks and in any case Landore depot was just a sea of mud with nothing yet to see. I'd just about got the answer 'No' out when I received the biggest drubbing of my life with no opportunity to explain anything. In hindsight I reckon he'd read my Old Oak report and decided that it was time I took as much interest in the new traction as in the old and had decided to shake me up - he must have known there was nothing to see at Landore - indeed, there was no access as it was a dangerous building site. Having threatened to remove me from the training scheme unless I bucked my ideas up, I was dismissed. Duly chastened, I returned to South Wales on the 11.35am relief train as far as Bridgend - with steam.

I spent a few days with the District Train Crew Inspectors. One of their roles was to examine new drivers and I was invited to join a day's duty in passing out a Llanelli fireman. We were to start with a freight to Margam, before taking over a Manchester – Swansea express at Port Talbot. We found our loco in the roundhouse at Llanelli, a 1910 designed Churchward 2-8-0T, 4279, but lost our trainee who failed to show up. The Inspector decided to continue with me in tow instead, and we made our solid and somewhat pedestrian way, bunker first, to the Hump Reception Sidings with a heavy and unfitted load of coal. Since there was no need to test the trainee on the passenger train, we ran down to the Knuckle Yard and picked up 50 empty cattle trucks for Fishguard, which we would run back as far as Llanelli and complete our turn for the day.

Once the passenger train we'd intended to test the fireman on was clear of us, we followed her out and took the Swansea Avoiding Line for a direct run to our destination. As we got into our stride (the train was now fully braked) I relaxed and enjoyed the passing scenery as we got well into the 50s with the old engine bucketing along cheerfully and in good voice. I peered along the running plate and watched mesmerised as the front end of the plate above the cylinders seemed to be having a separate life to the rest of the engine. I stared and sure enough, the plate above the buffer beam was jigging rhythmically up and down as we also shook and rattled to a different tune. Perhaps I would not have enjoyed my outing so much if I had realised that the maintenance staff would later find a total fracture of the front end of the plate which was apparently only held in position by the two struts from the bottom of the smokebox door to the top of the bufferbeam!

Swansea evenings progressed through August, September and October as before. I was now based in the District Office itself and undertaking a variety of duties both in and outside the office, including some small projects. In December I was summoned before the District Manager to be told that he wished me to act as Stationmaster at Pontardawe in the Swansea Valley to cover a five week gap before a new man was appointed. This outpost was on the freight route between Swansea East Dock and Ystradgynlais and involved the management of one colliery and a pit props yard, and a parcels sub-depot to Swansea itself. The office was Dickensian and I had just five staff, three of whom were Welsh speaking and had no English. The only clerk had been withdrawn the previous week so I was the lone occupant of this antiquarian office, which had had 16 staff in the early part of the century. I was still finding out where everything was when I received my first two visitors who wanted to use the parcels service - I was acting as a sub-depot of Swansea High Street. The first was an elderly gentleman who wanted to send a tin trunk to Mexico. The second was a scruffy young man who wanted to send a rifle to Ireland. Help!!! The phone was red hot between me and the Swansea Parcels Office. I wonder now if someone was setting me up but they seemed genuine and after long consultations with the distant clerk, money was handed over and the items collected by the parcels van that afternoon.

I amused myself by joining the signalman to watch the pannier tank hauled freights passing in the station (a crossing loop on the single line) and accompanying our daily shunt to the pit prop sidings to place empties and remove the loaded wagons, usually with 6754. Very conscientiously I decided to stop the practice of having a raft of wagons for the pit-prop works 'up my sleeve' and only ordered what was required immediately trusting that it would be delivered. I was immediately on the end of a diatribe from the manager of the plant who threatened some very nasty things that would happen to me if the ordered wagons failed to turn up. I'm relieved to say that I was not let down and therefore saved a fleet of about 20 wagons in the circuit.

Over Christmas in 1962 and the beginning of January 1963 it snowed. All the Western Region Traffic Apprentices were pulled off their current placements and closeted for 4 weeks at the Work Study School near Royal Oak station, where they subjected the two lecturers, used to compliant recruits intending to become Work Study practitioners, to a verbal mauling - to such an extent that no future set of trainees was allowed to inflict their criticisms through attending such a course ever again. After four weeks of hell, the authorities despatched the trainees to test their skills in real activity on the ground, and I found myself with three others in a foot of snow stop-watching maintenance activities in Laira Diesel Depot. The shed was meant to be steam-free but every morning a dozen steam locos could be observed queuing at the ashpits and coaling plant, rescuing the service from the frozen and damaged diesels.

From March to September 1963, I was attached to the Cardiff Divisional Office in Marland House opposite Cardiff General station. With fellow Traffic Apprentice, John Crowe, I lodged at 14, Dispenser Street, by the River Taff, right opposite Cardiff Arms Park. It was only a 5 minute walk to the office and I missed the daily commute on the many days where I was doomed to 'sit next to Nellie' when we were given files to read or told to watch what the clerk was doing instead of a more active role.

Meanwhile I had a new task. I was charged with designing and introducing Control Graphs to the Cardiff Valley coal desks and I spent a happy month travelling in brakevans up the Newport and Cardiff Valleys to Tredegar, Caerphilly, Barry to Ebbw Vale and the Cardiff Valleys via Pontypridd. I also covered the main line between Alexandra Dock Junction and Llanwern on an iron ore train and freights between Margam, Cardiff, Newport and Hereford. I meticulously prepared the graphs - I suspect a lot of my trips up the valleys were strictly unnecessary - I could have designed them from maps - but I learned the geography that way and got to understand more about coal and steel freight flows which stood me in good stead some five years later. Jack Brennan had moved from Swansea to Cardiff by this time and it was he who had charged me with the task and had grumbled fairly good-naturedly at the time I was taking over the job - I suspect he knew what I was up to.

During this period I was summoned to my next training interview with Lance Ibbotson and everyone had told me to prepare myself well and get my story in first. So when his first question was, 'Well, what are you up to now?' I was away and rhapsodised over the control graphs and the intent behind them - to move to short term planning of the local variable coal and steel flows using the graphs and to give a graphic daily picture of operations for dissection and understanding the effects of a lot of the track rationalisation that had taken place. There were too many round trips of less than twenty miles taking half a day of engine and crew time and certainly that sort of productivity for the new class 37 English Electric diesels (the 1,750 hp Type 3s as they were known then) was just not acceptable. I was not to know that I had struck gold. Ibbotson had come from the North East and before the interview was over he was arranging for me to spend a week in Middlesbrough and the surrounding area observing the North Eastern controllers using such graphs as they'd been doing for years. Ibbotson was an enthusiast for this process and my stock had now dramatically altered. Ibbotson was almost bubbling with enthusiasm at the interview and I was despatched back to South Wales glowing with relief and under orders to pack my bags and get myself to Middlesbrough the following Monday.

I spent a useful couple of days in two Control offices in the area watching the graphing of trains on the prepared scrolls as signalmen reported passing trips in the Durham coalfield and the North East docks, then a day watching train planners receiving coal production forecasts and using the 'pin and string' method of planning options on the graphs and finalising when all the Coal Board forecasts were in. The next day's train service was then sent out to depots with the crew and engine diagrams that had been optimised by the short term planning procedures. I resolved to spend the next day watching over controllers' shoulders to see how realistic the planning had been and the final day enjoying myself watching some of the trains in reality.

Early that Friday afternoon I was standing on a station with a four track layout – I can't remember where exactly now – when I heard the sound of the exhaust of a steam locomotive working very hard. Eventually clouds of steam and smoke appeared on the horizon and the exhaust now sounded like machine gun fire. The dot on the horizon gained ground rapidly and an ancient old NE Q6 0-8-0 pounded past me doing at least 50 mph with a full load of empty mineral wagons clattering crazily behind. I watched with some amazement – I'd never seen such rapidity in any South Wales freight activity – and on enquiry back in the Divisional Office before making my departure, I was advised that the crew would be on their freight bonus scheme and in addition, once the allotted pre-planned programme of work had been completed, the crew would be booked off with no hanging around at the depot to see if Control had found other work.

I reported back to Jack Brennan with some enthusiasm and advocated a similar short term planning methodology. He authorised the printing of the graphs and set up consultation arrangements with the Cardiff Divisional Office LDC to introduce the system. Surprisingly I was not invited to be present and I have no idea what went on, only that the project was shelved and never implemented. I was never told the reason for this –was it another case of the 'not invented here syndrome' that I found more than once on the old BR network? I got my revenge a few years later. Perhaps revenge is the wrong word. But I did use the Western Valley control graph in anger to some effect as I'll describe in a later chapter, I did become boss of the Cardiff Control in 1967 and I did introduce short term planning methodology for the South Wales coal working in conjunction with John Hodge and T.C.Baynton-Hughes' 'Blocplan' in the same year although not with 'pin and string'.

As the summer approached I was summoned by Bob Hilton, the Divisional Manager, and told that he wanted me to spend a couple of months as Assistant Terminal Manager at Fishguard Harbour during the peak tourist season. The 'St David', on the Fishguard – Rosslare route, had been refitted as a 'Roll-on/Roll-off' ferry and he gave me the job of designing the optimum layout for car and lorry parking to assess the maximum capacity and produce drawings for the staff involved in loading the ferry. This involved an overnight crossing to Rosslare on the St David during a force 8 gale and a meeting in a drab hotel in Wexford, but my work – conducted with some nervousness – must have passed muster for I was never called to account for any subsequent ferry capacity problems in operation. The rest of the time I spent helping the

Terminal and Harbourmaster with odd jobs – calling the vet to examine cattle after a rough crossing from Rosslare was one such task, to ensure that the cattle were fit enough to proceed to Smithfield Market. Often the vet would require the cattle to be given a 24 hour rest before further movement and I would need to liaise with Cardiff Control to change the train arrangements.

I took my first accident inquiry during this turn of duty when we had a crane slippage and dropped a load when the gears slipped. I'm afraid I didn't do very well and my report was inconclusive. I was faced with conflicting evidence between the crane operator and the maintenance staff and I was too inexperienced at that time - too gullible as well perhaps – to be able to make a judgement on the versions of what I was being told. It was made pretty clear to me that the crane driver was known to be a bit 'slap-happy', and therefore I was expected to find him the guilty party so he could be disciplined – clearly the desire of other management staff there, but I could not bring myself to find in that way as I'd been unable to uncover any evidence that would justify such a conclusion.

In other ways the assignment was a pleasure. Fishguard in summer was a delight, I went walking along the coastline, I had excellent lodgings, and took an occasional trip back to the main rail network at Clarbeston Road via the local connecting train of two coaches always hauled by the same pannier tank engine – the local 'Thomas'. I returned to the Cardiff Office for a last month or so and can't have upset too many people in the process for it was back to South Wales that I went at the end of my training with the full support of Bob Hilton and his team.

Two pannier tanks pass Pontardawe station with a raft of coal from Ystradgynlais to Swansea Docks, December 1962

Western Valley Control Graph

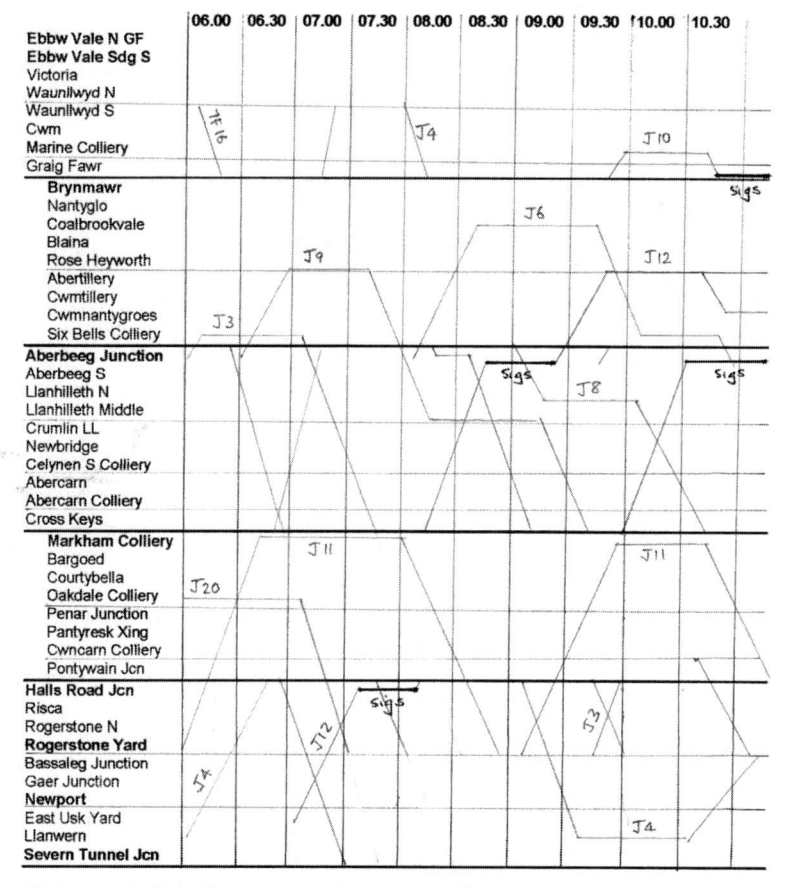

	06.00	06.30	07.00	07.30	08.00	08.30	09.00	09.30	10.00	10.30
Ebbw Vale N GF										
Ebbw Vale Sdg S										
Victoria										
Waunllwyd N										
Waunllwyd S										
Cwm	J16				J4				J10	
Marine Colliery										
Graig Fawr										
Brynmawr										Sigs
Nantyglo							J6			
Coalbrookvale										
Blaina										
Rose Heyworth				J9					J12	
Abertillery										
Cwmtillery										
Cwmnantygroes	J3									
Six Bells Colliery										
Aberbeeg Junction										
Aberbeeg S							Sigs	J8		Sigs
Llanhilleth N										
Llanhilleth Middle										
Crumlin LL										
Newbridge										
Celynen S Colliery										
Abercarn										
Abercarn Colliery										
Cross Keys										
Markham Colliery				J11					J11	
Bargoed										
Courtybella	J20									
Oakdale Colliery										
Penar Junction										
Pantyresk Xing										
Cwncarn Colliery										
Pontywain Jcn										
Halls Road Jcn										
Risca					Sigs					
Rogerstone N			J12					J3		
Rogerstone Yard										
Bassaleg Junction										
Gaer Junction	J4									
Newport										
East Usk Yard										J4
Llanwern										
Severn Tunnel Jcn										

This is a sample Control Graph compiled from memory of the graphs the author designed in May 1963 and used to highlight the delays caused by the revised layout at Aberbeeg Junction in May 1964.

The design of the proposed Control Graph for the Western Valley (used later during the author's time at Aberbeeg – see chapter 6). The planned freight service would be printed and the actual running graphed as it happened, with additional unscheduled services weaved between, using the graph as a short term planning tool.

Chapter 5: 1963 - 1964
Headquarters and Plymouth Division

During the previous eighteen months, our team of Traffic Apprentices had been spread over the four Divisions of the Western Region. For four months from the beginning of October 1963 we were gathered together at Paddington for the Headquarters element of our training. This was a convivial time and friendships were built from being together, but it was a bit of a headache for those planning our programme for we were all due to spend days in each section and we had to be rostered to avoid each other – although this meant some long suffering clerical sections received and had to occupy six young and demanding trainees in quick succession. Inevitably this led to even more prolonged and boring 'sitting next to Nellie' sessions – we may even have found a genuine 'Nellie' in this process!

A programme of weekend courses together in Cumberland Lodge in Windsor Great Park was also initiated when all three year groups were brought together to be indoctrinated by the Region's and Board's senior managers in the different functions – Marketing, Operations, Finance and Personnel in particular. Most memorable were the meals because this was also the training place for chefs and waiters for British Transport hotels. So we were the guinea pigs for meals to be delivered to American tourists and City businessmen staying at the likes of the Gleneagles Hotel in Perthshire. By day two we were leaving out courses, by day three some trainees were even opting out of whole meals, such was the rich fare to which we were totally unaccustomed. We were the bane of the French Chef's life who was responsible for the quality food produced by his charges and who took our abstinence from some of his delicacies to be a reflection on his standards. The other memorable activity took place in the gardens of the lodge where several of us were rash enough to play croquet with some of the visiting senior officers who came to lecture to us. Knocking Lance Ibbotson's 'balls' all over the lawn was greatly satisfying, but hardly a wise political move on our part!

One of my fellow trainees was Stan Judd with whom I was particularly friendly and we met frequently during lunch breaks or after work. Sometimes we managed to meet together to confer about some particular aspect of our training and on one occasion we had both been left to our devices in the file archives of Paddington (Nellie's grandmother?). I cannot remember if we were looking for anything in particular among the ceiling height shelves in the dimly lit office, but Stan pulled a sheaf of papers out and started an avalanche of loose files onto the floor. We both bent to gather the papers up and read a few headlines to try to get them back in some semblance of order, when Stan suddenly exclaimed and pulled out a couple of sheets of yellowing paper on which I could see copperplate handwriting. Further scrutiny gave us a real surprise and thrill, for we found that it was a memorandum to the Great Western Board signed by Sir Daniel Gooch, no less, dated 1866, proposing to take marketing advantage of the Paris Exhibition of 1870, by tapping the transatlantic trade from the USA route via Fishguard and taking the tourists to Milford Haven for embarkation for France, thus earning a small fee for every passenger so transported! The costs were to be part paid for by developing the wine trade from the south of France via Brittany, to be charged 1d a bottle 'to encourage the consumption of French wine by the British public'! I suspect nothing came of the proposal for I've not seen this idea floated anywhere else, but Stan took this to the archivist as it was of obvious historical value, not least in having Gooch's signature. I've no idea where this document is today – I would hope that it belongs to the NRM's collection of papers.

One personal memory from this time occurred when I spent a day in the locomotive record department where index cards held details such as mileages, heavy repairs, boiler changes etc., and building dates, costs and withdrawal dates. This was presumably where a lot of the data I collected at Old Oak Common in 1957 ended up and I began to browse through the files looking for engines whose details I might have provided. In the process I looked at the records of one or two 'favourites' and got a bit of a shock. Many enthusiasts develop an irrational affection for a particular machine, usually because of some personal reminiscence, and I was no different. Back in 1944 I remembered travelling from Bristol to London with my parents and the engine that pulled us had always stuck in my mind and when, as a trainspotter, I'd bought my first Ian Allan ABC, the only number to be underlined was 4087 *Cardigan Castle* .

I'd followed the career of this locomotive with interest ever since and saw it several times during my footplate training though attempts to ride it then had always been thwarted. During the first few months during my Cardiff Division training, it had been transferred from Laira depot in Plymouth to St Philip's Marsh in Bristol to cover a diesel availability shortage on the North & West between Bristol and Shrewsbury and it had appeared to be in excellent condition, with 4 row superheater and double chimney despite the fact that it was one of the oldest Castles built in 1925. I had expected it therefore to be one of the last survivors of the class and looked up its index card only to find with a sinking feeling that it had actually been condemned that very month. I can only assume that it had suffered some mechanical fault whose repair was not considered cost effective.

I suppose I had the same reaction as someone returning to the house they'd lived in during their childhood and found it demolished. The engine had certainly earned its keep running some 1.8 million miles in service having cost the GWR £4,000 when new in 1925. In the late 1950s I'd asked Swindon Works if I could purchase its name or number plate when withdrawn and they'd offered to reserve them for me for the price of £15 + carriage for the nameplate or £7.10/- for the brass numberplate. I had to turn down the offer as the price for even the numberplate was two weeks' wages. I had the chagrin of seeing 4087's nameplate go for £20,000 at a railway memorabilia auction a couple of years ago!

In December 1963 I was advised that the last few months of my training would, as expected, consist of filling supernumerary posts and that for this I was to be allocated to the Plymouth Division. I found myself once more in Plymouth itself in January when the mild weather contrasted greatly with the snowy spell I'd experienced at Laira the previous winter. Four weeks as Assistant Stationmaster at Plymouth North Road involved mainly trying to sort out some problems concerning the punctuality – or lack of it – of parcels trains in Cornwall and I was then sent as Assistant Yard Manager to Taunton, where frankly there was scarcely enough to occupy the Yardmaster let alone an assistant. I did spend some time learning from the new young manager of the just opened Coal Concentration Depot and even more time just trying to get warm for it was a raw freezing February and my lodgings had no heating in my bedroom. I tried going to the cinema during the evenings and found the only cinema in Taunton was showing a Western, a film genre that has never interested me. The second week, the same film had been retained 'by public request'! I was so cold I actually went to bed at 6 o'clock one evening as that was the only warmth I could find, then I started train excursions to Temple Meads or Barnstaple in the evening after eating out, to enjoy steam heating on the trains.

My next port of call in March was a total waste of time as being Assistant Goods Agent at Exeter St David's was a non-runner as far as local trade unions and management were concerned. The local management seemed scared to upset Chester Long, the Sectional Council Trade Union official who was a power in the NUR and came from Exeter Goods though he was rarely found at work there, being on trade union duties most of the time. Traffic Apprentices were anathema to the trade union officials there – perhaps there had been some insensitivity in the past by one of my predecessors – but the upshot was that no Traffic Apprentice was allowed to even put a foot onto the goods deck where all the activity took place. As a result I merely acted as a sort of relief clerk in the office - not the role that was intended for a trainee in those final months at all. I should have made a fuss – but I was too weak, just like the local management, I suppose. Whether the Divisional management team in Plymouth was aware of this situation and condoned it, I have no idea.

Which brings me to the final part of my training, an opportunity to act as a stationmaster in my own right, a chance to put into practice what I'd learned before moving on to a first permanent and established position, far away where one's mistakes in this last temporary appointment were not apparent to all. Firstly I had to satisfy the District Chief Signalling Inspector that I was sufficiently conversant with the Rule Book. My 90 minute investigation was not as searching as I'd feared for the Inspector talked more than I did and I was surprised later when talking to the District Manager to be congratulated on my performance in my rules examination. It was in late March 1964 therefore that I was due to finish my training with a spell as an acting relief stationmaster and I was appointed for six weeks to Gillingham station in Dorset. Having spent three years seeing modernisation at first hand throughout the

W.R. - traction, signalling, depots, marshalling yards and management methodology - I found in Gillingham that I was in a time warp untouched by the modern world. I spent the months of March and April 1964 there, with control also of Semley - and on arrival I was rung by the Plymouth Divisional office to ask me to assume command of Tisbury and Dinton as well, as the relief stationmaster there was wanted somewhere more important urgently. I shared 'on call' with the neighbouring stationmaster at Templecombe.

The Salisbury – Exeter main line had been transferred to the Western Region in January 1964, but I have to say that nothing had yet changed from SR days during my sojourn there – indeed, I don't believe anything had changed for twenty years or more! Perhaps this is not quite true, as a few 'Standard 4' 4-6-0s had infiltrated the Yeovil – Salisbury locals although the majority of trains serving my stations were three coach locals hauled by the inevitable Exmouth Junction unrebuilt 'West Country' or 'Battle of Britain' pacifics - somewhat excessive and costly power for the job in hand. I don't believe anything else had changed apart from the heading on the notepaper.

My main problem was that I had no transport (no stationmasters were allocated cars in those days) and as there was no road parallel to the old Southern mainline between my stations, there was no public transport other than the Salisbury - Exeter or Yeovil stopping services running at approximately two hourly intervals. As my duties involved supervision of staff at all four locations and the visiting of signalboxes and crossing keepers in my stretch of line, I spent a fair amount of my time travelling on a local to one station and walking through the spring flower bedecked cuttings and embankments to my next port of call. And it really was a gorgeous spring. The primroses were enormous!

There were other antiquated practices. The only way I could pay the crossing keepers on the main line was to clamber on the engine of the local pick-up goods (yet another Bulleid pacific) and hang out of the cab delivering the pay packets as if exchanging a single line token! The practice elsewhere of obtaining signatures did not apparently apply here.

The main event of the day at Gillingham was the stopping of an early morning express around 8.30 (it must have been the 7.30 Exeter) to take our commuters to Salisbury or even London. The train was heavily loaded - I recollect 13 coaches but my memory may be exaggerating - and was always hauled by a 'Merchant Navy' and for some reason I never fathomed in my six week sojourn, always pulled up twice as it hung way out of the short station platform. This was quite a rigmarole with a Bulleid, especially when it tried to pull away the second time as the engine was now over the dip and on the 1 in 80 climb to Semley, and what a palaver our light-footed pacific used to make of this manoeuvre, slipping and sliding, scattering cinders into adjoining cottage gardens and blackening the washing hanging on the line. The role of the stationmaster was to act as station announcer in charge of a battery operated loudhailer - although all the regulars must have known 'Salisbury, Andover, Basingstoke, Woking and Waterloo' off by heart.

The return evening service was the 6pm Waterloo although by the time of its arrival I was off duty enjoying a hearty meal at my lodgings overlooking the station. One evening, however, I was called out to Templecombe. I was nervous - this was my first 'emergency' - and on arrival at the joint station my confidence was not boosted by the discovery that the Somerset & Dorset signalling system was a total mystery to me. However, the problem was on the LSWR mainline - the 6pm Waterloo had disappeared in section between Gillingham and Templecombe and the last connecting trains for Bath and Bournemouth were waiting impatiently with their meagre passengers, both 'Standard 4' 2-6-4 tanks blowing off steam furiously. The express was an hour overdue by now, and we were just about to set off on foot to see if it had met with an accident in Buckhorn Weston tunnel, when the problem resolved itself and the train appeared on the horizon. The locomotive (unusually an unrebuilt 'Battle of Britain' rather than a 'Merchant Navy') had slipped itself to a standstill on the approach to the tunnel and had taken coaxing by the fireman hand-feeding the rails with sand to get it going again.

For me, the operation which epitomised the rural culture of the line was the late afternoon school train from Gillingham to Salisbury. We had a Grammar School in the town which served children from a wide area and every school weekday, the empty stock - four coaches - would arrive behind a tender first 'Standard 4' 2-6-0 from Salisbury depot, run round on the down side of the station yard and draw back into the up platform. The train would fill up with exuberant children - boys in the first two coaches and girls into the rear two, and the corridor gangway between them was locked (we were spoil sports in those days!). At Semley we gravitated(!) a loaded milk tank from the dairy private siding onto the back of the train for its connection at Salisbury to the main West of England – Clapham milk train. We never had an incident as far as I'm aware in the gravitational movement but I wouldn't like to propose such an operational ploy to the appropriate Health and Safety authorities these days!

At each station en route the station time varied from 6 to 15 minutes to enable the lone porter and train guard to load mountains of watercress punnets, no 'Brutes' or pallets here. The cress was grown locally in disused wartime underground storage bunkers. I often travelled on the train to assist, because at the peak times we could lose time even on this schedule. We would finish soaked through with sweat and water from the produce. All this activity was carried out under the bantering gaze of the schoolkids hanging out of the windows and cheering on the porter and guard as they flung the sodden punnets into the brakevan. You won't be surprised to learn that the train took its allowed 79 minutes to do the 22 miles to Salisbury (average 16 mph) – was this the slowest scheduled train on BR at the time? It was certainly an opportunity for the children to do their homework, but I never noticed any such activity on my patch.

The milk tank traffic got me into hot water during my brief stay at Gillingham. One of the porters told me that the Dairy was tarmacking an area round the loading point to allow the rail traffic to be replaced by a road tanker and during the first grand tour of his new domain by the WR General Manager (the affable but astute Gerry Fiennes) I mentioned this intelligence to him. He clearly took action because a couple of days later I received an anonymous phone call from someone - presumably in the Plymouth Divisional Marketing office - threatening my future career if I corroborated my statement to the GM. Clearly someone had been taken to task for not discovering this themselves. This was the only time in my railway career that I received such pressure and I am glad to say I stuck to my guns. In fact, we lost the milk traffic to road shortly afterwards.

Despite seeming to be from another age, there were aspects of the operation that were totally admirable. I remember the reliability with which the Brighton - Plymouth and Plymouth - Brighton through services used to pass each other at speed through Gillingham station with a regularity that was uncanny. I remember the sheer excitement of the down 'Atlantic Coast Express' thundering through our little station, whistle howling, at the foot of Semley bank hitting the dip under the road bridge where the gradient changed abruptly, and seeing the pacific appear to bounce several times vertically in reaction. My most vivid memory is of its extreme speed on one occasion - I was so startled that I assessed its speed by the rail joint noise as its train passed over and got a reading of around 96 mph!

At the end of April my three year training scheme came to an end six months prematurely and I was told to report to the Divisional Manager at Cardiff for appointment to a permanent job. However, a couple of months later, I had another encounter with Gerry Fiennes. It was customary for Traffic Apprentices to be interviewed by the General Manager at the end of their training, and although my session had been postponed, I found myself and my fellow trainee, Stan Judd, summoned to Paddington in June. My interview was at midday with Stan to follow half an hour later. When I was sent into the sanctum, I was greeted by the General Manager with the words, 'Do you like cricket?' When I affirmed this, Gerry Fiennes said, 'Oh, good!' and took a transistor radio from his top drawer and we listened to the Lords Test Match for twenty minutes. In between overs he plied me with very acute questions, then we were interrupted by a newcomer, introduced to me as his sister-in-law back from a Harrods shopping spree. After a ten minute pleasant three way conversation she left and he admitted that he was terrified of women like her who sat on school governing boards and ran half a dozen charities! We then checked the lunchtime score before Gerry Fiennes realised he had another interview to conduct and I was ushered out to allow poor Stan to enter who must have wondered what on earth was going on.

There is a postscript to this period of my career. In the summer of 2009, I saw an advertisement in the railway press about a proposed celebration of the 150th anniversary of the opening of the railway at Gillingham. I got in touch with the organiser and found myself invited, as a former railwayman employed there, to partake in a march from the town centre to the station along with the town band and other dignitaries. On arrival at the station, I was asked, with the mayor, to unveil the blue plaque on the station building commemorating the digging of the first sod with a silver shovel that still exists. After the ceremony I was introduced to a middle-aged lady, whom I'd known 45 years previously. She was then the very shy granddaughter of the couple with whom I lodged and I'd developed a rapport with the auburn haired four year old involving surreptitious hide and seek games to reading her bedtime story. Afterwards I had a stall for the charity Railway Children in the old goods yard alongside the other stalls and displays by the local townsfolk and their children. I recognised the pathway from my digs to the station and the station building and signalbox were familiar, but everything else had changed - in particular the 159 series diesel units bore little resemblance to the thundering restaurant car expresses and the wastefully overpowered stopping services of yesteryear.

The author's favourite railway engine, 4087 *Cardigan Castle*, in store at Plymouth Laira during the harsh winter of 1963, just before its 'swan song' on the North & West main line working from Bristol St Philip's Marsh, February 1963.

> ON
> APRIL 3rd 1856
> NEAR THIS SPOT
> THE HON MISS SEYMOUR
> DUG THE FIRST TURF FOR
> **THE SALISBURY**
> AND
> **YEOVIL RAILWAY**
> WHICH OPENED ON
> MAY 2nd 1859

The blue plaque, which I helped unveil on Gillingham station in May 2009.

45 years on - my Gillingham landlady's four year old granddaughter in May 2009

Chapter 6: 1964 - 1965
Stationmaster, Aberbeeg

After completing the BR management training scheme in April 1964, my colleague, Stan Judd, and I appeared before the Cardiff Divisional Manager, Bob Hilton, who informed us that he intended to appoint us to two stations in the Western Valley pending the replacement of the yard managers, shedmasters and stationmasters by a Western Valley Area Manager some ten months hence. I'm not sure whether he really wanted two young ex trainees, but he was obliged to place us somewhere. The two vacancies, which for some months had been covered by relief stationmasters, were at Ebbw Vale and Aberbeeg. Bob Hilton drew a half crown from his pocket, tossed it, Stan called correctly and chose Ebbw Vale because he'd heard of it. I became Stationmaster Aberbeeg, the 'Operating' job, by default. This choice coloured the rest of my BR career, leading ultimately to four years as Chief Operating Manager of the London Midland Region in the mid '80s and my last years before retirement as Head of Safety Policy for BR and Railtrack.

We were sent, the two of us, to have a look round Aberbeeg and Ebbw Vale and search for lodgings. We found a public house right opposite Aberbeeg station, the Hanbury Arms, abutting the Webb Brewery in the V junction of the valley overlooking the small yard, junction signalbox and station and enquired within, thinking that we could stay temporarily and we might get some advice about something more permanent later. Of course, we stuck out like a sore thumb – two strangers, not one. 'Londoners from their accents. They said they work on the railways. They asked for lodgings so they're staying in the valley. Ask Islwyn, he'll know.'

Islwyn, the 60 year old relief stationmaster, who'd been covering the vacancy at Aberbeeg for eighteen months or so, didn't know. The office hadn't told him, so our arrival was a shock, an incomprehensible shock. He thought he'd be there until he retired. He didn't believe us. Stan went to Ebbw Vale to break the news there before the valley drums beat out the message but in vain. The relief stationmaster there found it incredible too. They reacted in disbelief. The two clerks at Aberbeeg station swore that no-one had advised them and opined that it must be a mistake, we'd come to the wrong place. I sat and listened, while they rang the Personnel Office in Cardiff and asked where these two young men should be. 'It's madness!' they said. 'What can you know about running a station in a place like this. You're just a boy.' They went on and on about the stupidity of the office and told me how difficult the job was, how could I be expected to cope. 'Oh, it's not your fault, how were you to know the set-up here.'

Stan came back and we decided to go back to Cardiff and get our things from our lodgings there and we called in the Personnel Office to explain our predicament. The Chief Clerk was horrified. 'You went and introduced yourselves? We told you just to go and familiarise yourselves with the area. We hadn't advised the staff there yet.' What had they expected us to do? Surely they should have guessed that two young men 'familiarising' themselves with the railway infrastructure there would raise questions? We'd not been told to lie low or keep our presence and purpose a secret. We both assumed that local staff would have at least been made aware that new stationmasters were arriving even if they didn't know which of us was to go to which station that morning.

The damage was done now and there was no further reason to stay away so we returned with our belongings the following morning and took the only unoccupied room which was in the front of the hotel overlooking the railway, having ascertained that there was little likelihood of other accommodation in the village. Although the stationmasters and clerical staff now accepted that we were there to stay, it did not stop them passing comments about our unsuitability and the grave injustice to the present incumbents until their depression spread to us and made us feel guilty. Then the next day, the relief man at Ebbw Vale whom Stan was replacing, had a heart attack and died. They didn't say we killed him, of course, but the implicit accusation hung in the air: 'It was the shock to the poor man, how could the Cardiff Office be so insensitive.' They never blamed us directly; it was always 'they' and 'them'. At the end of the week they had worn me down and I called into the Divisional Office and asked to see the Personnel Manager. I told him I could not take the job, the morale at the station was rock bottom because of my arrival and I didn't want to be part of it. I wanted to see Bob Hilton to explain. The guy took me aside and told me not to be so foolish. 'Go home for the weekend. Relax, travel back on Monday, don't rush back. You'll see it in a different light then.'

Thankfully I took his advice and rescued my career. Had I gone through with my intentions and confessed my reluctance to Bob Hilton, it would have been the end. I would never have worked in South Wales again and I'd have started my career with a huge 'black mark' that I'd have found very difficult to shake off. On Monday, after a rested weekend away from this stress, I returned to Aberbeeg and it did look different. I met some of the other staff in the yard and signalbox. They didn't immediately dismiss my appointment as crazy or catastrophic. In fact one of the signalmen confided to me in a whisper – when Islwyn was out of earshot – that I was most welcome and that perhaps I'd stir things up a bit, because it was needed.

Islwyn, after his initial apparent distress and patronising comments, decided that he had better help me and changed from one extreme to the other, so that whatever I tried to do, he was always at my elbow explaining to me, as if I were a child, how it should be done. He promised he'd remain to help me as long as I wished, but during the second week the staff office rang and asked me how much longer I needed his assistance and with my huge sigh of relief, he was reassigned to another post the following week. Islwyn lived in the neighbourhood – which was why he'd been so put out by my appointment – but once he'd accepted me, we became friends, although he took early retirement shortly afterwards.

Stan and I shared a huge room at the hotel. I asked Stan if he wanted to find somewhere in Ebbw Vale, but I think at that stage we both needed the companionship and support of the other, so we stayed put. In fact, there was so little to do of an evening – one of us was always 'on call' anyway, so we couldn't go far in the days of no mobiles or bleepers – that we spent hours after the evening meal in the hotel playing canasta or discussing the experiences of the day. We each had a half day off during the week, and covered one another for 'on call' purposes, so the one who was free would climb the local mountains and look over towards Abergavenny and the Sugar Loaf or down the valley to Crumlin Viaduct or Newport. Later, as it was already the beginning of summer, we found a local tennis court and joined the cricket club at Llanhilleth whose ground ran alongside the railway line, within loud hailing distance of Llanhilleth Middle signalbox. Sometimes we would walk the line together. I would take the 'Jones' bus to Ebbw Vale and we would walk the five miles back to Aberbeeg along the sleepers, calling off at various locations where Stan had staff at the steel company's sidings and colliery outlets. We were both good walkers but Stan outshone me and would often arrive back in Aberbeeg a hundred yards or so ahead of me as his rhythm seemed to match the distance between the wooden sleepers better than mine!

We got gradually used to the eccentric routine of the hotel. It was a barn of a place, the bar spit and sawdust and much to be avoided. There was only one other permanent occupant of the hotel, an elderly and clearly sick Irish gentleman – a former tipper truck driver with whom it was difficult to converse sensibly without getting involved in a political argument – inhabitants of Welsh lodging houses seemed to have extreme political opinions which they were wont to air and we were an obvious new audience. The hotel was owned by an 80 year old but the power was his 50 year old wife who ran the hotel with her rod of iron, countered only by one other soul, a woman on whom she depended, but the two of them always seemed to be in perpetual strife and each breakfast or dinner we would become the confidants of one or other woman regaling us in a fierce whisper about the iniquities of the other. Each night we entertained ourselves until late, listening to the night noises emanating from the railway opposite. Any attempt at sleep was abandoned until after midnight when the last raft of coal empties for the early morning trip to Marine Colliery was safely berthed in two portions in the little yard, until the clanging of buffers ceased and we were convinced they were not 'off the road' again!

The passenger service had been withdrawn a year or so previously and the track layout around Aberbeeg rationalised and the stations left to rot. My office was in the middle of the V shaped station between the branches to Ebbw Vale to the West and Abertillery and Brynmawr to the East. The office was dingy, lit by gas mantles, with two buckets strategically placed on the floor to catch the drips from the incessant rain through the leaky roof. The telephone was archaic, hung on the wall (until one evening a spectacular lightning strike surged through the power lines and it exploded into myriad fragments). Filing appeared to be by carbon copied memos speared onto a forbidding looking spike on the desk.

My pessimistic encounter with the office environment and systems was countered by the way I was welcomed by the seventy operating staff outside. Charlie Sargeant, Secretary of our LDC was a signalman in the Junction (Middle) Box, Jack Shepherd his burly mate and Relief Signalman Terry Parsons, the Trade Union organiser, were superb and shared their problems and ideas in a constructive and enthusiastic way. I was encouraged to instigate a number of changes to improve the working and their lot, a win/win situation, which bolstered my credibility with both the staff and the Divisional Office and I started to spend long periods tramping around my territory, getting lifts from our local pannier tanks and occasional new 1750 hp English Electric diesels (later class 37) which were infiltrating from their Newport Ebbw Junction home.

A number of factors helped me to get accepted, little things, but they impressed the locals and I was grateful for any help that chance gave me. All the local trips to collieries berthing empty wagons and clearing the loaded coal had 'target numbers' by which the trains were known by signalling, train crews and shunting staff. It was a silly thing, but about a week before we had arrived the Train Planning Office, for some reason best known to themselves, had changed all the target numbers from K + numeral to J, with the numbers changing without any link to the old number to make it easier for the staff to remember. I, of course, coming afresh, only learned the new target codes and thus was able to refer correctly to our trains before any of my staff had mastered them. This soon got me an undeserved reputation of understanding the workings better than they did.

A second and more significant event, which I in all ignorance drew great kudos from, occurred quite early. A few days after our arrival there had been some rationalisation of the layout at Aberbeeg Junction and the four tracks from Llanhilleth had been reduced to two, by the closure of the Up and Down Relief lines, leaving just the two main lines all the way from Llanhilleth, past the engine shed outlet to the junction itself at Aberbeeg station. This meant that no train could take the line to Ebbw Vale, the more heavily used line, until a train on the Abertillery and Brynmawr side had cleared well beyond Six Bells Colliery. We observed very quickly the trains now waiting at Aberbeeg Junction to get line clear and Jack Shepherd mentioned to me that if he had authority to change the clearing point on that side to a spot a couple of hundred yards or so clear of the junction, much delay to trains bound for Marine Colliery at Cwm, Waunllwyd Sidings and Ebbw Vale steel works would be avoided. I talked to him for a few minutes about the safety implications on which this very experienced signalman reassured me, went back to my office, handwrote (we had no type-writer) a 'special instruction' authorising a revised clearing point and took it to the signalbox and pinned it to the notice board there. Jack looked at me with eyebrows raised and said, 'You mean that, boss?' and I replied, 'Well, you assured me it was safe. It is, isn't it?' 'Well, yes, of course...' he said, so I left it there and word ran round the depot like wildfire that they had a boss not afraid to take decisions.

A few weeks later I got the only visit from any officer from the Divisional Office in my ten months there – Jack Brennan came. I received a call from Charlie Sargeant saying he'd had a visitor, hadn't a clue who he was, he looked like a farmer. He'd stared at the track diagram displayed in the box, read the notices, signed the Train Register with an indecipherable scrawl and was now coming my way. It was a dreadful evening, the clouds were low and the rain was pouring. Jack Brennan pushed the door of my office open, tripped over one bucket and dropped his matches with which he'd been lighting a cigarette into the other bucket that was catching the steady drips from the ceiling, swore, and settled himself opposite me to say he'd come to see how I was getting on. He never let on that he'd seen my special instruction – I can't believe that he didn't notice it. It was only in later years that I realised the authorisation of special instructions was the prerogative alone of the Regional Operating Manager – a task I had in later years when a sheaf of such instructions would be placed before me for signature by the Rules & Regulations Officer in Rail House at Crewe.

Whilst the revised rule at Aberbeeg Junction relieved the pressure a little, we were still bothered by the amount of delay being suffered by trains in the valley. Having little to do in the evenings, Stan and I called in all the signalbox registers from Crumlin to Ebbw Vale, I got the control graphs I'd designed for the Western Valley which were gathering dust on top of a cupboard in the Train Planning Office and we spent several evenings graphing the passage of trains over a three week period. Every signal stop was denoted by a red horizontal line indicating the number of minutes delay and our finished artwork laid across our hotel room floor was peppered with so much red that calculating the total amount of delay was almost superfluous. We took the finished graphs to Jack Brennan and unfurled them on his desk (see sample Western Valley control graph on page 54).

Three weeks later, on the 30th July 1964, there was an emergency blockade instituted, cranes and track specials arrived and the closed Down Relief became a loop from the Junction a train length to the south and the Up Relief (now renamed Up Loop) was restored from Llanhilleth to Aberbeeg Junction with trailing spring points open to the engine shed enabling the closure of Aberbeeg South signalbox to remain. This third line between Llanhilleth North and Aberbeeg Junction was ready for opening at 9 o'clock on the Monday morning. This was unprecedented and sealed Stan's and my reputation with our staff. We owed a lot to Jack Brennan for the speed with which he reacted was unprecedented too. I've a suspicion that – as well as eliminating a lot of costly delay – he realised how much this would boost our confidence and obtain the full support of all our staff.

My southern border started under the impressive Crumlin Viaduct and included the derelict station at Llanhilleth and the colliery, which were under the watchful eye of Charlie Corfield, my Inspector there. Charlie supervised the workings so efficiently that I soon learned to leave things in his capable hands. Llanhilleth station was a mess, the only resident being a large and vicious ram, which later was the inspiration for a 'Thomas the Tank Engine' video (our railway had permanent trespassing sheep - there was no point in stopping trains to warn of animals on the line). This ram appeared to have the old waiting room at the station as its residence and one day Charlie went in to shoo it away, when he slipped on loose floorboards disturbed by vandals, and being a large and heavy man, unfortunately fell through and broke a leg. This accident gave rise to a Court case for compensation, when BR's lawyers tried to argue, against my advice, that he shouldn't have entered the room, whilst I maintained he had a perfect right, and indeed duty, to protect our property from trespassers (and marauding animals). I don't think my evidence was very popular with our lawyer and I'm glad to say Charlie got his compensation.

Another personnel issue, which much exercised me, concerned my relief porter. He'd been rostered to Crumlin station on the morning shift and word reached me that he'd failed to show up. This was not unusual as the man had the reputation of having days off after a particularly heavy drinking session and when I asked to see him the following day, he turned up with a sick note from the local doctor dated the previous day. When I scrutinised it closely, I observed that in fact the note had been dated today, but it had been clumsily erased and the previous day's date inserted. He had obviously visited the surgery before coming to see me and I discovered that it was the practice of the local doctor to leave a pad of signed and dated blank sick notes with the receptionist for her to write in whatever the caller complained of – the number of miners and others reporting sick were too many to be all seen by the doctor, so he'd allowed this practice to grow up. When I challenged the man, at first he tried to lie his way out but finally in some confusion confessed, so I sent him home while I took advice from the Divisional Office on the action I should take. Someone from the Personnel Section phoned back a couple of hours later to say that the man had been sacked a couple of years earlier for theft and had somehow evaded discovery when he'd applied for a job again only a few months later.

I was instructed to sack the man a second time, which the individual seemed to accept stoically and I thought little more about it until that night somewhere about 3am there was a thunderous rapping at my bedroom door and as my eyes opened this man stood over me, his hair dishevelled, eyes wild and I thought my last hour had come. In fact, sanity returned when I discovered he'd only come to call me as we were off the road again in the yard opposite and my presence was required. I only started later to wonder why he had called me after he'd been sacked, and in the morning I discovered that he'd immediately sought employment as a part time handyman around the hotel. Goodness knows what sob story he'd told Mrs C, the hotel's 'mistress' and she never sought my input on why he'd lost his railway job.

The main activity centred around Aberbeeg Yard and Engine Shed. At that time there were still six working collieries in the area and the provision of empties to the colliery sidings was made by the Aberbeeg trip engines, by May 1964 predominantly Class 37s, although we still had two Churchward 2-8-0 tanks, 5214 and 5218, to cover our 8 o'clock 'anywhere' turn, used to mop up variations in coal production, and stand by for diesel failures. The loaded coal trains made their way down the valley to Rogerstone Yard, still under the iron grip of a Welsh Yardmaster who viewed our goings-on with considerable suspicion. Our engines and Aberbeeg men would return with empties from Rogerstone, or even East Usk if they managed to slip past the Rogerstone border controls, and bring them up to our yard for breaking down into manageable loads on the fierce gradients to Marine or Six Bells Collieries.

We had a fleet of pannier tanks - the preserved 9682 was one of them - and three 94XX (9493-5) for banking the heavy coal and ore trains up the five miles to Ebbw Vale steel works, and for shunting the yard between turns. One of my first managerial actions was to replace our 350hp diesel shunter, which spent most of the day idling, by a steam banker awaiting its next turn, a move so obvious that the staff had no argument about the loss of a turn and the Divisional Office rejoiced because they'd been trying to persuade my predecessor to give it up for years. I was therefore uniquely congratulated in the post 'Stanley Raymond' era for replacing diesel with steam traction (for a few months anyway)!

Stan and I shared 'on call' duties for the Western Valley from Crumlin northwards in the days before mobile phones and bleepers which meant we were tied to the valley for a week at a time, one or other of us escaping alternate weekends on the 'Jones' bus (never the Western Welsh option) and the main line to London at Newport. Minor derailments were common - the 37s were a nasty shock to the local S&T lineman whose maintenance of signals and points had to cope with constant colliery subsidence. It was apparently very common for a steam engine to mount the guard rails at points and either drop back on again or be swiftly rerailed with ramps from the yard without bothering the Newport breakdown gang. The diesels had a habit of splitting the points and derailing a bogie and we only tried driving it back on with ramps once. The damage to the under bogie traction motors was not well received.

I had a propensity to invite call outs for some reason - indeed during our stay, Stan was only called out three times, while I had sixteen emergency calls. Within days of my arrival, a diesel and the Guinness tanks from the brewery were on their side fouling three of the four lines approaching Aberbeeg Junction (shades of

'Whisky Galore') and I had to open up single line working over a complex junction layout with red-padlocked points now out of use littering the remaining single line open. Charlie Sargeant saw me nervously looking at the mess and said 'Follow me, boss, stick this red armband on as pilotman, and do what I say'. We never looked back.

During one night of torrential rain, I was called out to an earth slip opposite Marine Colliery on the Ebbw Vale section. Not only the bank, but a large mature tree had slid down the cutting and was now residing in the middle of the line from Ebbw Vale behind which stood a large 2-8-2 tank, 7249, and a full load of 50 vanfits of steel tinplate. We opened up single line working and then had to get the tinplate train to reverse its load up the 1 in 73 gradient to the crossover at Marine Colliery about a mile to the rear. We were way over the load for a 72XX and there was no engine north of us to assist, so we had to try. I shall never forget the crashing and very deliberate exhaust and the rocking motion of the engine as it propelled its heavy train in slow motion without the trace of a slip through the stormy night.

Our constant 'emergencies' had their humorous side. Stan and I could occasionally venture out together provided our inspectors knew where we were and we were not too far from reach. Adjacent to Llanhilleth station was a little cricket ground and we had both joined the club and played an occasional match. I can remember vividly one sunny afternoon being at the crease and had just snicked my first runs through the slips when a thunderous voice came from the Llanhilleth Middle Box loudhailer 'Mr Maidment, you're needed, they're off the road at Ebbw Vale'. The scorecard read 'Maidment, derailed …4'. Turning up at Waunllwyd Sidings in cricket whites was apparently another first!

The Aberbeeg Shedmaster retired in the autumn of 1964 about two months before the depot was due to close when full dieselisation would be completed. As there was little point in filling the post for such a short time, I was asked to take over the reins there for this interim period and had one brief moment of glory when I managed to persuade the diagramming people in Cardiff to let our Aberbeeg men learn the road and go through to Gloucester with a Mondays Only tinplate train with one of our two 52XXs. I don't think the route learning costs amounted to anything - the men were so keen, I think they learned the road in their own time! So I vividly remember bowling down the valley in the cab of 5214 on our inaugural run and whistling rudely at Rogerstone Yard as we escaped into the big wide world outside the Valley. I baled out at Newport but rumour has it that some of the signalmen on the Newport - Gloucester line had never seen an old 52XX in such a hurry.

The 37s reigned almost supreme - an occasional Churchward 2-8-0 tank or BR Standard 9F would foray up to Ebbw Vale from Alexandra Dock to the end of our time there. Our trusted panniers were replaced by Paxman engined Class 14s, D95XX, we must have had some of the first, and they were totally unsuited for the terrain. Their attempts at banking heavy trains to Ebbw Vale were farcical. Around Marine Colliery, halfway up the 1 in 50, the engine would often overheat and trip out, and the class 37 train locomotive would be left to haul the dead D9501 or one of its sisters all the way to the top. I have to say this for the 37s - they were man enough to do this without falling down, so I began to wonder whether they really needed a banker.

One consequence of the switch from steam to diesel was the sudden shortage of coal at all the signalboxes on the patch. We had to start actually ordering domestic coal and the Aberbeeg Junction Box asked for a coal store as they could no longer replenish themselves from the bunkers of pannier tanks. I ordered a breeze block coal house from the District Engineer at Newport and got a quote of £465. I remember being horrified as there was a terraced miner's cottage in the road just below the box going for £325 and I offered to buy that instead. I don't think my irony was appreciated, but we did get our coalhouse.

Just before I completed my turn of duty at Aberbeeg - I was made redundant on the introduction of Area Management and was moved to Bridgend as Assistant Area Manager there - I was host with a member of the local press to witness the last steam turn from Aberbeeg depot. It was a Saturday lunchtime turn, a set of coal empties from Marine Colliey at Cwm, to be stabled in our yard. The pressman set up his tripod and 9494 duly appeared round the curve from the Ebbw Vale branch with its string of 16 ton mineral wagons. It had just reached the underbridge at the end of the platform when the pannier tank derailed all wheels and continued to run towards us hitting the paving slabs at the edge of the platform and throwing them like frisbees across the deserted station. The noise was incredible and I backed away quickly out of the line of fire, only to see the reporter haring out of the station. He never did get a photo! Miraculously all the wagons stayed on the line and we were faced with a pannier tank at the signal protecting the junction sitting upright in the fourfoot. Saturday at midday when Newport County was playing at home was not the best time to call out the Ebbw Junction breakdown crew, so our foreman got a set of ramps from the yard and with much creaking and splintering of wood, we drove 9494 back onto the rails. And the local press missed their story!

I often look back at the ten months spent at Aberbeeg as the time I learned most about human nature - not just in the railway activities, but also from the experiences in the Hanbury Arms, now no more. However, that would need a whole new book to describe… The Western Valley not only provided such valuable experience and a rich encounter with some marvellous and generous characters, but it shaped both Stan's and my railway careers for years to come, in that Stan became a 'Marketing Man' and I became an 'Operator'.

The collieries closed in the 1980s and the valley returned to the rural state that existed before the coal and steel industries arrived. It became a commuting area for people working in Newport and Cardiff and in 2008 the passenger service between Cardiff and Ebbw Vale was restored and Stan and I made a pilgrimage to see what remained. The Hanbury Hotel and Aberbeeg station were gone. But Aberbeeg Junction signalbox was still there, derelict amongst of forest of trees that had completely overrun the former marshalling yard.

Aberbeeg Junction signalbox, station and the Hanbury Hotel in 1964

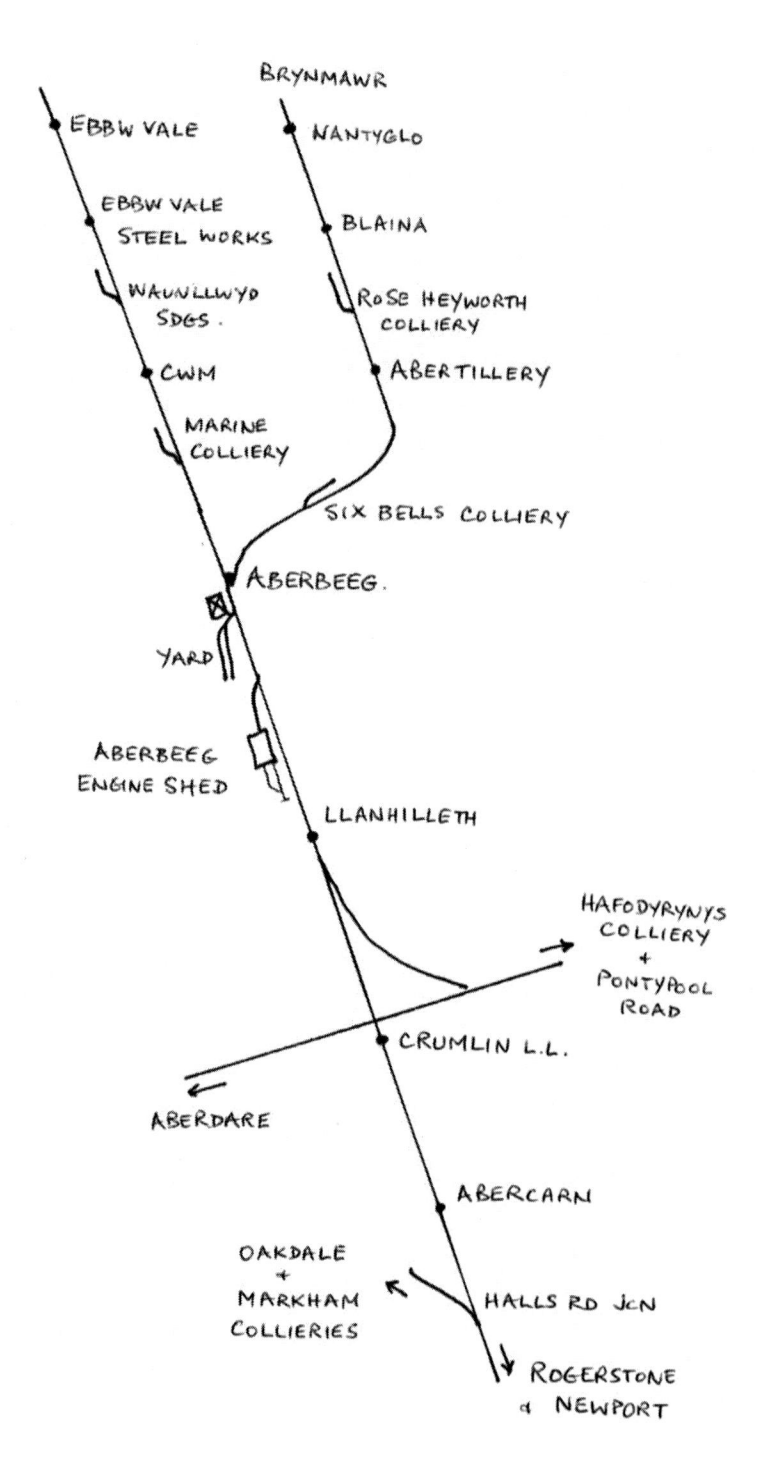

Western Valleys, 1964 – 1965.

The revised layout at Aberbeeg South implemented to reduce the delays to northbound trains – 30.7.64

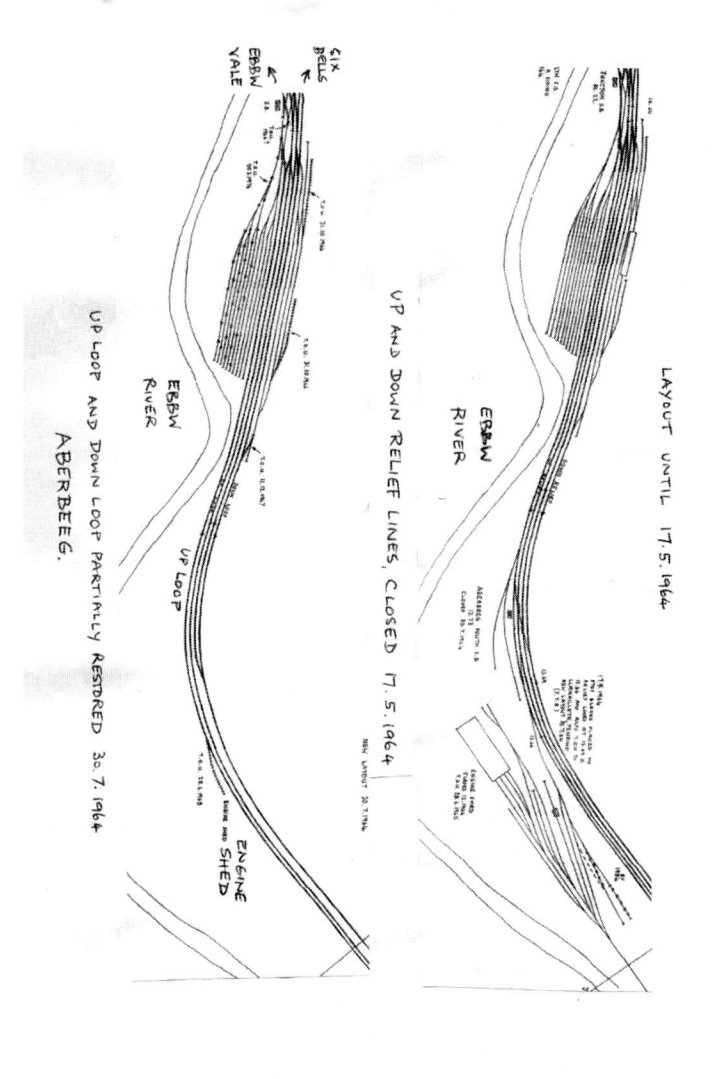

The track layout at Aberbeeg South, before and after our intervention

Llanhilleth station in 1956 while passenger trains still ran: photo
– Michael Hale/GW Trust

0-6-2T 6693 calls at Llanhilleth on an excursion from Aberbeeg to
Cardiff Ninian Park, 14.10.61: photo R E Toop

A Newport Ebbw Junction 42XX starts out from Aberbeeg with a load of iron ore for Waunllwyd Sidings at Ebbw Vale, June 1964

The mature tree that slid down onto the Aberbeeg – Ebbw Vale
line at Cwm , near Marine Colliery, Autumn 1964

Pannier tanks 8778 and 3647 shunting Aberbeeg Yard, c 1963: photo Colour Rail

Two of Aberbeeg's 94XX pannier tanks stand at Aberbeeg South Box awaiting trains to be banked to Ebbw Vale, 7.11.63: photo R O Tuck / Rail Archive Stephenson

Aberbeeg Yard from the Llanhilleth Road, circa 1964

An iron ore train from West Mendalgief to BSC Ebbw Vale with class 37 diesels fore and aft, shortly after replacing similarly positioned 9F 2-10-0s, 7.11.63: photo R O Tuck/ Rail Archive Stephenson

The culprit that derailed on the last day of Aberbeeg's steam shed, pannier tank 9494, on the 5.35pm Newport – Blaina on 7.11.63, just before closure of the Western Valley passenger services: photo R O Tuck / Rail Archive Stephenson

Aberbeeg Junction's derelict signalbox surrounded by trees, July 2010

The author and Stan Judd at the reopened Llanhilleth Halt, July 2010

Chapter 7: 1965 - 1967
Area Management, Bridgend

I arrived at Bridgend as Assistant Area Manager in the winter of 1965 and had to find lodgings. I was recommended a semi-detached house about half a mile from the station in North Street with a widow and her teenage son and installed myself, noting that my main heating (a key issue for me as a soul suffering acutely from the cold) was an old 'Valour' oil stove. There was also no sign of a telephone and as I would be 'on call' every other week I advised my landlady that I might get called out any time of day or night, which would mean being 'knocked up' by a taxi driver sent by the station inspector.

'That won't be often, will it?' opined my landlady hopefully, and I reassured her as best I could, remembering my reputation as a 'Jonah' at Aberbeeg – having been called out sixteen times in ten months compared with Stan's three times! Sure enough, I was called out every evening or night that first week to some minor derailment. I discovered later that the Area Manager and I had replaced eight stationmasters who liked the overtime to supplement their 'on call' allowance, and therefore encouraged their staff to call them however minor the incident. As 'management staff' neither Eric Warr, my boss, nor I would receive any additional payment.

On the Friday evening we did have an accident, which warranted my attention. Our '08' shunter in Bridgend West Yard managed to derail and turn over and we had to summon the Canton breakdown crane. We toiled all night and I arrived back at my digs just before six absolutely exhausted. I had thrown off my clothes and flung myself into bed and had fallen into a deep sleep, when, at just twenty past six, I heard hammering on my bedroom door. It took me a long time to make sense of the noise but in the end I realised that I was being called out again and that a taxi was waiting for me. It took me straight to Tondu loco shed where they had managed to derail a pair of wheels of a wagon of loco coal inside the shed limit and clear of the running lines. It only needed a pair of ramps and a pannier tank to give it a shove, and as I stared stupefied in the steady drizzle at my feet, I realised that in my brain fog I had put on one brown shoe and one black. The inspector looked at my misery and said, 'I think you'd better go home, guvnor, you'll not be much help to us here.' From then on we made it clear that we expected the supervisory staff to deal with minor incidents that did not affect running lines and managed to reduce call outs to a more reasonable level, although there were plenty of derailments in the Welsh Valleys in the early years of dieselisation.

My new domain was a big one geographically. The Area Management team of which I was now a part had responsibility for the Cardiff – Swansea mainline between St Fagans and Stormy Sidings, near Pyle; the passenger branch to Tondu, Maesteg and Cymmer Afan and colliery outlets to Glyncorrwg and up to Abergwynfi Colliery and the Rhondda tunnel, to the west of Treherbert; the Garw and Ogmore Valleys with their coal mines; and Llantrisant Yard, near the village of Pontyclun and freight only branches to a colliery, iron ore mine and a Ministry of Defence depot. There were two loco depots and train crew signing on points at Tondu and Llantrisant and, of course, the main line station at Bridgend itself.

The Area Manager's office, which I shared, was in the former Goods depot at Bridgend. The Area had 534 staff and one of the most difficult jobs I found was to remember everyone's name. Some managers I've met have an extraordinary capacity to do this. The most remarkable example I ever encountered was my former Headmaster at Charterhouse, Brian Young, a brilliant scholar who became head of ITV at one stage. He used to gather in house photographs of all eleven houses (700+ boys in total) and deliberately learn every boy's name so that within a fortnight of the new term starting he could greet every boy he met by name. I'm afraid I was very weak in this department. The fact that so many of my staff were on shifts did not help and there's a limit in time on how long you can keep asking someone their name. Of course, as the new boy, everyone soon knew who you were, which didn't help.

With such a wide area, a car was essential and initially I was very dependent on the Area Manager or taxis. Later the railway management took it upon themselves to teach me to drive and supply me with a brand new 'Mini', my first car whose identity I've never forgotten, a little grey number, JLE 406D. But first I had to be taught to drive and I was sent to the Western Region Driving School at Taplow where there was a private road layout adjacent to the station, which had all those ingredients needed, traffic lights, a roundabout, a hill start. I arrived at 9 o'clock on the Monday morning and was put in the driver's seat of a little pale blue Mini, shown the controls, handed the keys, whereupon the instructor got out and told me to get on with it and teach myself by trial and error. Little wonder that you could virtually change gear without depressing the clutch. When I got my own brand new Mini and took my foot off the clutch for the first time, I nearly shot through the windscreen! Anyway, that Monday morning I had the track to myself until about 11 o'clock when learner parcel van drivers began to appear and I had to cope with traffic, drivers who might do silly and unexpected things as they had two hours' less experience than me. By this time I thought I was Stirling Moss and was tearing round the circuit seeing how many seconds I could clip off my best time (inclusive of the compulsory hill starts). By day two I was driving in Burnham Beeches and by day three I was driving up Slough High Street with its notorious number of traffic lights (accompanied by the instructor, I hasten to add).

When I received my new Mini I received further necessary instruction on how to change gear with a car whose clutch was not life expired from the efforts of a new unsupervised learner every week and I passed my test first go and was let loose on the hills of South Wales. The car was splendid if I was on my own, but when on occasion I had visitors from the Divisional office or NCB to transport into the hills, I found I was having to drop down an extra gear – even to first gear for some of our remoter steeply graded lanes.

Eric Warr, the Area Manager, was the former Shedmaster of Southall, an extrovert Londoner with a very practical and at times, unorthodox way of dealing with problems. On one occasion we had a problem with the ground frame that controlled the entrance to Bridgend West Yard from the Up Main Line. It had failed with the points set to the yard causing a stoppage on the main line. Eric took me down with him and I watched as he dismantled the ground frame mechanism and clipped the points to allow trains to start running again. 'Don't let me ever see you doing that!' he said, 'I know what I'm doing, it's against the rules but I'm taking responsibility. You can only do that sort of thing when you've a lot more experience under your belt.'

One week that winter it rained – as only it can in Wales – and at 4am there was a loud knocking on the door, which woke the whole household. The taxi driver said, 'They say it's serious, you'd better come quick!' With some foreboding I arrived at the station, the night pitch black, the wind howling and rain lashing on the station roof and platform. There were coaches standing on the Up Main - luckily, as I discovered shortly afterwards, empty stock as the Fishguard Boat Train had been cancelled because of storms in the Irish Sea. I fetched my Bardic lamp from my office and ventured out into the eerie darkness and came across a sight I shall never forget. My way was blocked by mangled wreckage some three vehicles high filling the cutting just where the Vale of Glamorgan line parted from the main line to Cardiff. Underneath the angular jagged metal of coaches and wagons I could just see the rear of a Class 47 burrowing under the snout of a class 37 that had clearly met it head on.

There was obviously nothing I could do to rescue the train crews before the fire brigade arrived with cutting gear and within minutes the darkness and silence had been transformed as fire engines, police and ambulances converged on the station. As dawn broke I could see the scale of the disaster – the cutting was filled to the brim with 12 coaches, 52 wagons, and three diesel engines, for the coal train had been double-headed by two class 37s. The torrential rain had loosened rock from the cutting just east of the station and this had spilled onto the track in the storm and darkness and had derailed the empty stock, which had been travelling at around 60 mph. The loco had been derailed and unfortunately had slewed foul of the Down Main and had met the double-headed coal train travelling at around 35 mph head on. As the class 47 was on the trackbed, the front 37 rode over it crushing the cab, killing the second man immediately and severely injuring the driver who died later. The crew of the freight were lucky and survived with comparatively minor injuries.

The line clearance in appalling weather, cutting strengthening and track renewal – including the whole double junction – took nearly two weeks during which time trains to West Wales were diverted via Pontypool Road and the Vale of Neath. However, the rain continued and lines became flooded and at one stage the only way we got the Down Fishguard Boat Train through was to send it, with its 'Western' diesel hydraulic, via Treherbert through the tunnel to Cymmer Afan, then down the Llynfi Valley through Maesteg and Tondu to Pyle and back onto the main line. Cliff Rose, Divisional Movements Manager, was in my office when the decision was taken – he had no idea whether the diesel was cleared for this route, but he took a chance and it crept down the valley successfully as we all held our breath. This was a time of great stress for all concerned – I spent most of the period on twelve hours nights and by the end was so shattered that the Assistant Divisional Manager, Jack Page, seriously wondered if I was up to the job. I survived and my lack of fortune continued, becoming host to more than my share of mishaps. As a painful reminder of the accident the mutilated corpse of D1671 *Thor* stood for several weeks in my goods yard right beside my office, shrouded in tarpaulins to screen it from the sight of passengers as they passed.

I also got more than my fair share of Sunday engineering work to supervise. Many were the winter nights spent putting in single line working between Bridgend and Stormy Sidings – a very apt name – or near the Cardiff end of my patch, between Llantrisant (now more correctly called Pontyclun) and my border at St Fagans. For some reason the track formation under the main line in the River Ely valley was 'fragile' and we had a number of plain line derailments there, culminating in a spectacular incident when the empty gunpowder van forming part of the brake force behind the locomotive jumped plain line when travelling at around 45 mph and the train of coke behind it reared up on end and deposited several hundred tons into the river just after Miskin. A local coal merchant was granted the franchise of emptying the river of the coke and I shudder to think how many householders received a motley collection of ballast with their fuel! This was one of a series of derailments involving plain line, when all the ingredients were near to their limit – speed, track voiding and uneven wagon loading or stiff springs. After several such derailments and analysis of each by the Derby derailment research team, it was decided to restrict the large number of short wheelbase freight wagons to 35 mph.

It was during one of my engineering possessions in yet another steady downpour that we actually caught a fish – and a decent size one at that – from between the sleepers in the main line where the

Llanharan Colliery workings had caused subsidence and a 40 mph permanent restriction was in force. It was around this time that I enjoyed one of my last steam footplate runs in BR service. Tondu depot had closed although men remained stationed there and our Churchward 2-8-0 tanks at Llantrisant for the iron ore trains to Llanwern had been replaced by the new 37s. However, the engineering Sunday turns would sometimes produce a steam engine, and I enjoyed one Sunday managing affairs from the footplate of 0-6-2 tank, 5691.

In the middle of my spell at Bridgend I was summoned to attend BR's Middle Management Course – six weeks at the former LMS Training School in Derby. A couple of dozen budding senior managers were bombarded with outrageous ideas – 'thinking the unthinkable' was doubtless the remit the lecturers had been urged to deliver to shake us out of any complacency we may have had. My abiding memory of the course, however, was the 48 hours we spent in groups on a specific project. My team, which included (deliberately) no engineers, was sent to Crewe Works to devise ways of reducing the downtime of Class 47s in the Works by at least 24 hours. Our confidence what not boosted by the news that our project presentation would be assessed by the Board's Chief Mechanical & Electrical Engineer, R.C.Bond, no less. We were further dismayed to discover that one of our number, an architect by trade, had wasted a whole day minutely recording the activities of a group of fitters on a large blue locomotive which turned out not to be a Class 47 but A4 pacific 4498 *Sir Nigel Gresley*, and one of us went to Crewe station that evening and bought him an Ian Allan ABC to try to teach him the difference between a steam and diesel engine! In the end we did produce some suggestions and Mr Bond was very kind to us – whether Crewe Works management ever implemented any of our ideas was never fed back to us.

About this time my landlady became ill and had to go into hospital and for a week I resided in a local hotel while I searched for new lodgings. I found a newspaper advertisement for the winter occupation of a holiday flat on the Glamorgan coast at the village of Southerndown, about five miles from Bridgend and reachable by an hourly bus service, for I was still a few months off getting the Mini I referred to earlier. I was pretty desperate because I couldn't really afford to continue at weekly hotel prices so I rode out to Southerndown on the east side of the Ogmore river, after dark (it was November) and when I'd negotiated a rate of 3 guineas a week with the elderly couple who owned it, I took it at once, returned back to Bridgend, picked up my meagre belongings in one suitcase and moved in that night.

Next day was one of those perfect blue sky days that you sometimes get in winter, and I got up early – even though it was a Saturday and my day off – and went to explore where I had come to. The cottage – a whitewashed stone simple building whose walls must have been at least a foot thick – was high above the cliffs and a five minute walk took me down the lane that led to the beach. I got to the ridge where the lane dropped dramatically and held my breath in awe at the landscape laid out before me. The wide sandy beach was framed by magnificent jagged cliffs that some past volcanic eruption had twisted into a geologist's dream. The sea was calm and blue and the beach was empty. I ran headlong down the little road and gambolled on that beach in sheer exuberance. I fell in love with the place there and then, and when, in March, the couple asked me if I wanted to stay on, as they now felt too old to cope with new holiday-makers every week, I jumped at the chance and stayed there very happily until I got married three years later and we bought our own house back in Bridgend.

Later in a second winter there after I'd moved to a temporary post in Cardiff and had exchanged my railway Mini for my own Austin 1100, I was driving along the coast road still in darkness when I saw a number of dim lights twinkling ahead of me. I was mystified, thinking perhaps my headlights were catching the frosty outlines of grass on the roadside when suddenly my lights picked out dozens of sheep lying on the tarmac – apparently the roadway was warmer than the fields and the sheep had found a hole in the fence and settled on the road for the night. I braked heavily, skidded on the frosty road and slammed into some of the sheep sideways – thump, thump, thump – and came to rest with one wing crushed against a stone wall and the headlight shining upwards into the sky. Shaken, I got out, surrounded by loudly bleating sheep – the low skirts of the 1100 had knocked the sheep out of the way and none had gone under the car. I found, despite the awkward angle of the headlight, that the car was still drive-able and I crept on into Bridgend and reported the accident to the police before catching the 'Blue Pullman' to London, which had been my intention.

When I called back at the police station that evening, the police reported that a constable had visited the site, had found all the sheep safely ensconced in their field and the farmer had reported no sheep being injured in any way. The policeman advised me that the farmer had probably removed any that were injured or dead, patched up the hole in his boundary fence in case he faced a claim from me for the damage to my car. The police said they could prove nothing. However, it may be that the Welsh sheep, who seem to be a hardy lot, had just got up, shaken themselves, and got on with life. I'd seen sheep hit by cars in the Aberbeeg and Tondu valleys and get up uninjured. Not the case if we hit them with one of our trains, but trespass by sheep in the valleys was so widespread that it was impracticable to stop trains and warn them of animals on the line.

After 18 months or so, Eric Warr was promoted to the Divisional Office in Marland House, Cardiff and I took over as Area Manager. My problems in the valleys above Tondu continued unabated. A loaded train of coal –18 unfitted wagons – ran away down the 1 in 33 gradient from Abergwynfi Colliery with its Paxman D95XX (class 14) despite 12 of the wagons having brakes pinned down and derailed at the trap points protecting the Treherbert – Cymmer Afan single line, damming a stream in the process which then flooded the track. Before the wheels stopped spinning, doors of the miners' cottages on the hillside above the line opened and dozens of small children descended on the train stripping it of anything removable and filling their buckets with coal dust (destined for Margam Steel Works) even though they were all entitled to free coal from the mine.

A few weeks later another D95XX was propelling four empty wagons up the 1 in 27/36 to Glyncorrwg Colliery when it buffered up to another wagon left foul over the entrance to the colliery siding. These five wagons overpowered our weak tool and the train ran back down the gradient accelerating rapidly, the locomotive brakes inadequate to slow the runaway. The train crew decided discretion was the better part of valour and jumped before the train reached the catch points protecting the junction at Cymmer and the D95XX made a spectacular somersault at an estimated 35 mph and lay in the ditch between track and cutting bank.

Our most horrendous and indeed, miraculous, runaway was in the Garw Valley. A class 37 had hauled 52 empty mineral wagons up the valley and stopped at the ground frame controlling the entrance to the Glengarw colliery. The guard walked forward to operate the frame and called the train forward. The train started with a bit of a jerk and the coupling between the first and second wagons snapped and 51 wagons and brake van set off down the hill with the guard in hot and vain pursuit. It was a hopeless quest and the entire train of unbraked wagons quickly accelerated to a frightening speed, down the 1 in 45 for the first mile, and still accelerating down three miles of 1 in 67 to Llangeinor. It smashed through crossing gates just missing a bus and I received a phone call from the signalman at Brynmenyn Junction at the foot of the bank and about a mile from Tondu, saying 'Listen to this guvnor!' and in my office I was treated to the roaring sound of the runaway train then estimated at 70 mph! At the inquiry the signalman was criticised for not turning the raft of wagons through the trap points into the river in order to protect Tondu Junction, depot and village, but the signalman claimed that he was unsure whether the guard was still on board and did not want to condemn him to certain death.

By Tondu after a mile on the level, speed had reduced to about 60 mph, but the four way junction ahead had double reverse curves and a speed restriction of 5 mph. Staff had already cleared the terraced cottages in the line of fire and later described how the train seemed to scream round the curves on two wheels. How it did not spread itself all over the junction no-one knows, but it sped off up the 1 in 132 gradient to Pyle and Margam with two quick witted shunters in pursuit in their old banger. They correctly surmised where the train would have slowed sufficiently to pin down enough brakes to stop the train rolling back to Tondu and having another go at demolishing the junction. When it was eventually stopped and the train was examined, 37 of the 52 wagons were found to have smoking axle boxes.

Another source of vexation, although not nearly so serious, was the constant theft of the tiny oil lamps, which lit the wooden platforms at Nantyffyllon, one station north of Maesteg Castle Street, – the line served by a 'Bubble Car' single-powered unit shuttling between Bridgend and Cymmer Afan. We were worried that someone would slip or fall from one of the platforms in the darkness and kept replacing the lamps only to find they would disappear again within days. Eventually we discovered that these lamps were highly prized by local entrepreneurs for hatching out baby chicks!

Gerry Fiennes was General Manager until 1966 and he was getting increasingly dissatisfied with what he considered to be the lack of sufficient horsepower on WR expresses - certainly compared with the Deltics on the East Coast. He therefore directed that a pair of 37s in multiple were to be tried out on the South Wales - London expresses with the prototype XP64 stock and I rode on the 8.20am Swansea to a London meeting one day in May with a pair of Newport Godfrey Road engines, D6877 and D6892. The acceleration from scratch was phenomenal and we sustained 100 mph on level track but after a couple of weeks, the experiment was called off as the heavy freight locos were unsuited to continuous high speed and began to develop serious traction problems.

Near the end of my time at Bridgend, I was alarmed to hear that I was to be host for a full day's saloon tour by the new General Manager, my bugbear, Lance Ibbotson. I had to report to the saloon arriving in Bridgend West Yard at 08.00 and present myself for breakfast. I was so nervous that I was physically sick just before climbing into the vehicle and I doubt I did justice to the eggs and bacon served up. At least there were no kippers. This time I'd done my homework well and having been in the area for nearly four years, I was able to answer all the GM's questions or bluff successfully. A couple of years later my successor had a similar tour, which he told me was going pretty poorly until they got to Llantrisant Yard. The General Manager had been scathing about the need for Llantrisant at all and its few wagons from the Ministry of Defence Depot and iron ore mine above Mwyndy Junction. My colleague was fearing another diatribe when the saloon arrived back in the yard expecting to find it empty. However, the place was a hive of activity dumbfounding Lance Ibbotson, with two iron ore trains and a coal train awaiting the road. After the General Manager, somewhat appeased, had gone on his way, Ken Shingleton asked Bill Heard, the area inspector, how come the yard had been so busy.

'Ah, we've been holding them here since lunchtime. We thought you deserved a show for the General Manager!' Llantrisant depot survived a few more months.

Not all memorable activity took place on the railway. As in Aberbeeg, social history was being lived out. I was in 'chapel country'. In the 18,000 population town of Maesteg, there were said to be 32 different chapels (I didn't count them) – doubling up because there was an English and Welsh language version of each denomination. In the Ogmore Valley there were two Methodist chapels a hundred yards from each other, but rivalries were such that they wouldn't merge. One chapel was apparently praying for children for their Sunday School – they had potential teachers. The other had so many children they were praying for teachers. That condition continued without either prayer being answered! When one was in financial trouble, the other chapel, which was well endowed, paid their bills to save them having to join up.

Down in Bridgend I was prevailed upon to act as an 'auxiliary preacher' although I felt my calling was to youth work rather than taking Sunday services. When the quarterly plan came out I discovered that I was allocated to take the services at the chapels at the heads of the valleys, only because I had my railway car and I could drop the other preachers off as we passed the chapels as we went up the valley. Then I knew why I was 'called to preach'! If you looked at Welsh Sunday bus timetables you could understand why I was in such demand. In the end my performance before the General Manager paid off or someone from a village chapel said they'd had enough of me (I was probably too radical/liberal in my beliefs for traditional Welsh chapel Methodism) and I found myself promoted to be Train Planning Officer at the Divisional Office in Cardiff. At least my on call duties would be less frequent, I could get home more often or conduct my long distance courting with greater ease (my girl friend and subsequent fiancée and wife was at college in Ealing). I now became a commuter from Bridgend.

Bridgend station platform nameboard, 3.5.58:
photo – David Lawrence /Hugh Davies Collection

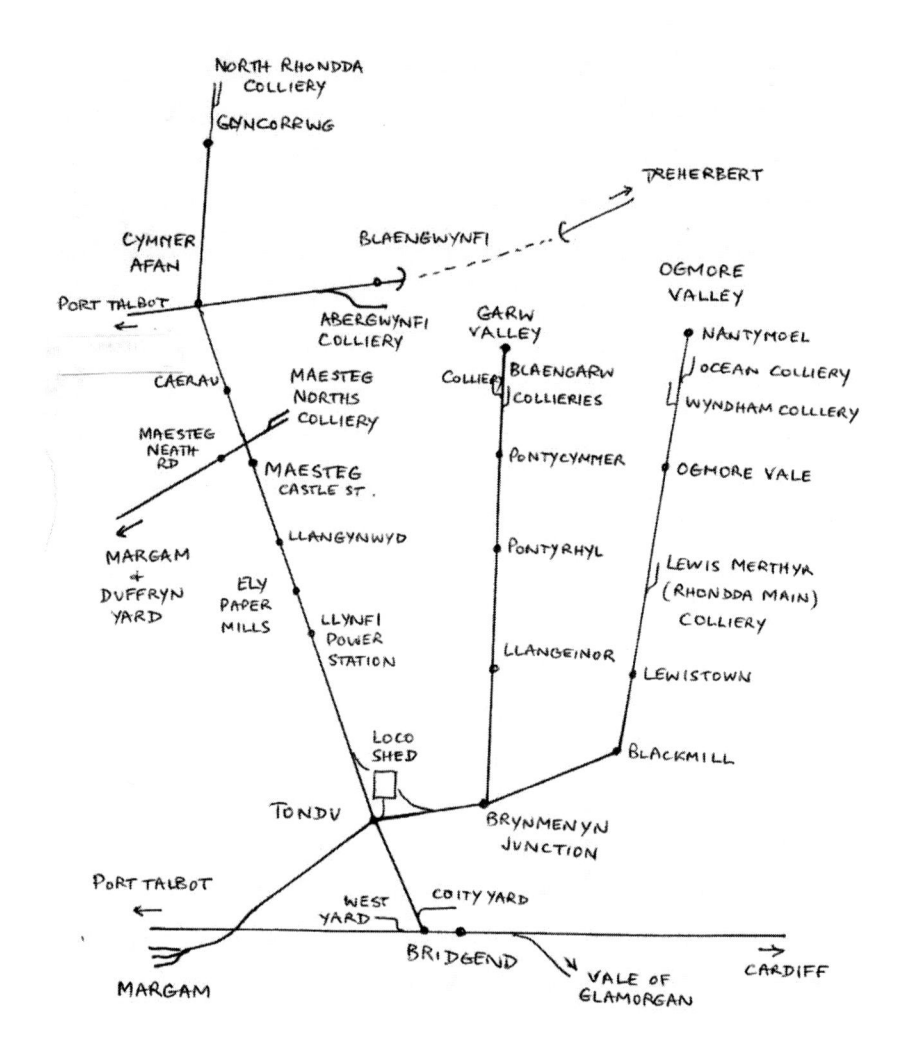

Tondu and the Llynfi, Garw and Ogmore Valleys, 1965 – 1967

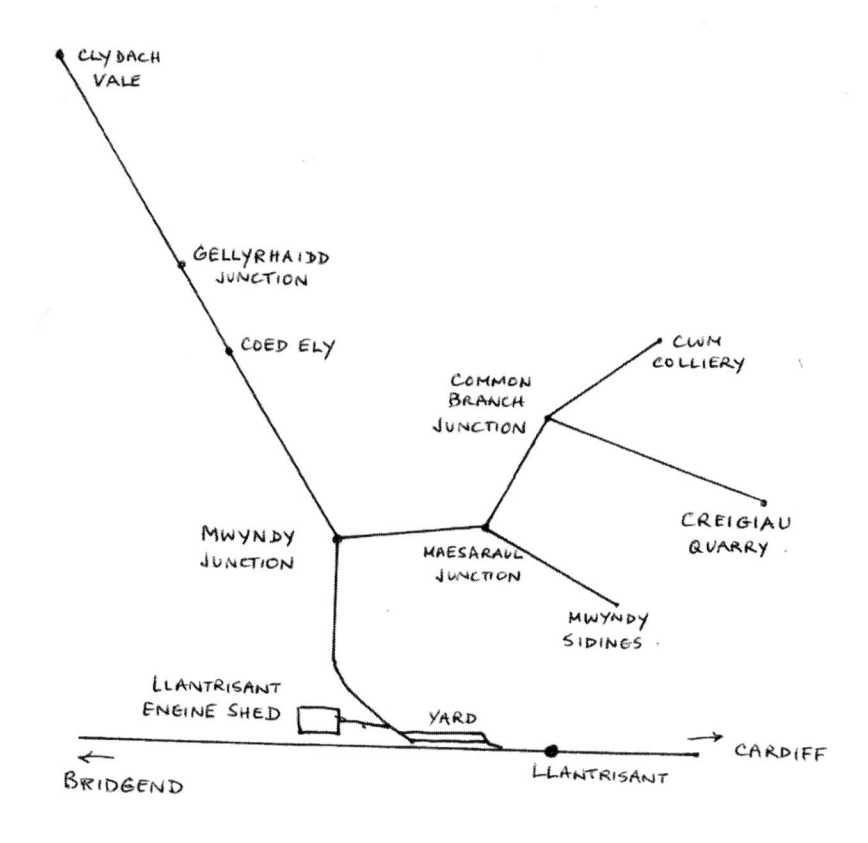

Llantrisant and Ely Valleys, and the freight branches feeding into Llantrisant Yard, 1964 – 1965

The Derby Middle Management Course of 1966, with the Principal, H.B.Samuel in the centre, and tutor Bill Latham, later to become the author's manager at the Parcels Business at the BRB, two places to the right. The author is the youthful looking guy in the light jacket and black hair in the 2nd row, left of centre.

Picture Postcard of Southerndown and bottom left, 'Seaview', the holiday flat, which the author rented for three years

A 57XX pannier tank with a loaded coal train from Abergwynfi Colliery crosses the Afan river between Blaengwynfi and Cymmer Afan where the runaway with the D95XX Paxman diesel occurred, 5.8.59: photo – Robert Darlaston

North Rhondda Halt just below Glyncorrwg where the runaway occurred, pannier tank 7744 with the miners' train, 24.8.53: photo – anon / John Hodge Collection

2-8-0T 4243 snakes a train of 21t Minfits, loaded with coal from Ogmore Vale Central Washery to Margam Steelworks, across the 5mph restricted reverse curves over Tondu Junction, 1.6.62: photo – B W L Brooksbank /Initial Photographics Collection

Nantyffyllon station, with wooden platform and oil lamps, circa 1964

The Bridgend – Cymmer Afan Single Power Car ('Bubblecar')
at Cymmer, 5.8.59: photo – Robert Darlaston

The author with fiancée Patricia Kemp, 1968

Chapter 8: 1968 - 1971
Cardiff Divisional Office

I was sent for by Divisional Manager Bob Hilton in the Spring of 1967 and told (people didn't ask in those days) that I would be covering the post of District Terminals Superintendent in Swansea for a while as there were a number of temporary officers' moves taking place. The previous incumbent had moved to a similar role at the Cardiff Divisional Office in Marland House. My main priorities seemed to be to keep an eye on the summer sailings and trains at Fishguard harbour – bearing in mind my experience some four years before during my training – and the taking of a number of consultation meetings with the trade unions over the closure of goods and parcels facilities which were coming thick and fast as the Beeching proposals began to bite.

As Fishguard had no regular train service from Swansea and was a good 2-3 hours drive by road, the post was furbished with a chauffeur and car, previously supplied to the District Manager Swansea before the abolition of that tier of management. The District Terminals and Operating Superintendents were the last remnants of that organisation. The idea was that I would be able to undertake work en route if I was driven, but we discovered on my first two journeys to the port that I became car sick as soon as I attempted any reading work in the back of the car, and that I was even queasy being driven that distance anyway. So I regret my travel sickness became the reason for the chauffeur's redundancy and I was allocated a self-drive Cortina. And a pretty awful car it was too. It had a disconcerting habit of dying the moment I took my foot off the accelerator and I lost count of the number of roundabouts I free-wheeled round frantically trying to 'cough' the engine back into life. It was a flimsy thing too. I kept the car later when I moved to posts in Cardiff and the following winter was innocently standing at traffic lights when I was rammed from the rear by a Morris Oxford that had skidded on ice. I could find no scratch on the latter car, but the rear end of my Cortina crumpled like an accordion, it went to the garage and I never saw it again.

Before I breathed a sigh of relief, however, I was ironically provided with a company Morris Oxford, a venerable machine that nearly caused me to come to grief one evening on the A48 as I was obeying a 'call out', when suddenly without any warning the bonnet flew open and completely obscured my vision. An emergency stop luckily prevented me colliding with a bus that had halted in front of me and I'm glad to say that they let me use my own 1100 after that and claim mileage expenses.

I was moved to Cardiff to cover the absence of the Terminals Manager for three months, a man who seemed terrified every time he received a summons from Bob Hilton. Hilton was a manager of the old school, autocratic but decisive and forceful, embracing the new 'management thinking' that was de rigueur under Richard Beeching. He was only interested in solutions, not problems, and expected his managers to get on and do things – as long as they were 'on message'. This was fine as long as his management instincts were right – and they usually were – but occasionally things would go badly awry when he pushed something and his managers were too timid or fearful to argue. I was not particularly happy as Terminals Manager finding myself required to confront a very militant set of Trade Union representatives covering the terminal and freight staff – Sectional Council D. As often as not I had the unhappy role of negotiating closures of depots or stations, and it was with some relief that I was transferred to the Operations side where I had more support in the powerful and gifted Cliff Rose, who became a Board Member at an early age and died of cancer tragically young.

After another temporary period as an Operating Assistant, the Train Planning Officer's job became vacant and I was appointed on a permanent basis. The main line services between Severn Tunnel Junction and Swansea, Carmarthen and Fishguard were timed and diagrammed by the Western Region HQ staff in Paddington, but I was responsible for the passenger services in the Cardiff Valleys and all the internal South Wales freight services. After a few months, my job was amalgamated with that of the Trains Office Superintendent who was responsible for the Cardiff Control Office, so I found myself having to implement my own plan and correct any of its shortcomings on a daily, even hourly, basis.

This was my first experience of managing in the office environment and I quickly noticed a couple of cultural issues that needed tackling – one successfully, the other I'm not so sure about. The train timers and diagrammers in the Train Planning section were competent, indeed, dedicated to their work and we got on fine with our mutual interests. I had always prided myself on my enlightened and forward thinking staff management attitude and policy and had welcomed participation in a scheme developed by the Personnel section that took newly recruited clerks and gave them a taste of working alongside experienced staff in different sections for a few weeks before permanent employment. I had chatted to a few of these clerical trainees, mainly women, and was both surprised and taken aback when I received a complaint from the Personnel Manager that a number of these trainee clerks felt neglected or ignored when working in my department and as all the complaints were from women, I was accused of running a sexist organisation. I was certainly unaware of any overt hostility to the women and made my own enquiries with the staff, who seemed as bemused as I was by the complaints.

We eventually came to the conclusion that most of the Train Planning staff were so engrossed in the minutiae of their jobs and so interested in it, that they assumed the new clerks would be as interested. But of course, not many of these new recruits were train enthusiasts and the women missed the rapport and conversation they experienced in other sections where the issues were more about 'people' than 'things'. Having persuaded the Personnel Manager that no intended slight or prejudice had been present, he concluded that such staff would find it difficult to change their approach – indeed the company valued their dedication – so he decided to avoid sending many of the new clerks to Train Planning in future unless they showed an obvious aptitude and interest in that type of work.

A more successful intervention on my part was the lead I took in trying to persuade controllers that I did not measure their success by the amount of manipulation of resources – crews and engines – that they indulged in. There seemed to be an attitude that they must look busy or management would shut their post, a constant fear at a time of drastic cost reductions being sought by Beeching and his new officer recruits. However, with my responsibility for the plan, I took it personally if Control spent most of the time wrecking it through constant changes and I told them that if they had to make changes other than to reflect revised traffic flows or emergencies, then the Train Planning Office had failed. As manager of both, I encouraged a closer understanding between the two departments, getting train planners to go and discuss proposals with the Chief Controller or asking the controllers to report working that needed adjustment instead of grumbling under their breath and changing the plan without giving proper feedback. I think I convinced most controllers that I would genuinely like to see them with feet on the desk reading the Mirror when I visited Control for that would indicate everything was running as planned!

By and large, the Cardiff Valley passenger service needed little action unless the whole timetable was to be recast and I found that I spent many hours each week negotiating requirements with the Coal Board Transport Officers in Cardiff and Neath. There were large flows of coal moved internally to the steelworks at Margam and Llanwern and also for export via Newport, Barry and Swansea Docks. I would agree longer distance coal flows with the NCB and then negotiate paths with the Regional Office – my first achievement of note was to run a coal train to Newcastle, albeit a specialist train of anthracite that was only mined in West Wales. On a daily basis we received forecasts of tonnages available at the pitheads and my job was to ensure a sufficient provision of coal empty wagons to clear the tonnage and not, in the worst case, to hold up the mine production as the coal could not be loaded. We had a number of locomotives designated to cope with the daily variations under 'Control Orders' and these would be diagrammed by roneo notice to depots only the afternoon before implementation.

It soon became apparent to me that we were having to improvise far too much on a daily basis and every weekend we were running a special expensive programme to tackle backlogs to avoid NCB criticism and penalty payments. Under the 'slash and burn' principle that had been in operation since the Beeching/Raymond era, some yards and depots had closed and spare resources of track, trains and men severely restricted, but it had been done piecemeal without any overall strategy. By now we had a new Divisional Movements Manager, Gerry Orbell, who joined us from the Eastern Region and Cliff Rose had been elevated to Assistant Divisional Manager. We were having crises nearly every day, exemplified by the congestion in yards like East Usk, Alexandra Dock Junction and Radyr, which were often so full that we could only move a train towards them if Control simultaneously took a train from them for somewhere else. It was all very wasteful, made worse by the fact that the longer distance diesel engine diagrams were so complex that once we were out of the plan, chaos reigned. We had the stray ends of Tinsley or Toton engines booked for trips from Margam to Severn Tunnel Junction and similar, engines that were rarely traceable and never in the right place when you wanted them. Gerry and I decided that something drastic and radical needed to be done and the concept of the South Wales Freight Strategy was born. Our mantra was 'keep it simple'.

We decided to involve senior Operations staff from Paddington Headquarters as we wanted to analyse and review all freight working in South Wales including flows of traffic into and out of the Principality. This was a brave move on behalf of my manager as some senior officers, including the Divisional Manager himself, were paranoid about any potential interference from HQ in their affairs and we had to keep their involvement under wraps. We built a Divisional team including train planners and productivity staff from Management Services and the HQ team with Ray Fox, Train Planning Officer, Vic Gregory, Freight Officer, Dennis Mann the Diagramming Officer and others led by the Regional Operations Manager himself, Leslie Lloyd. I - under direction from HQ - arranged overnight stays at seaside hotels in Barry and on the Gower for the team to have a meal together, and spend a couple of hours preparing the agenda and key issues for the next day's discussions. We were joined by the HQ Projects Manager, T.C.Baynton-Hughes and John Hodge from South Wales who together were persuading the NCB to rearrange their transport requirements to put out the wagons in block loads for one destination, but varying daily, the start of the so-called 'Blocplan'.

These evening sessions invariably started with sport of some sort – bowls, croquet, a golf driving range on one occasion – at which we all made sure Leslie Lloyd, an ardent competitor, won. After dinner and the real work, around 11pm we would adjourn over pints to a fearsome game of 'Liar Dice', which again Leslie would win and Baynton invariably lose as I don't think he ever fathomed the rules. At 1am, most would retire to bed, while I had to drive round the Vale of Glamorgan back to my home – the former summer-rented seaside cottage balanced on the cliff top above the sands of Southerndown Bay, near the dismantled

Dunraven Castle (dismantled apparently in days of yore so that the owner could avoid paying tax on it!).

Next day we would assemble at some secret abode out of the sight of spies from the Divisional Office and bring together the evidence and analysis we had been gathering in our South Wales team. We reviewed the role of every marshalling yard, got Management Services with local management to draw up consistent siding allocations in the light of the Blocplan proposals, which took a lot of coal tonnage out of the yards, and simplified the engine and crew diagrams. When we were sufficiently advanced in our thinking, I was delegated to spend time with every local trade union representative group (LDCs) explaining our proposals and seeking staff ideas and input. The only proviso was that I was accompanied by a senior Trade Union official from Sectional Council to see fair play and ensure no local group put forward biased proposals that would unduly benefit their depot at the expense of others – a highly contentious issue. All LDCs except one – Margam – agreed to meet me on this basis and we benefited enormously from the staff input coming up with finalised plans that local staff believed were practicable and were 'owned' by them.

The upshot was when we held the 'grand' consultation meeting with 150 LDC representatives and Sectional Council staff from all over South Wales in the Cardiff 'Temple of Peace' (usually given a very ironic cheer when large controversial meetings were held there), it lasted just under an hour and a half. I spent the first 45 minutes going through the proposals explaining the staff ideas we had accepted and included in the strategy and which ones we had had to reject and why. Instead of a longwinded and protracted argument from staff representatives that was usual, one LDC member after another stood up to confirm their agreement and express their satisfaction with the way this huge and potentially controversial plan had been developed and consulted on. Only Margam, who had held out against co-operation, found any argument with the plans and the other LDCs soon made it clear to them that they had turned down the opportunity to influence things, which was their loss and got little sympathy.

What the plan did was to rationalise the piecemeal changes that had taken place over the previous years, make the freight flows work with reduced yard and locomotive resources, meet the NCB's justified criticisms and reduce the overall cost considerably without any substantial staff redundancies. As an example of the changes we made, we designated Severn Tunnel Junction to be the starting place for wagon-load traffic to England, with increased frequency of trains round the clock for English destinations, instead of spreading them over Margam and Severn Tunnel. We diagrammed two 2,700 hp diesel hydraulics to do nothing but round trips from Margam to Severn Tunnel and back reducing the shunting need at Margam and giving the wagons a faster and more frequent service from Severn Tunnel Yard. The network of steel high speed freight services to the Midlands and North East we concentrated on Alexandra Dock Junction and East Usk became our main collection and dispersal point for coal empties in the Newport and Cardiff Valleys. When the plan was implemented with the vast changes, we all expected teething problems. They did not happen – why not? Because the local staff made sure it worked; it was their plan as much as ours. I'm astonished that this method of staff consultation was never picked up and copied by other Divisions and Regions. I subsequently wrote a 4,000 words thesis on 'Simplicity in Railway Operations' based on this experience, which was accepted as my qualification for membership of the Institute of Transport.

I had been courting a student from Ealing University since meeting her on holiday in 1965. At first continuation of the relationship was very difficult as Pat came from Fakenham in Norfolk, about as far from an open passenger railway in England as you could get. However, when she moved to London in the autumn, I was able to use the occasional half day to see her. Initially it was a long journey for a couple of hours at most, with a 40 minute bus ride from Aberbeeg to Newport, then a two hour train journey and the same home in the evening. It became a bit easier when I moved to Bridgend and even easier when I would start my journey from Cardiff. Despite this Pat was accused of fending off other would-be suitors by feigning an imagined boyfriend – in fact I gather I was known as a 'figment of Pat's imagination' as I was so rarely seen in her college digs.

We got married in 1969 and I reluctantly left my 'paradise' by the sea for a chalet bungalow ten minutes' walk from Bridgend station. When a couple of years later our first daughter, Helen, was born, I was fortunate that my 'on call' commitments had fallen to one week in five, shared among the other Divisional Operating Officers, as after an initial misleading few weeks Helen began to have long sleepless periods. On the other weeks I could occasionally be found at 3am motoring round Bridgend and Porthcawl with Helen in the carrycot on the back seat, as putting her in the car and driving aimlessly around was the only certain way we knew of getting her back to sleep.

Chapter 9: 1972 - 1974
222 Marylebone Road

Hints were being dropped that I should be looking for promotion, so I started scouring the weekly vacancy sheets with renewed interest. I put in for a few management grade 5 posts somewhat ambitiously (my Cardiff job was range 3) and it was with some surprise that I was quickly successful and was appointed as BRB Assistant Parcels Planning Officer with the specific role of undertaking a strategic review of the Board's Parcels Business and its future options. I reported to the Parcels Planning Manager, Bill Latham, whom I'd last seen as one of the tutors at the Derby Management School and he quickly briefed me on the project I was required to lead.

I lodged during the week with my parents back in Woking, resuming daily commuter journeys on the now wholly electrified railway, thus escaping the sleepless nights that my wife suffered as by now Helen was teething and probably missing me as well, making her even more unsettled. This put some urgency into house-hunting and within three months we had bought a modest house on an estate in Hazlemere, between High Wycombe and Amersham – much more affordable than Woking. By now Helen's nightly waking had become ingrained and it was some relief that my new job had no out of hours 'on call' responsibilities. I drove each day through the Buckinghamshire beech woods of Penn to Beaconsfield station and caught the DMU service directly to Marylebone and straight into the BR Headquarters building opposite.

I was required to look at the business options available for both Red Star and Collected & Delivered Parcels from scenarios ranging from drastic downsizing involving the rejection of much costly activity to a scenario requiring major investment. To help me with this major project, I was allocated a full time team consisting of a manager from the parcels business of each Region – including Ron Mendes from Crewe, David Allen (who reported directly to Gordon Pettitt in York), John Blyth from the Western and Bill Lamport on the Southern. Each week I would hold a team meeting and we would decide the data to be collected and analysed by the regional representatives while I planned the next moves working closely with the IT department who had been engaged to model the scenarios under consideration. This meant that I had to plan carefully for the data gathering for several options at the same time, to minimise data input and computer time, and in consequence I constructed a massive Critical Path Analysis which adorned my office wall and which became the object of much comment – a mixture of admiration, confusion and cynicism.

As the project progressed and I ticked off elements of the CPA that had been completed and rubbed out and redrew aspects that changed through time and experience, I began to test some of the emerging conclusions with the Regional Parcel Managers and we eliminated some of the options fairly quickly, as we were in danger of sinking beneath the reams of computer output that began to emerge purporting to show likely transit times, costs and resources for the different scenarios. By the end of year 1 of the two year project we had virtually concluded that a scheme to concentrate the business on some 65 main stations for the C & D traffic was the most likely runner and were given the go-ahead to develop this in detail with train plans, vehicle diagrams and detailed 'Brute' traffic transfers simplified as far as possible to minimise the need to tranship – learning much from the principles of the South Wales Freight Strategy that we'd implemented in 1968.

Crucial to these bulk flows and the maximum through working without excessive shunting or Brute transfers was the dominance of the mail order traffic particularly from the Lancashire depots of Manchester Mayfield, Bolton and Oldham. I seem to remember that some 55% of parcels at this time were from mail order firms and it was desperately disappointing that just as we obtained the Board's approval to significant investment, the mail order business decided that it could cut costs and be in charge of its own destiny if it operated a road fleet and companies like TNT began to appear and cream off the most profitable flows of traffic that would have been the mainstay of a national plan, leaving the railways – as so often – with the unprofitable remnants.

However, at the time we were unaware of these companies' plans and soldiered on taking the completed report to the BR Board for approval. It recommended significant investment at a number of the future parcels concentration depots, justified by massive savings in train mileage and resources and staff reductions at terminals through some mechanisation and the bulk handling of much parcels traffic in through 'brutes' to destination avoiding much of the double and triple handling that then took place. The plan postulated a very significant improvement in average parcel transit times – one of the main grouses of existing customers and part of the reason the Mail Order companies eventually put to us for their change of transport policy. If I remember rightly, the computer simulation of our plan produced a next day delivery for over 90% of the parcels put on rail.

As I said, the Board approved the plan although I do wonder sometimes how much scrutiny they gave the papers – I presume they had misplaced confidence that all the detail had been checked elsewhere. We'd all missed a simple typing mistake of a decimal point in the wrong place, so that the Board approved an investment of £11.1million in its Scottish depots instead of the intended £1.11 million! I assume this would have been picked up when and if contracts for the work had been prepared.

Before anything could be put in hand to implement the proposal and commence consultation with the trade unions, the blow fell and significant flows of traffic from the Lancashire depots were transferred to road. A rapid reassessment of the plan showed that without the bulk flows from the Manchester area, many of the main services forming the core of our proposals were not viable and if they were withdrawn or radically reduced, the impact on quality of service and average parcel transit times plummeted dramatically. We had built some contingency costs into every option that we'd studied but the sudden dramatic switch to road of the mail order traffic forced us to one of the options that had been rejected early in the analyses. The way was now set for that increasing decline through loss of volume that puts rail at a disadvantage and was the beginning of the end of 'C & D' parcels, pushing us to the option that retained and developed the Post Office and Newspaper businesses' traffic and the Red Star station to station traffic only.

What lessons should we have learned from this abortive work? Was our marketing intelligence so poor that the Board was unaware of the probability of the mail order companies' plans? Were we just too late? Did we not tell the companies the steps we were taking to meet their quality and cost objectives? Or did they not believe us? Or were they not prepared to wait 2-3 years for the change? If I had used my experience of bringing about successful change to the South Wales freight working which owed much to our preparedness to take the unions into our confidence and get their input, should I not have pressed for one or two representatives from the mail order firms to become a part of our study team? I suspect such a suggestion would have been quickly rejected for fear of exposing our costs to the companies and therefore putting pressure on the rates we charged. However, in hindsight I think such openness might have evinced co-operation and confidence in our intentions, but it was already probably too late.

Was this a disaster for my career? I think not, for someone had seen the derided Critical Path Analysis covering one wall of my office and had studied it in some depth – not to learn about the Parcels business but to consider the potential of the artwork's author. That person was Alan Englert who was Head of the Board's Productivity Services, the organisation that included the Regional Work Study and Organisation & Methods (O&M) teams. It was a 'critical path' to the next stage in my career.

Chapter 10: 1974 - 1982
Management Services, WR and BRB

I returned to the Western Region in 1974. I still think that my move came about because of the analytical nature of the work I was engaged in on the Parcels Business Strategic Plan. Alan Englert cannot remember my giant Critical Path Analysis, but remembers my interview. Of that I have no recollection. Such is our respective selective memories. On all Regions bar the Western, Management Services was the name by which the Work Study and Organisation & Methods (O&M) practitioners went. However, my predecessor, Geoff Goldstone, was a visionary and had developed the WR Work Study and O&M teams into an effective internal management consultancy organisation working with the senior Regional Management team. Geoff had transferred his expertise to the Board where his enthusiasm for technology in the office was to be given free rein. I still remember his repeated mantra of the 'paperless office' and the cynicism this provoked, born out I'm afraid over the years as only too true a reservation.

The Western Region Management Services department was around 35 strong with a small office at the Paddington HQ and outbased staff in the three Divisions in Cardiff, Bristol and Reading. However, they were all HQ staff and could be deployed in any of the Divisions. As well as deputies with Work Study and O&M backgrounds (Sidney Manning and Richard Fortt) I had a number of middle range management graded staff with functional rather than productivity professionalism supported by a balance of staff with line management experience and trained Word Study or O&M practitioners. I reported directly to the Assistant General Manager, Jim O'Brien, and had a position in the Western Region General Management 'cabinet', unlike my opposite numbers on the other Regions where the department was seen as a fairly low level support group.

However, before I could get my feet under the table and size up my new task, I was nominated to attend the eleven-week BR senior management course at the railway's Woking Staff College. This was indeed a sign that I'd made it as the course was designed for the mid-career development of those fortunate enough to be destined under the Board's sophisticated management planning process to be elevated to top management in due course. On arrival at Woking – still the home of my parents – I found that two of my contemporaries and close friends, Stan Judd from Western Valley days and Ken Shingleton, my successor at Bridgend, were not only members of course 36 as well, but were actually allocated to the same syndicate for a lot of the group exercises we were to undertake. This was totally at odds with the college intention, which was to mix experience and skills as far as possible, but because we now did widely different jobs on different parts of BR, there was no recognition of our common background. The other members of our syndicate sussed out very quickly the rapport between the three of us, which did lead to some fairly efficient division of labour in the various tasks we were given to do, based on our knowledge of each other's strengths. At 35 I was nearly the 'baby' of the group, although I had to give way to the 28 year-old Chris Green already pencilled in for higher things.

I remember that one of the skills we were taught was public speaking and media presentation and each of us had to deliver a five minute talk from a rostrum on a subject of our choice while being videoed and then watch (painfully) the playback whilst being subjected to critical comments from both staff and our fellow students. I have no recollection of what I spoke, but I do know that my experience as a preacher in the pulpits of Welsh chapels provoked much comment as did my habit of flinging my arms around and wandering about which gave the video camera operator a very difficult task. The session was immediately after a heavy lunch and the college Principal, Gordon Beard, came in and sat in a chair at the back of the auditorium to listen. At some stage in my oration, I paused and thumped the lectern to drive home my point and there followed a tremendous crash as the Principal woke up with a start and fell out of his chair. The other students were convinced that I had noticed Gordon slumbering and had woken him on purpose, but frankly I was far too carried away by my own imagined eloquence to have noticed that.

The main highlight of the course and looked forward to eagerly by all participants was the one-week overseas tour, where we would visit a mixture of railway and other business enterprises. We got Switzerland in mid winter and were based at Berne for most of the week. On the first Sunday we had our only 'day off' when we were guests of the SBB and the Gornergrat private railway, travelling to Zermatt and then high into the mountains, with spectacular views of the Matterhorn. At the top of the Gornergrat Railway, our Zambian member, Michael Banda, Assistant General Manager of the national bus company, stepped out of the train into more than a metre of snow and disappeared chortling into the stuff as he'd never seen snow before!

The syndicates split up for a number of tours and our group was scheduled to visit Zurich to be guests of the Swiss Credit Bank to learn something about the Swiss economy in the morning and after lunch we were due to have a session with the SBB Zurich Divisional Marketing people. We suffered one of those very rare Swiss train delays en route because of a freight derailment at Olten and subsequently arrived in Zurich an hour and a half late. We were escorted into the stained glass windowed boardroom, given the full and unabridged presentation and then sat down to a sumptuous lunch at which – and I can still see them – our places each had eight (eight!) glasses of various shapes and sizes of which only one was for water. When, eventually we finished the meal, about 3 o'clock, our hosts, instead of hurrying us to the SBB HQ, insisted on taking us on a walking sightseeing tour on the basis that they would deliver us to the SBB personnel in exactly the same lateness as SBB had delivered us to them. I saw the only revolving cathedral I'd ever experienced and a number of photographs that eventually were exposed and printed I had no recollection of taking. This was very unfortunate for our next host sat us down at a table and delivered us a talk in broken English on the Swiss Rail marketing strategies. Four of the eight of us fell asleep and our tutor, Charles Underhill, actually slipped gracefully under the table although the Swiss Rail manager politely pretended not to notice.

Whilst the Swiss railways are generally held to be the model of efficiency, we did see some surprising things, especially during a half day visit to Lausanne marshalling yard, a huge brand new hump yard that stretched as far as the eye could see from the Hump Tower where we were assembled for a briefing on the SBB freight business strategy. We were astonished to learn that Lausanne was just one of 28 brand new yards under construction – years after the yards built under the BR Modernisation Plan were already under threat of closure because of the emphasis on developing block train working. Because of its geography and laws limiting the size of lorries using Swiss roads, there was clearly more wagon load traffic than in the UK – but 28 modern yards for a country smaller than the UK? We thought we had misheard or that something had got lost in translation, but we were assured this was the case.

Back in London I got down to the task of marketing my new department to potential users from the functions. The Operating Department had been the major user of the organisation's services and Jim O'Brien encouraged me to make some inroads into the engineering functions, which had been resistant to my predecessor's offer of help to achieve their productivity and cost reduction targets. Neither Leslie Lloyd, the General Manager, nor Jim O'Brien were engineers and they suspected that all three main functional managers used their technical expertise to baffle general management and protect their budgets from the Board targets being imposed. We had some success with the Mechanical & Electrical Engineer as the Region was on the brink of introducing the highly successful diesel HSTs and depots had to be designed and the number of required maintenance staff assessed. A team on this liaised closely with our opposite number on the Eastern Region who were similarly poised and their manager, Tom Greaves, and I met occasionally to compare notes and help each other. The idea was to meet on neutral ground between our Regions, although on one occasion we met in a Liverpool pub renowned for its 'Black Puddings' (not my choice) and on another occasion we met at a railway model shop in Eastbourne, where we had common interests, as well as enjoying the sun on the promenade where we laid out our depot diagrams for mutual inspection.

The S&T Engineer was also co-operative, but I do remember that it took us a long time to persuade the Regional Civil Engineer, Philip Rees, to let us anywhere near his Department and I remember vividly his defence of the civil engineering budget at meetings chaired by the General Manager where he challenged anyone to question his professional judgement. The result of this stout protection could be appreciated when I moved to the Board and used – when under pressure – to take myself off to write an urgent paper closeting myself to work in isolation on a train going to Bristol or Preston or York. My secretary would complain bitterly about the legibility of my handwriting if I'd been on the West

Coast Main Line, the East Coast was acceptable, but she always encouraged me to go west to provide a perfectly written piece of work on Brunel's billiard table and Philip Rees's 'gold plated railway'.

The staff in my department were formed into appropriate small teams for each project, based on their functional background and the specific skills we – Sidney Manning, Richard Fortt and myself – thought necessary. The grades of the staff denoting their salary ranges were based on the experience they had to offer us when recruited and which we widely ignored when selecting the right team for each project. Sometimes we deliberately assigned a junior member of staff as team leader, to give them experience and because of the relevance of their background for the task. Once a fairly new member of the department used this to claim upgrading for the duration of the project. He was promptly persuaded by other staff members to withdraw his application as the other more junior staff relished the flexibility we had adopted and the occasional chance they had to demonstrate what they could do.

We soon found that we had plenty of work in the West of England and South Wales, but the Reading Division was very reluctant to ask for our assistance. This was in part due to the attitude of the Divisional Manager, Albert Barnes, who felt his own staff should make the improvements without outside help and avoid credit going elsewhere. I countered this by offering Albert some of my staff to be seconded to his Division to work with his staff so that the Division could claim the credit for results achieved. This approach was so successful that within six months the Reading Division had commandeered 60% of my resources and I had to look seriously at recruiting more staff. The Region's top management, of course, knew what I was up to.

The Head of Productivity Services at the BRB, Alan Englert, had been keen to replicate the Western Region model on other Regions and when he was appointed to head the Staff Management College at the Grove, Watford, in 1978, I was asked to move to the Board to replace him and fashion the five Regions' Management Services resources into a powerful internal management consultancy organisation, reporting directly to a Board Member, James Urquhart.

From the mid 1970s the government had been increasingly concerned about BR's worsening financial position and the Board was under pressure to introduce major productivity improvements to cut costs. Top management was therefore keen to beef up its capacity to identify and help implement significant changes. Another department, the Board's Strategic Planning and Research organisation, had upped its profile by appointing former General Manager, Geoff Myers, as its Director and Jim Urquhart wanted the same for his emergent Consultancy Services unit. I know he was seeking to interest people like Jim O'Brien, but most were cautious as the advisory nature of the structure was feared to be a career risk taking a high flying manager out of direct personal line responsibility.

The appointment of a Director was therefore delayed and as the Manager, I was asked to get on with the job of recruiting suitable people in the Regions to head up the restyled organisations. I was given General Management support and we appointed a powerful team, which included Paul Watkinson on the LMR, Mick Newsome on the Eastern Region and Paul Winder on the Western. We held a series of meetings to ensure that we had a common vision and then the Regional Management Services Managers set about recruiting appropriate people for the new roles, retaining some of the best Work Study and O&M practitioners who were felt to have the capacity for development.

At Headquarters I started recruiting some senior consultants from the functions – Operations, Marketing, Engineering – at the same level as George Tidy who was very experienced in the whole Work Study and incentives philosophy and Geoff Goldstone continuing his campaign to bring management into the technological age. Jim Urquhart also wanted a senior officer to measure the impact of efforts to improve productivity and to devise key performance indicators (there was a Finance Act Requirement for nationalised industries to include indicators in their Annual Reports about this time) to identify good practice, targets for measurable improvement and the ability to compare like activities – which led some managers to fear that they were to be judged by a 'league table' approach. This 'policeman' role did not sit easily with the consultancy 'advisory' role and when eventually a Director was appointed, the Productivity Manager, John Craik, was shifted to report to the Director leaving the consultancy wing reporting through me. By the time a Director had been recruited from private industry the organisation had been formed and key people appointed which meant that the new man, Michael Ferrand, who'd been a senior IT man in an American owned company, had had no influence in shaping the organisation he was to head.

I shall always remember my introduction to Michael – we met on the morning of his appointment in his office and his first words to me were 'Can you show me your Procedure Manuals?' I hadn't a clue what he meant, revealing the wide culture clash between a nationalised industry in which the managers knew one another and had worked together for years, developing an informal but effective structure based on the knowledge of, and trust in each other, and private industry – especially American owned ones – where formal management systems were necessary because of the frequent movement of managers in and out of the company. Michael's expectations and priorities were at odds from the word go and I know he had a hard time developing sound relationships especially with the five powerful Regional General Managers.

He didn't help himself by being overly concerned with what many railwaymen saw as peripheral status issues – his office equipment and furniture, chauffeur provision. He and I went to many meetings jointly in the early days as he picked up the key parts of the job, and jokingly we often separated, Michael insisting on taking the chauffeur driven car whilst I plumped for the quicker underground invariably arriving at our destination first. This was not just about scoring points off Michael – I still had a tendency to be car sick if driven, especially if I tried to read anything while we were driving and Michael would want to open papers and discuss them with me en route which caused such problems to arise.

Michael Ferrand wanted to build on his own expertise in the IT area and he and Hylton Craig, who led the BR IT development unit, were soon vying for the leadership of BR's pilot studies in these areas and choice of equipment. This left me to carry on building the teams on the Regions and establishing good relationships with Regional General Management – essential if we were to be effective. One consequence of the competing drive to introduce new technology was that I found myself the guinea pig to have the first word processor to be used in general administration. It was believed that the extra capacity and productivity of the new equipment would enable my secretary to take on additional managers, certainly one, perhaps even two.

Events soon proved this a major mistake. Certainly my secretary's productivity improved, but so did mine. In consequence, my secretary found her work increased threefold and this was proved invaluable during a major exercise mounted in 1979, which became known as 'The Challenge of the Eighties'.

In the late seventies government policy had been to restrict the annual pay increases in the public sector, with general rises above inflation to be funded only by demonstrable productivity improvements. This led to annual increasingly bitter arguments between management and trade unions over decimal point percentages. Fearing the impact of a potential Conservative government after the May 1979 election, the trade unions hastily entered into a 'Pay and Productivity' agreement in April 1979, and then found after the election that other nationalised industries achieved better pay deals with no strings attached. Sidney Weighall, General Secretary of the NUR, reported to the Board that he was finding it difficult to deliver on the agreement and in some exasperation, challenged management to 'think big' and put on the table substantial productivity improvements they wished to see in exchange for a significant general pay rise – aiming at 10-20% improvements on both sides. Peter Parker, the Board Chairman, took up the challenge and Cliff Rose, by then the Board Member for Personnel, took charge of the studies and subsequent negotiations. Five management teams were to be set up mirroring those of the trade union groupings – Operations (Signalling), Operations (Train Crews), Operations (Terminals), Engineering and Administration.

The BR Consultancy Services senior staff were heavily involved in the Working Groups for each theme and were given the task of identifying potential productivity improvements in their area and costing them ready for negotiations with the unions. We were set the target of identifying a 20% reduction in costs without any significant reduction in the business. There was to be a co-ordinating group and I was charged with acting as secretary and organiser of this group bringing together the daily results from each team and identifying any duplication or possible complementary savings.

This is where my word processor paid off. Every evening I would receive the day's deliberations from each Working Party and would add anything new to the existing lists modifying changes that had occurred. Of course, it was easy to build on the work already done without having to retype everything and at 9am every morning the five team leaders found a complete up-to-date list of all identified schemes and an estimate of cost savings against each. We had just a fortnight of intensive work and I can well remember the last night when the final document was drawn up – some 40 or 50 pages of typed proposals. At 3am Cliff Rose and another couple of us could be found photocopying the completed document and laying the pages in piles round the boardroom large table, then circling the table gathering a sheet from each pile to provide a separate booklet for each manager and each trade union representative engaged in the exercise.

The results formed the basis of a significant number of productivity agreements in the early 1980s – single-manning of modern traction units, flexible train crew rostering, one man operation of suburban and local passenger services, removal of ticket platform barrier staff and encompassing ticket examination on train within the guard's duties where guards were to be retained. These were the biggest and most controversial of the many ideas put forward and eventually agreed. It caused a row between the two major trade unions because the initiative came from the NUR but the most significant job cuts would come from ASLEF members.

There was some disappointment that no great productivity improvements had been identified in administration, but the team felt there was scope for challenging the necessity for some of the work, rather than trying to do it all more efficiently – mainly through investment in technology which did not release sufficient savings to fund the investment and offer a large pay increase to clerical workers. Therefore in 1981 we embarked on what was known as the 'Discretionary Cost Analysis' where every single clerical unit had to work with Consultancy Services to identify and quantify all work carried out and rank it in order of importance. Then the sections concerned had to justify why the bottom 20% was required at all – or if needed, whether there were other simple ways of achieving the same end.

I worked closely with Leslie Soane, General Manager of the Scottish Region, on this and one of the key findings was the amount of duplication between the departments in different tiers or levels of the whole organisation. We began to look at the options of eliminating at least one tier and hotly fought debates took place about whether the Regions or Divisions should be abolished. There was even a school of thought that wanted to eliminate both and, with stronger functional lines, go straight from Board to depot or area level. This would come about as the new Chairman, Robert Reid (Mark 1), began to push the concept of business management strongly, but the railway was not ready for this yet and the Regional General Managers fought a fierce battle to retain their Regional structures.

The Discretionary Cost Analysis teams had done their work by this time and the organisational structure debate took place under the aegis of Jim Urquhart with my Consultancy Services well to the fore. I can remember before one crucial meeting on this with the General Managers, which Jim Urquhart chaired, Michael Ferrand was due to make the presentation. However, Michael's relationship with the General Managers was not good and as I had done most of the work behind the paper we were presenting, I was asked to take over ten minutes before the start of the meeting. This mollified the GMs to some extent as I had a good working understanding with the two General Managers that were most vociferous in their opposition, Frank Paterson and Leslie Lloyd, but I did feel as though I was taking a particularly difficult trade union meeting. The die was cast and the Divisional structure was doomed – part of which process I found I now had to implement in my next job.

Between the Board's 'Opportunity for Change' report in late 1976, proposing investment and workload changes, BR's total staff was to reduce from 190,000 to 150,000 and by 1982 this was being achieved through the implementation of the 'Challenge of the Eighties' and the 'Discretionary Cost Analysis' – or was embedded in the budgetary and planning systems. The Consultancy Services Department had played a significant role in this and by the time I was offered a new role back in Operations, Jim Urquhart was concluding that the time was ripe to move the department's key resources from an advisory to an executive role, as the issue was now one of implementation. In January 1983 the department's staff were dispersed back to the production functions mostly within the developing Business Sectors, the productivity monitoring role becoming part of Finance & Planning and the Director's contract expired in 1984.

Woking Staff College Course 36, March 1974 – Principal, Gordon Beard, and his wife, Elizabeth in the centre, the author's syndicate tutor, Charles Millard in the light-coloured suit in the front row and next to him, on the right, Hugh Jenkins, another tutor and later Assistant General Manager LMR, when the author was Regional Operations Manager. The author is near the centre of the photo nearly at the back, still with a good head of black hair!

Chapter 11: 1982 - 1986
Regional Operating Manager, Crewe

Jim O'Brien, London Midland General Manager, sent for me in the summer of 1982 and offered me the post of Chief Operating Manager of his Region. I was astonished, as I think were many others, but he had known me when he was Assistant General Manager of the Western Region and I was the Region's Management Services Manager. We had maintained contact during my higher profile time at the BRB when I led the Board's Productivity team during critical negotiations with the top trade union officials. My High Wycombe neighbours were similarly impressed until they heard that I was to be based at Crewe amid what they imagined were the North's dark satanic mills. I had to point out that outside the immediate confines of the town there were cows and grass and trees and that generally Cheshire was acceptable as an abode, even for those who had never ventured north of the Watford Gap M1 service station.

It was acknowledged that my 'Rules & Regs' knowledge might be a little rusty and even out of date, so I was sent secretly to spend a couple of days with a friendly opposite number on the Western, Fred Walmsley, who spent time bringing my knowledge of Track Circuit Block Signalling up to scratch. Thus equipped I ventured to appear at Rail House at Crewe and was promptly taken under the wing of Peggy, my new secretary, who had doubtless mothered my predecessors. Then began the process of acquainting myself with the Region's geography and my 25,000 staff – at least as a railway enthusiast I was not ignorant of the former, although the railway geography of northern Manchester including the network of services radiating from Manchester Victoria was a bit of a mystery to me. I now had to curb my outings and pay close attention to the responsibility I had for train running on the West Coast and Midland Main Lines.

The Region's management was dispersed – Operations in Crewe, Mechanical Engineering at Derby and General Management at Euston, so the GM's Monday morning 'Prayers' were essential for all of his team. After my first meeting I returned to Crewe on the 18.05 Euston – Preston and Blackpool and noted a/c electric locomotive 86.259 *Peter Pan* at the head end. We got only as far as Wembley before we came to a halt and an ominous silence reigned. Eventually after a delay of 70 minutes 87.028 appeared from Willesden Depot only a mile away, coupled on ahead of the failed locomotive and we continued north. Leaving Rugby, we suddenly ground to a halt again and it transpired that 87.028 had now expired, and worse, had experienced brake problems that proved impossible to release. Eventually we were hauled back into Rugby by an 86/3, leaving the two disabled electrics on the Down Main just beyond the Birmingham line flyover and the new loco ran round and got us to Crewe just before midnight. Enthusiastic in my new duties, I offered help to the guard and went through the front half of the train explaining what had happened and offering to take messages – it was before the days of mobile phones. By the time I alighted at Crewe I had 58 messages to pass on from the Crewe booking office phone – the front coach was full of French schoolchildren going for exchange visits to families all over Cumbria and two gentlemen implored me to advise their wives of the reason for their delay, as they would not otherwise be believed!

The next Monday evening I caught the 18.05 again and 86.259 was once more the loco – and it failed en route yet again. Crewe Control realised that this loco was becoming my bête noir and started warning me (and my wife) when that loco was in danger of appearing on a train I was due to take. When, a couple of years later, the Great Eastern Section demanded four 86s for crew training to Norwich, Crewe Control with some irony selected 86.259 and 86.416 *Wigan Pier* and I gather one of them pulled the wires down in Liverpool Street station the first time the loco set foot in it. I subsequently had a number of perfectly adequate runs behind 86.259, including cab rides as I made it my principle to ride with drivers as much as possible – they used to complain that they only saw management when they were 'on the carpet'. *Peter Pan* has since metamorphosed into the preserved heritage locomotive named *Les Ross* after the Birmingham DJ who now owns it, via some ridiculous interim name dreamt up by the marketing people, and I had the pleasure recently of supplying Les with the details of its nefarious past.

The unreliability of my first two return journeys from the LM management conference caused me to consider the risks of missing the starts of key meetings held in London and I was informed of the availability of a flat on the top floor of Euston House, then the LMR headquarters – later to become the Board headquarters when 222, Marylebone Road was sold. Although this accommodation was primarily for the General Manager's use, it was frequently used by myself and Doug Power as we were both outbased at Crewe and Derby respectively. There were of course early morning trains from Crewe including the overnight sleepers from Scotland, but they were not as frequent or as fast as the current early morning Pendolino services now. Once the decision had been taken to sell 222 and move the BRB to Euston, the Regional team moved to Birmingham and I had no alternative but to take an early morning service.

My first cab ride in my new post was on a London – Liverpool train, non-stop to Crewe scheduled in an hour and three quarters and I was surprised to find one of the 1959 series electrics, 85.030, in command. We ran hell for leather and kept time, but I kept looking at the driver to see if he showed any signs of alarm, for I had never experienced such a rough ride before. I saw that the driver seemed unperturbed, so I jammed my knees under the second man's desk and held on tight. The track south of Rugby was in poor condition with many wet spots and the loco seemed to bury itself in these, then bounce violently. The Civil Engineer eventually got budget funds to address the state of this stretch of track although the number of p-way restrictions while this was done was very damaging to punctuality in my first year in the post.

I was of course responsible for train and passenger safety on the Region and it was not long before I was tested with my first serious emergency. Despite the gap of over ten years since I'd last been 'on call' it appeared that my capacity to act as 'Jonah' was undiminished. A night sleeper had derailed in Linslade tunnel near Leighton Buzzard and on emerging from the tunnel in a derailed state at about 50 mph, its class 81 electric had hit the overbridge just outside and killed the driver.

Although most of the train was derailed, we were fortunate that no passengers suffered serious injury and I took charge of the site and diversionary arrangements for the next day's business. The LMR had a series of 'contingency plans' already timed and diagrammed that could be put swiftly into effect and I decided to implement CP1, covering a total line blockage south of Rugby, necessitating Birmingham services starting from Paddington, Scottish services from Kings Cross and other services diverted to St Pancras and back onto the West Coast Main Line at Nuneaton. The reason for the derailment was obvious. A piece of new switch and crossing trackwork being transported to site had come loose from its wagon during transit of the tunnel on the Up Slow Line and had fallen, being picked up by the bogie of the locomotive. It was more difficult at the internal inquiry, which I took, to establish the root cause and culpability for the slack loading and inspection before the freight left the private sidings at Long Eaton between Derby and Nottingham – whether the load had ever been properly secured, or whether it had suffered a rough shunt loosening the ropes and straps before it was marshalled into the service from which the crossing work fell and whether the guard of the freight had been lax in not observing the risk before train departure. As so often, it was a case of conflicting evidence between the individuals involved each seeking to lay the blame elsewhere.

In my first summer we ran a couple of interesting tests for the InterCity business. The Passenger Manager wanted to accelerate trains to Scotland so we ran a high speed test with 87.005, the Royal Train engine at that time, and a ten coach train. We sought to climb Shap without falling below 100 mph, but there was a slight drizzle on the fells and try as we might we could not get it above 92 mph as every time we opened up further wheelslip began. Another more successful test was carried out with a motley collection of Mark 1 stock to sample the ride when exceeding the speed limit on certain curves between Euston and Manchester via Stoke, as most restrictions were unnecessary purely for safety purposes. Volunteers agreed to ride in various vehicles at the critical points and report on their experience. One poor soul was consigned to the toilet – presumably someone kept up a suitable supply of liquid to him to make the test realistic! I had a more congenial task of drinking interminable cups of coffee in the buffet car. The only point at which we were severely discomforted by the ride was passing the Weedon ground frame at 100 instead of the normally allowed 80 mph. Other restrictions were raised although the Weedon slowing stayed until track renewal many years later.

I mentioned that after the first failure on the 18.05 Euston, our train was rescued by a class 86/3. These twenty AL6 locomotives were from the 1965 built group of electrics that had not had their springs modified although allowed 100 mph – a further nineteen, the 86/0s, were restricted to 80 mph and were used almost exclusively on freight. The rough riding of the 86/3s at speed was notorious among drivers and it became pretty obvious to me quite quickly that they were called upon for top link passenger work too often. I struck a deal with Bert Jones, the Board Director of Operations' Resources Manager, that we would offset other cost savings to invest in the modification of all the 86/0s and 86/3s and they became 86.401-439 and worked turn and turn about with the 86/2s until the advent of the 90s when some were further modified for the Freightliner business and became 86/5s and 86/6s.

I often rode the 86/4s, which I considered 'my' engines and remember one particular journey from Crewe to Glasgow in the cab of 86.434 *University of London* (my college). All was normal as far as Preston where we changed crews and the London man gave way to a Polmadie driver. The latter was a cheery soul who chatted to me all the way to Glasgow. Unfortunately his Glaswegian accent was so thick that I hardly understood a word and kept nodding or grunting at appropriate places hoping that I was causing no offence. I kept my eyes skinned on the signals in case I was a distraction to him – I didn't want to be the first Chief Operating Manager served a Form 1 for incurring a SPAD (Signal Passed at Danger).

In the early 1980s we were testing the three Advanced Passenger Train (APT) sets – one based at Crewe for crew training and tests and one at Glasgow, which, with the London set, initiated passenger trials. I travelled in the cab of the Crewe train with members of the ASLEF Trade Union and we had an excellent run – in fact comfort in the cab seemed superior to that in the train. At least we were not subject there to any of the signs of nausea that some early passengers and press complained of – it was suspected that the sickness experienced by some of the press during a demonstration run may have been exacerbated by over-indulging in BR's liquid hospitality! Cyril Bleasdale, Director InterCity, asked us to run a non-stop high speed run to Glasgow to demonstrate what the unit could do and I was the Operator in charge of the run, saddled with the responsibility of ensuring no signal delays. All was going well until we approached Stafford when we came to a halt before a red signal protecting the line from Birmingham. I was about to be subjected to a barrage of banter from the engineers present when Ken Burrage, the Regional Signal Engineer, discovered that the stop was caused by a track circuit failure and I was let off the hook. Despite this, we raced north in a record time of 3 hours 52 minutes from London to Glasgow, a time still to be beaten by a Pendolino unit.

Unfortunately the Glasgow unit, which seemed more prone to problems than the others, failed due to a frozen brake system shortly after leaving Glasgow on a press demonstration run, and bad publicity followed the APT around after that, with every incident getting reported in the press. Political and managerial pressure to introduce the APT prematurely to passenger service mounted and the units started regular running in 1984, when continuing problems reduced both passenger and Board management's confidence as costs rose. A final straw was when an APT unit broke an axle at speed near Lancaster during a high profile test run and shortly afterwards the tilt train system was abandoned in the UK until the Italians picked up where we had stopped.

I found myself in charge of a different sort of special in 1984 when the Central Electricity Generating Board commissioned us to carry out a 'test to destruction' - a high speed collision involving a rail-mounted nuclear flask. There had been public and media concern about the safety of movement of nuclear materials by rail and so with engineers at Derby research, we set up a demonstration on their Old Dalby test track. The CEGB purchased two redundant class 46s for the project and they were wired to accelerate three Mark I coaches to 100 mph at the point of impact with a derailed nuclear flask wagon, tilted so that its theoretically weakest point would take the main impact. The train would be set off by a driver who would then dismount leaving the engine in full throttle. If the train had not reached 60 mph by a specified point, the trial could be aborted through application of some sort of track based trip mechanism.

After initial tests, a public demonstration was arranged and grandstand seats were set up in an adjoining field to the impact point for the CEGB and BR officials, media and the CEGB's critics. 46009 duly collided with the nuclear flask at 98 mph, was itself destroyed (although the Mark I coaches were remarkably undamaged externally) and the flask itself was completely intact. Even despite this, critics were not satisfied. Some people will only see what they want to see. As far as BR was concerned, it was a highly successful and profitable event. I understand the CEGB paid a substantial sum for the test and I calculated our costs, suggesting that this was much more profitable than many of our activities then under financial scrutiny. I mooted that expansion of this was a more profitable line of business for BR!

One area where I inherited a really poor service was the St Pancras - Luton - Bedford suburban service, run with first generation DMUs, then in a very unreliable condition. Electrification was taking place, but punctuality performance had dropped to 27% in the last year of DMU operation. We were struggling with trade union negations over the proposed 'Driver Only Operation' ('DOO') of these trains - one of the productivity principles agreed at the 'Challenge of the Eighties' described in the last chapter. We eventually succeeded and in 1984 I was present at the opening of the new service at Moorgate. The improvement was immediate and spectacular. The first year's operation saw 94% right time performance. It is interesting to note, however, that when this dropped to 87% the following year, we received more complaints than when the service was only 27% punctual. Such was the effect of the heightened expectation!

I was in charge of operations over the Settle & Carlisle and in March 1983 I was invited by John Peck, the Hon CM&EE for the Friends of the National Railway Museum, to join his party in the support coach behind LMS 'Princess Coronation' pacific *Duchess of Hamilton* at Leeds and ride the footplate from Hellifield to Garsdale. Theoretically I was checking the safety of such steam specials for myself, and in reality I couldn't resist this invitation and had a splendid day out - and got paid for it! We had a heavy 14 coach load of 565 tons gross and - with Driver Ken Iveson and Fireman John Brown of Skipton and Inspector Arthur Morris of Preston - we left Hellifield 14 minutes late. We accelerated to exactly 60 mph at Settle Junction and held a steady 38 mph through Stainforth and Horton-in-Ribblesdale, accelerating to 45 mph and holding that on the long 1 in 100, easing to 30 mph over Ribblehead viaduct. We drifted down to Dent and Garsdale arriving just one minute late. It was most impressive, performed without any fuss, steam pressure rock steady, the engine riding like a Pullman coach.

I had an enthusiastic Loco Inspector, Phil Bassett based in Birmingham, who persuaded me - again, with not a lot of difficulty

- to make an annual check on the safety of these trains by riding on the footplate from Banbury to Marylebone. In March 1985 the motive power was a former Southern 'Merchant Navy', *Clan Line* with 11 coaches, 360 tons gross. We had Driver Brian Axtell and Fireman Brian Tagg of Marylebone and Inspector Peter Crawley of Euston. We took on 5,000 gallons of water at Banbury and set off 10 minutes late. We freewheeled the downhill stretch from Ardley summit with liberal interpretation of the speed limit despite my presence - I think they wanted to demonstrate to me the ridiculousness of the 60 limit - touching 75 after Bicester, when I was handed the shovel. I fired from Bicester to Ashendon Junction, and maintained pressure at 220 pounds per square inch, during which time we'd observed a 20 mph p-way slack, then opened up achieving 42 at Brill Tunnel at the summit of the 1 in 200 gradient. After Ashendon Junction the steam pressure took a nose dive to 170 psi - was it belatedly my fault? However, we were on time at High Wycombe where we stopped to take on a further 1,600 gallons of water. The fireman, after discussions with the Inspector, altered the damper setting and we had no trouble with steaming for the rest of the journey, arriving at Marylebone 4 minutes early.

Later that year, in November, Phil Bassett took me himself on LNER A4 *Sir Nigel Gresley* with a heavy 12 coach 460 ton load. We had Driver Trevor Barrett and Fireman Brian Tagg once more. The train arrived very late from the Eastern Region at Banbury (it had started from York) and we left 69 minutes late after filling the tender with 4,250 gallons. We crawled to a stand at Bicester waiting for the 17.40 Paddington DMU to come off the single line. Departing 91 minutes late I was offered the driver's seat and regulator and to this day I'm convinced Phil was anticipating that I'd exceed the 60 limit and strengthen his case for that limit's abolition. I had my college friend, train timer Alistair Wood, in the train behind, so I knew every speed would be meticulously recorded. I quickly adjusted the cut off to 15% with full regulator as we accelerated to exactly 60 mph at Ashendon Junction, brought the regulator back to half to maintain this speed to Phil's obvious chagrin and then opened up to full regulator again as we hit the rise after Haddenham. I must admit we slightly exceeded the limit just reaching 64 at that point but I increased the cut off to 25% as we approached Princes Risborough at 58 mph and I enjoyed myself in the darkness pulling the chord for a long blast on the chime whistle as we hurled ourselves through the waiting crowds on the platform. The steam pressure was solid at 225 psi and we maintained 54 mph on the final part of the climb to Saunderton. I had gained 15 minutes on schedule from Bicester to High Wycombe without excessive speed and I was very proud of myself! I handed the driver's seat back to Trevor Barrett after Wycombe and just enjoyed the pleasure of the effortless run into London.

There were other enjoyable occasions to which I was invited as the LM's senior Operations representative. My family were guests at the Crewe Works Open Days when my children particularly enjoyed climbing aboard the various locomotives displayed. I was also introduced to Ian Allan's Great Cockrow 7¼" gauge railway at Chertsey - over four miles of track fully signalled to BR standards. I was told that new signalling innovations, including the 'flashing yellow' indication, were first tried out there. I was given charge of Richard Stokes' GW 'Mere Hall', Mike Johns' K3 and John Butt's unrebuilt 'Royal Scot' on various visits - all by courtesy of colleagues alongside whom I'd worked. This could be quite a test of enginemanship when it was possible to really mess up the busy schedule by running short of steam. I'm please to say I did not disgrace myself apart from giving John Butt a scare when on the first trip with 6100 I discovered rather late that the brake valve operated in the opposite direction to the other locomotives and we sailed round the first curve rather too near the safety margin for comfort. I also have a shot of my 12 year old daughter, Helen, driving a model 'Black 5' with Malcolm Southgate, the LM General Manager, and Cyril Bleasdale, then InterCity Director, as passengers (unfortunately too blurred to reproduce here)!

Throughout my time at Crewe I was Officer-in-charge of the Royal Train when it started on the LMR and when the Queen herself was on board. The arrangement between Regional Managers was that the Officer from the originating Region would see the train through to destination, so most fell to me (London/Euston departures) and the Western Region man (for Windsor starters). For other members of the royal family, I could and did delegate the 'mini-royals' as they were known, to one of my other officers. I was assured before my first royal trip that a uniform bowler hat was 'de rigueur' for the royal officer but I was reluctant to buy such a headpiece just for that. I solved the problem by borrowing a bowler from an elderly widow at our local church.

It didn't fit - it was too small - but I did not have to wear it, only tuck it under my arm and doff it on appropriate occasions. Margaret Halden, whose late husband's hat it was, used to retrieve it after the trip and place it back in its immaculate box with the inscription 'This hat has been doffed to the Queen x times'. After each tour of duty she would cross x out and replace it with x+1 and so on.

I would average 5-10 royal trains a year, usually starting from Euston in the late evening, stabling overnight at some remote and secret siding location and proceeding unhurriedly in the morning to the nearest station to the Queen's first engagement. Timekeeping on this last leg was absolutely essential and I took pride in the train drawing to a stand as the second hand crept towards the twelve of the appointed minute. I only failed once – I'd gone north to Glasgow with 87.023 as our engine (that and 87.024 were my regulars – 87.002 and 87.005 were also used from time to time). We were timed via Birmingham New Street to spend some pathing time and avoid the rush of West Coast night mail and newspaper trains, and when we drew punctually to a stand, I was informed that 87.035, waiting to drop on our rear, had just failed. 87.023 therefore ran round and we departed 6 minutes late, which we soon made up and arrived punctually at our stabling point, some half hour from Glasgow Central.

It was in January and there was an extremely heavy frost overnight and I was alarmed to see that our relief train crew had not arrived at their rostered time. When they did arrive they found they were unable to raise the pantograph of the electric loco and soon there were men in orange jackets swarming all over it. Then we found the semaphore signal controlling the exit from the siding was frozen in the on position and no-one could free it. I lost patience with the efforts to release 87.023's pantograph and decided with the Scottish Inspector that we'd recouple the Class 47 that had drawn us into the siding and get it to propel us to Central station, with the main crew in the front loco to control the brakes. We eventually set off and I calculated that we'd be at least 20 minutes late at our destination. This was relayed to the Queen's secretary and I awaited events, my heart in my mouth. I suddenly noticed that we were being propelled at a fair pace – the speedometer in my saloon indicated 75mph, whereas I had thought we were restricted to 40 mph in propelling mode. Before I could take breath, I realised we were crossing the Clyde and just managed to get a message to the Queen that we were now arriving less than ten minutes late. I was told subsequently that Prince Philip was totally unready, still in his shirt sleeves at a computer although apparently the Queen riposted that she was ready as she had her hat on!

My predecessor, John Gregory, had told me of an incident when he was in charge of the royal train which was a precursor to a speeding upset of my own. The Queen does not like high speed (although her 'coasting' comfortable speed of 70-80 mph is double that which her ancestor, Queen Victoria, permitted in her lifetime). The royal train vehicle bogies had been modified to permit 100 mph although this capability was not normally used. However, on one occasion Prince Philip had been delayed at an evening commitment and the royal car arrived some 20 minutes after the train should have departed from Euston. At that time there were still several important 100 mph night postal and newspaper trains and one was due to depart only about five minutes after the royal was ready to go. The police told John that they were not prepared to stand letting the newspaper train precede so arrangements were made for the royal train to be diverted via Northampton for the mail and newspaper trains to overtake and the royal train would use its capability to run at 100 mph as far as Hanslope Junction. Apparently John, so he said, was sitting relaxed in the officer's saloon thinking he'd solved that problem, when the phone rang and he heard one of the Queen's Ladies in Waiting shouting 'For God's sake slow this train down! The Queen's bath water is hitting the ceiling!'

John Gregory refrained from asking if Her Majesty was in the bath at the time or even suggesting that a body in the bath might have a calming effect on the water, but I remembered his anecdote when later I provided a few incidents from a 'Fat Controller's viewpoint' to the storyteller writing the 'Thomas the Tank Engine' books after the death of the Rev. Awdry. I wonder if the Queen ever sat with her grandchildren watching the video in which the Fat Controller's mother attempts to have a bath in her VIP saloon but Thomas is going too fast and her bathwater is splashing the ceiling in her coach and realises where the story originated! I was also told of another occasion when John Gregory managed to give the signal for the royal train to depart from Liverpool Lime Street and somehow failed to board the train himself. He had to commandeer a car and chase the train joining it at a suitable location half an hour later.

I managed to avoid such a misfortune, but I had my own 'speeding' problem. We'd left our stabling point in north Cheshire on time, but had to run the gauntlet of the West Coast main line at line speed between Warrington and Wigan before bearing off to Southport, our destination. This meant our class 47 had to sustain 80-90 mph on this stretch and I had not realised that the Queen was taking breakfast during this period. We hit the 70 mph curve after Warrington at Winwick Junction at just over 60 and got an immediate frantic phone call from the royal dining saloon imploring me to slow the train as the Queen thought we had been derailed. A few minutes later we hit Golborne Junction at 84 mph against the permitted 90 and I got a further irate call to say that the Queen had spilt coffee down her dress and was having to change to a new outfit. The dining table in the royal saloon ran lengthways down the centre of the coach and so she rolled with the curve. The expected visit to the Tower did not materialise but I soon obtained an understanding with the Queen's officials that they would advise the train planners when the Queen would be having a meal so that the train schedule took this into account and did not require the train to exceed 50 mph. In this case, it would have been difficult as the Sovereign does not like delaying ordinary passengers and we couldn't have occupied the main line at the lower speed between Warrington and Wigan in the morning peak without substantially affecting other trains.

We had one royal trip, which had the potential of a number of things going wrong. The Queen was attending the Royal Show in Builth Wells on the Central Wales line and the royal train was routed from Euston to Crewe and then across to Shrewsbury and Craven Arms, the eleven coach train being topped and tailed by two class 47 diesels. There had been considerable apprehension about taking such a cavalcade down the Central Wales line where we would have to cross at least one normal DMU service. All went well, however, until we arrived at Builth Wells station. The engine drew up correctly to the white marker board, but I noticed that the red carpet did not match the door of the royal saloon from which the Queen and Prince Philip would alight. The Queen stepped out as normal and walked unobtrusively to the carpet but Prince Philip took an enormous 'John Cleese Ministry of Silly Walks' step of about two metres to the carpet and remarked to all present that they must have a learner driver on this morning, a most unfair remark because it transpired that the Western Region station staff had measured up wrongly - perhaps the Welsh used an ancient Celtic measuring system.

I have to say that the duty of the Officer-in-charge of the royal train was usually an easy task, as certainly everything on the LMR was planned down to the last detail. However, I was never relaxed until we had deposited the royal party at their destination in case anything went wrong and urgent high profile decisions had to be made. On one occasion I had to get Jim Summers, my Scottish Region counterpart, up at 2am to check our route availability from Carlisle to Aberdour via Perth instead of via Edinburgh as the police had had a phone call advising that there was a bomb on the Forth Bridge. Having got the all clear from Jim and told that the engine would run round outside Perth station, a footman rang to ask when the royal Corgies would be able to uncross their legs as the stabling time had disappeared with the diversion. We therefore rerouted the train into a Perth platform at 5am to allow the footman to walk the dogs. When we stopped the still air was rent with howling dogs for the police had turned up with Alsatians who were having Corgies for breakfast!

It was pleasant on the home run. After the royal party had alighted I would travel back with the empty stock as far as Crewe (the train went on to Wolverton where it was stabled). On one occasion returning from Glasgow in mid morning, we ran into Carlisle station middle road just as I was being served lunch on a silver platter by the royal restaurant crew. The platform at Carlisle was full of passengers awaiting the London service that was due to overtake us, and seeing me in state everyone began to wave to me. I practised my royal hand wave – I've no idea who they thought I was, but I'm sure most told their children that they'd seen royalty.

Much of my time as Chief Operating Manager, later renamed Regional Operating Manager, at Crewe was taken up with coping with various organisational changes, an obsession of BR management since the early 1960s. Gone were the days when Philip Rees, the WR Chief Civil Engineer, could say to the 14th Minister of Transport since nationalisation that he was the 14th Chief Civil Engineer of the Great Western Railway and its successor since Mr Brunel. In the last chapter I referred to the proposed elimination of the Regions' Divisional set-ups from a Board point of view. Now I had to implement it. One essential if we were to lose this 'middle' tier of management was to strengthen the ground level by ensuring that the Areas had the right people running them. We were reviewing their boundaries and trying to find an optimum size, which would justify the sort of manager we needed for the future. Between 1982 and 1984 I was appointing men like Jan Glasscock, Gordon Ford, Sam Reed, Adrian Shooter, John Mummery, Iain King, Colin Hamer and Mostyn Goodwin to Area Management positions and setting up direct lines of responsibility between me and them, cutting out the Divisional structure.

In the initial stages, I needed some support in the former Divisional geographical areas - to be my eyes and ears, not to have any sort of administrative life. I therefore retained three Operating Superintendents, Alec Wise at Preston, Brian Scott succeeded by Bob Owen at Birmingham and David McKeever on the Midland. Their role was to ensure safety and train performance and assist me in the day to day dealings with the Area Managers. We set up regular Area Managers' conferences to tackle some of the key issues and then I turned my attention to the Divisional Control offices, which had been retained for a temporary period after the demise of the Divisional Managers' organisations. Much of my Headquarters Control in Crewe had outdated equipment due for renewal and we seized the opportunity to go for the latest touch screen technology with the opportunity in future to hold so much more data required for decision-making by controllers on-line instead of in the myriad booklets and bits of paper that traditionally littered Control Office desks. I appointed a brilliant S&T specialist, Richard Stokes, to lead the small team, a man whose eccentric sense of humour (he told jokes in Latin on one occasion) and intellectual capability did not easily fit into the robust and forthright culture of day to day Operators. There was a lot of scepticism about whether our high tech vision for the new HQ Crewe Control would work, but we persevered and I held the doubters at bay and the transition was implemented remarkably smoothly in 1985.

I remember the large consultation meeting with representatives from around seven of the Controls being displaced. One member of the Manchester Control was especially vociferous and foretold chaos if their organisation did not remain to sort out the daily failures and DMU manipulations they had to resort to, to keep the trains running in the Manchester, Preston, Liverpool and Chester area networks. My experience at Cardiff came back to me and I realised that by their manoeuvrings the Manchester Control was prolonging a bad plan by covering up its deficiencies. When I investigated their claims, I found the situation even worse than I thought when the degree of unit failures that they had been trying to cover was way outside any standards held by the M&EE function. When Douglas Power studied my concerns he found a major problem at Newton Heath depot, which was only solved by making significant changes there. Thus Manchester Control, in what the individual controllers thought was the best interest of the customer, had managed to prolong the problem which could have been addressed much earlier had the root cause been identified.

During my tenure of office, there was concern that management of the Midland Main Line as well as the West Coast was too much for any one individual and there were suggestions that the Midland might be transferred to another Region. I was horrified - the Midland was no trouble - indeed its punctuality record kept the average of the LM Region punctuality statistics up the Regional InterCity table! Once I had a strong Area Management team at Derby, Nottingham, Leicester, Toton and St Pancras, I told David McKeever and the Area Managers to get on with running the Midland patch without interference from my Crewe Headquarters and they did just that revelling in the authority they had been given. We went one further - Roger Williams, my ER opposite number, and I with support from AGM Ivor Warburton and Freight Manager, John Edmonds, enlarged the Toton area to include both LMR and ER territory and made the Area Manager virtually self-sufficient. Whilst technically responsible to me - I still did his annual appraisal - to all intents and purposes he reported to the Freight Business thus anticipating the full introduction of Business Sector Management, which was the next major organisational upheaval on the horizon.

The development of Business Management had significant implications for the production functions and general management. Five businesses – InterCity, Network SouthEast, Provincial Services, Parcels and Freight – would assume the leadership role in decisions about investment, running costs and standards of service, with Operations and Engineering functions having an interim tricky period in which they reported to the new businesses for policy and to general geographical management for the plan's efficient implementation. Some routes were clearly the responsibility of one of these businesses but my Region – and particularly the West Coast Main Line – was very much a mixed traffic railway, and the interface with the new businesses was complex, especially while the Regional General Management structure remained.

One of the issues I had to face, therefore, was the relationship between the Operations Planning organisation and the increasing clout of these businesses. The Crewe Train Planning Office, especially the Train Timing Section, had developed a reputation for being inflexible and procedure-bound, unacceptable to the business management now beginning to flourish and flex its wings. There was a growing tension that I saw could easily cause a shift to the opposite extreme when the operating disciplines could be ignored with much grief as a result. Therefore I made it my priority to understand the objectives and needs of the business sectors and try to wean my train planners to a more positive approach to see how things could be done rather than find the obstacles. At the same time I had to caution the businesses to consider the realities and not to assume that the tightest and cheapest solution without any contingency cover would work in practice. We were being pushed hardest initially by the Freight business, then even more severely by the Provincial Services sector, which was under enormous pressure to reduce costs and saw the advent of new DMUs in the 150 series as the ideal opportunity to achieve 100% availability and utilisation. The realism of planning the minimum maintenance required to the hours and locations when the sets were not actually in use was fine theoretically, but did not hold good in practice and some compromises had to be made on both sides. I like to think that we managed to avoid the extreme conflict, which had threatened at one stage.

During my time as Regional Operations Manager I had to think hard about our systems for managing safety and the culture surrounding it as we had a number of train accidents, some with serious potential, around 1984-5. I was becoming aware that BR's traditional reliance on the 'rules' culture was inadequate and did not take into account often enough the context in which rules were applied or ignored, an issue to which I was to return in much greater depth after the Clapham Junction accident in December 1988. This weakness was highlighted for me by an accident at Dorridge one Sunday to an express rerouted because of engineering work. A cross-country train hauled by a class 47 with Mark II coaches, was derailed and turned on its side when it ran through a cross-over at 60 mph instead of the permitted 20 mph. Luckily, despite the train being crowded, there were no fatalities or very serious injuries, but the inquiry identified a number of disturbing factors. There had been confusion over which set of points was being used as part of the single-line working resulting in the driver not being properly instructed. I identified errors by seven different Operating staff which was bad enough, but the entire site was under the supervision of a comparatively young and keen Movements Supervisor who had prided himself in his 'Rules & Regulations' knowledge, had taken the R&R exams three years running, coming top of the Region and earning monetary rewards. The raft of mistakes stemmed initially from the inability of the man, who knew what should happen, to counter the culture of an experienced signalman who persuaded him 'that we always do it this way, boss'. The result - modification of plans being implemented, confused briefing, poor communication.

I felt that knowledge of rules was too often tested 'parrot fashion', ie there was more emphasis on getting the words right than understanding the situations in which certain rules became vital or looking at the application of rules in problematical situations. Later, when I was evaluating BR's safety management systems after the Clapham Junction accident, I spent time with James Reason, Professor at Manchester University who was an expert in understanding human error. He shared with me his belief from research he and others had carried out that decisions were routine, rule- based or problem-solving and made in normal or stressed environments and times. In each of these situations the percentage of errors could be anticipated. I'd already been well aware of signals passed at danger (SPADs) as a key risk and whilst the 'routine' error level postulated by Professor Reason was only three errors per million decisions, what if a driver sees a million red signals in the 25 years of his driving career? For rule-based decisions the error rate was much higher - it was not just a matter of remembering the rule, but also which rule was appropriate in the circumstance at hand. If this decision was required in a stress situation the error rate doubled. In the circumstances at Dorridge with out of course working, engineering and business pressures to complete on time on a Sunday afternoon and the confusion caused by the doubt over the crossings being used, there is no question but that this was a stressed situation and most of those involved made understandable errors - understandable that is from the academic point of view, but unacceptable if running a safe railway.

I was also concerned about the increasing involvement of the civil police and their reaction of turning an incident site into a crime scene, with consequent escalation of train delays, and the way in which this inhibited railway managers and staff uncovering the causes to learn, modify and implement revised safety measures. This came to a head after the Wembley accident in 1984 when an evening commuter train from Euston passed a signal at danger and collided with a freightliner train leaving Willesden Yard. The driver, wandering in a daze, admitted responsibility immediately and was then reported by the police and threatened with a court case, so that he was advised by his solicitors to say nothing at the BR internal inquiry or even at the one instigated by the Railway Inspectorate. It was only 18 months later after the prosecution case was dropped that we learned of omissions in the process of examining the driver when he returned to work after a serious fall at his home. This had failed to discover occasional mini black-outs that might have accounted for his lapse. Had we known this earlier we might have been able to plug a gap in procedures that could have led to other incidents.

Serious rail accidents are usually caused by multiple factors coming together, some bizarre as in the case of the collision at Eccles between a Liverpool – Newcastle express and a standing oil tank train and the ensuing fire. The bald facts were clear enough. The Liverpool train, hauled by a class 45 with Mark II coaches, overran signals at danger and ran into the back of the tank train which itself was held at signals. We discovered that three weeks earlier the local authority had renewed a road bridge over the railway in red brick, thus spoiling the visibility of the red semaphore arm of the signal that was immediately in front of the bridge parapet. Attention was then focused on the sighting of the distant signal, which was clearly on. We learned at the inquiry that the distance from the signalbox controlling the distant signal was nearly a mile, the lever in the box was a very heavy pull and that one of the signalmen, a small man, was unable to clear the signal. The regular drivers, faced with that distant signal 'on' would jump to the conclusion that 'Joe' was on duty and not take the aspect of the signal seriously as no train was ever normally brought to a stand at that location! In fact, on this occasion the oil train had stopped with a suspected hot box. No driver had ever thought to bring this to the attention of management – protecting the signalman presumably – and although drivers had grumbled about the difficulty in seeing the aspect of the home signal since the local authority bridge work, again no-one had told management. And local management had been too office-bound to get out and about and pick up the concerns or see the problems for themselves.

We had monthly Operations conferences chaired by Maurice Holmes, Director of Operations at the Board, which were held alternately at 222 Marylebone Road and at a Regional location organised by the relevant Regional Operations Manager. When my turn came I had arranged a visit to the new suburban network and control system in Dublin, courtesy of the CIE, and we had the GM's saloon at the front of a Euston – Holyhead train to convey the participants. As we passed Rugby at speed I glanced out of the window and saw a train of hoppers in the process of derailing and tipping on their sides in a cloud of dust on the Up side. To this day Maurice accuses me of arranging this purposely to drive home the importance of the conference addressing some of my safety concerns! My Southern colleague, Alec Bath, topped this a few conferences later by organising the meeting to see air traffic control and British Caledonian operations at Gatwick followed by a visit hosted by the SNCF in Paris to observe their new ticket barrier installations at the Gare du Nord. The trip was packed with useful things to see and learn, but Alec forgot to allow any time for the conference itself and we had to beg a small meeting room from the SNCF to squeeze in a quick discussion, and spend the time on the return ferry in conference instead of at the bar!

A major event during my tenure of office was the Crewe remodelling. Most engineering work had traditionally been carried out at weekends with severe disruption to traffic and over long periods of time, as the access to the lines by the engineers was extremely limited. However, in 1966 the resignalling of Paddington station had been carried out during a several-weeks-long 'blockade' with trains terminating at Ealing Broadway and passengers continuing their journeys into central London by underground and this had been deemed successful. The amount of change planned for the complex Crewe layout implied widespread disruption over several months, especially at weekends, and it was decided to close Crewe station completely for a limited period when the station and junction complex would be handed to the engineers entirely, minimising substantially the length of the disruption and significantly cutting the costs of the redesign and renewal.

Luckily we had succeeded in persuading the freight business, against their instinct, to retain the Crewe station avoiding lines, so we were able for a couple of months to route all through trains via the freight lines using Stafford as the railhead for the Crewe area. There were teething problems of the revised arrangements in the first week. The first night of the closure was a disaster - the DMU taking the post office staff to Stafford failed on the remaining open single line for two hours and not all the post office staff turned out anyway. By the time adequate resources reached Stafford, trains were queued back and lateness of the night trains grew to hours. This was unacceptable and several of us spent some uncomfortable nights putting things right.

These issues, however, were quickly resolved and the engineers completed the new layout, resignalling and rerouting all the overhead lines inside the allocated time. Unfortunately we then nearly spoilt the reopening. My Train Crew Manager, Bob Breakwell, had agreed with the relevant drivers' LDCs that they would learn the new route and signalling through the station by observation of videos of the new layout. Three days before the reopening ASLEF officers at HQ got to hear of this and stuck their oar in, fearing the precedent for future route learning and we were faced at the last minute with Crewe drivers and those from some other depots refusing to go through the route into the station without the traditional form of route learning – impossible in the timescale. We opened with the absurd anomaly of seeing Crewe drivers piloted through their own territory by drivers from Bescot or Saltley or other foreign depots! I can remember the reopening of Crewe station by our local renowned MP, Gwyneth Dunwoody, in which she proclaimed that she was now required to eat her hat as she, informed by some local railway trade union doubters, had expressed the view that we would never reopen on time. She was gracious enough to concede she'd been wrong, but it was a damn close thing and it was the Operators who nearly spoiled it after the superb work by the infrastructure engineers.

In 1985 I was contacted by Dr Alan Wickens, Director of Derby Technical Centre's research facility. For sometime he'd believed that the Operating function had insufficient technical support in running its activities and that a lot of operating knowledge and decision-making processes should be amenable to IT modelling and assistance. We debated this at length, especially as at the time I was in the throes of the application of modern IT equipment to Control, and we agreed that this was an opportunity that should be explored further under Dr. Wickens' 'blue-sky' budget as opposed to that set by the businesses and functions to overcome particular technical problems. The railway timetable planning process was already computerised, but the day to day decisions around its implementation had a myriad more perturbations and options than could be modelled under the conventional programming used. Dr Wickens thought that the application of heuristic methodology might provide a means of developing more useful decision-making assistance to Operators in the field and together we decided to recruit an academic to explore this in depth. A Research Fellow from the USA was duly recruited and briefed by the two of us, but Dr Wickens retired and his replacement cut the budget to exclude the more risky speculative research and the development of this particular opportunity disappeared.

Concern over reliability and punctuality of our train services continued to plague everyone. The General Manager in 1985, Malcolm Southgate, got fed up with the weekly bickering at his Monday morning conferences between the three chief engineers and operations over whom to blame for poor punctuality performance and asked me to sit down with them and thrash out the root causes of our problems. I started with the allegation that each engineer made, that they were achieving the targets for reliability that had been set them. I therefore decided to take them at their word and work out the implications of the achievement of such targets on train punctuality.

I started with Doug Power, the Chief Mechanical & Electrical Engineer who told me that the target mileage per casualty for the class 87 electric, the most reliable locomotive, was 36,000 miles, a casualty being defined as a delay of 10 minutes or more caused by a locomotive or rolling stock failure or defect. There happened, by chance, to be 36 locomotives of this type and crudely they were averaging nearly 1,000 miles per day when in traffic, so even a poor mathematician like me could calculate that we were accepting a failure every day. The much larger class of 86/2s was targeted at 24,000 miles per casualty, 85s and 47s at 10,000 miles and other lesser breeds even lower. I estimated that we were building at least a dozen engine failures into the train plan every day by accepting these targets.

I found allies in the newly appointed Bob Brown, the Regional Civil Engineer and Ken Burrage, the Signal & Telecoms Engineer and we calculated the impact of the previously agreed reliability standards in their functions. When I added the targets in mean time between broken rails, structure failures, track circuit, points and signal failures, and the average daily occurrences of incidents over which we had little control (suicides, police incidents removing drunk or aggressive passengers, dealing with trespassers, animals on the line, etc) I calculated that if the Operator was perfect (!) we could achieve 62% absolute right time or around 85% within 10 minutes against the overall punctuality BR target of 70% right time and 90% within ten minutes. However, the more disruption and out of course running was caused by these failures, the greater the likelihood of operational delays caused by train conflictions and staff errors. We assessed the lost time from the various causes and using values developed by the InterCity business with Cranfield College, we could build an investment case to reduce some of the highest risk factors.

Bob Brown, who had only recently been appointed as Regional Civil Engineer, was extremely concerned about the condition of the track on this very busy main line, especially south of Rugby, and accompanied by appropriate Divisional Engineers, walked the track from Euston to Carlisle in 1985 and set himself reliability targets, managing an 8% improvement over the three years from that period. Ken Burrage accepted that there was a major problem with the reliability of track circuits at the south end of the WCML when in the original resignalling the practice was to install relatively short (400 yard long) track circuits, resulting in a large number of insulated block joints causing problems for the Civil

Engineer and the probability of individual track circuit failures. By the 1980s improvements to track circuit technology had enabled signal engineers to use much longer track circuits and Ken therefore proposed to double their length at the London end of the WCML thus halving the probability of failure. The General Manager – by now InterCity's Cyril Bleasdale, who had taken my punctuality model to heart – accepted this with alacrity but it needed additional investment and track possessions and the money was not forthcoming, so the improvement had to be achieved gradually during normal maintenance and renewals. Changes in the maintenance regime of the electric locomotives took place when Willesden depot was selected as one of the key pilot applications of 'Total Quality Management' (TQM) described in the next chapter.

Malcolm Southgate had gone to Eurostar and Cyril Bleasdale looked for other ways of using the cost of failure information we had developed to see if there were opportunities to invest modest amounts to improve reliability and therefore punctuality. After one particularly dreadful weekend when the overhead wires came down between Hest Bank and Carnforth on an exposed stretch of line, we calculated that the delays incurred cost the business a potential half million pounds in lost revenue. Very quickly a £62,000 scheme to strengthen the overhead wiring on this stretch was approved. This gave the business a more positive tool for improving revenue through quality improvement.

I guess as a result of this study, I was sent for by David Kirby, Board Member for Operations and Engineering, and asked to accept the position of the Board's first Quality & Reliability Manager. 'Why me?' I asked in some innocence, to receive the riposte, 'Well as Operations Manager of the West Coast Main Line, you know more about failure than anyone else.' I hoped he was joking.

The preserved 86 259 *Les Ross,* formerly *Peter Pan,* at Preston after hauling a railway enthusiasts' special handed over to heritage steam traction, 9.5.09

The wrecked sleeping car train at Linslade tunnel, 9.12.82

The Crewe based APT set 370.006 (now preserved at Crewe Heritage Centre) at Crewe station on a test run, 1983

Official photo of the impact of the test train with the nuclear flask, July 1984

The aftermath of the staged collision on the Old Dalby Test Track, July 1984

The first train of the new electric service (nicknamed the 'Bedpan' route) arrives at Moorgate station, 1984

35028 *Clan Line* on arrival at Marylebone with the special the author rode, 3.3.85

The author at the controls of 4498 *Sir Nigel Gresley* at Marylebone, 23.11.85

John Butt and his 7 ¼ " gauge model of 'Royal Scot' which he was rash enough to let the author drive, 1985

The author in the loaned 'royal' bowler hat

The royal train at Crewe headed by 87024 *Lord of the Isles*, 1984

The officer's saloon 2911 (formerly 45000) in the royal train

The interior of the royal train officer's saloon

The office section of the officer's saloon used by Winston Churchill as his mobile office in World War II

Operating Conference visit to Düsseldorf to see the DB suburban push-pull services, 1985

German Railways hospitality to members of the BR Operations Conference – left to right: Director Maurice Holmes, ER Regional Operating Manager Roger Williams, Adrian Bulkyn-Rackowe, ScR Operations Manager Jim Summers, Les Singleton and in foreground, Peter Whittaker.

Chapter 12: 1986 - 1988
Reliability management

So I knew more about failure than anyone else, did I? I hoped he meant 'the causes of failure'. I discovered that my appointment owed much to pressure from non-executive Board Members who came from industries where reliability and quality management was accepted as routine and a basic management concern. Apart from the application of reliability management techniques in some technical design departments, most BR managers was not conversant with the latest thinking on these issues and it became apparent very quickly that I was being left to discover for myself what might be relevant and of value to the industry. Go to France and Germany, I was urged. Find out what they do!

It was strange to move from the responsibility for an annual budget of £35 million and a constant series of events and pressures to which I had to respond, to a situation where I had a part time secretary only, an empty office with no files and the ball in my court to determine how to fill my days. In fact it was suggested that as I would be travelling extensively, I could work from home using a Euston House office as a 'pied à terre' and postal point.

So I acted on the suggestion given to me by David Kirby and made arrangements to meet up with operations and engineering managers in the SNCF and DB. Arrangements were made for me to ride in the cab of an electric locomotive from the Belgian border to Paris and then to travel in the cab of a DB locomotive on the left bank of the Rhine to observe the impact of cab radio. The SNCF loco was one of the ten quadruple system Co-Co electrics, 40110, described by the inspector as 'très fragile', but we performed perfectly with the strict adherence to absolute punctuality that SNCF was known for at that time. I tried in vain to establish the techniques SNCF management used to ensure their punctuality performance, but my question did not seem to be understood. It was apparently self-evident that trains had to run to time, but SNCF managers could point to no analyses or justification of reliability investment. It was just taken as a 'given' without question.

As I stepped from the cab of 40110 at the Gare du Nord, the Inspector asked if I was free the following day. I was not returning to the UK until the 'Flèche d'Or' the following afternoon, so he suggested I showed up at the Gare de Lyon at 07.00 and he accompanied me in the cab of a TGV to Lyons and back with a one hour coffee break in a city café there. I was back in Paris by midday! This precision was exemplified by his statement that there were six seconds of recovery time between each signalling section, which allowed the TGV to run on less than full power for over 50% of the journey if there were no delays. The driver used the switchback nature of the high speed route (ruling gradients of 1 in 28) to power uphill for about two thirds of the way falling to around 220 kph at the summit and freewheel down the gradient to the maximum speed of 270 kph. We only ran with the controller open for 48% of the journey. In fact, the SNCF deliberately left power control in the hands of the driver rather than automating it to keep the driver active and alert, and I was told that some drivers competed to see how much of the journey to Lyons they could accomplish in 'freewheeling' mode.

I had an enjoyable trip in the cab of Co-Co electric 103.128-5 from Mainz to Cologne and the value of the radio system was shown when we received a message about the failure of level crossing gates approaching Bonn. As a result, we were not stopped to be warned, but acknowledged the message and proceeded over the crossing at 5 mph losing only a couple of minutes in consequence. However, I found little supporting evidence of calculated justification in the DB for their quality policy, which seemed to be based on building in substantial spare capacity regardless of cost. As well as the provision of spare stock and locomotives to cover unforeseen incidents, equipment was utilized way below its capacity or over-engineered. As an example, I was told that the V200 diesel hydraulics built in 1953 were normally only run by drivers in notch 4 (of a 7 notch controller) except on an InterCity or EuroCity train running late. As a comparison with the British culture, the WR 'Warships' based on the DB design spent most of their journeys from Paddington to the West of England being worked to their limit in notch 7. Although there are no V200s still in service on the DB, examples can still be found – sold to the Swiss, Greek and Saudi Arabian railways. In contrast, the British examples were all withdrawn from service by the early 1970s, even though they were built four years later than their German precursors. The British were famed at getting a 'quart out of a pint pot' and this was exemplified in the lesser subsidy that BR received from the taxpayer compared with its continental neighbours, and the passenger business wanted to extort the maximum advantage from its new resources to boost revenue, but BR paid the price in significantly reduced reliability and lack of standby cover.

An interesting and novel interlude occurred in May 1988, which was the 250th anniversary of the conversion of John Wesley, the founder of Methodism. Although Methodism was still strong in the UK, most global adherents were in the USA and some 1,000 or more were coming over for a special commemorative service at St Paul's Cathedral to be attended by the Queen. Their tour company wanted to take these 'pilgrims' to Wesley associated sites in the UK - his father's rectory in Epworth, near Doncaster, Lincoln College at Oxford where he was an undergraduate, and the New Room at Bristol, one of the earliest Methodist chapels. A proposal was made to run a couple of special trains for the American tourists over three days and two nights to these sites and I was asked as a person wearing two hats (a Methodist and Train Planner) to join the committee planning the event to liaise with BR and the Travel Company. It gradually became more and more ambitious, until we'd planned two trains travelling round the London - Doncaster - York - Leeds - Bristol - Oxford - London circuit in opposite directions, meeting for a service in Gloucester Cathedral on the second day. Then the BBC 'Songs of Praise' team got involved, with choirs singing hymns on the two trains, the Methodist Youth Association put 500 youngsters on an HST from St Pancras to Bedford and back, with a Methodist Lay Preacher who was a Crewe engine-driver naming one power car 'Charles Wesley' (John's brother and a prolific hymn writer) and the President of the Methodist Church naming the other, 'John Wesley'.

There were several 'interesting' meetings with the BBC culminating in one at St Pancras with the BBC Programme Producer, the three 'Songs of Praise' presenters - Sally Magnussen, Cliff Michelmore and Roger Royal - joining BR staff and demonstrating moves required with coffee cups and sugar bowls while Sally breast fed her baby around the meeting table. I finally put my foot down at one request - to film from a helicopter one USA special passing the HST on the four track section just south of

Bedford, while a John Wesley look-alike rode a horse parallel in an adjoining field! We did get the two trains running parallel, however, and Sally shouting the next hymn request across the track to the moving special with Cliff.

A further opportunity to look overseas at reliability and quality management came in the latter part of 1986 when I was invited as BR's representative to a Quality conference being hosted by the Swedish national railway, SJ, in Malmö. This put me in touch with Professor Ăke Claesson of Stockholm University who invited me a couple of years later to lecture to students at the Stockholm Technical Institute on the value of reliability, the work I had commenced with Cyril Bleasdale on the LMR and developed further during the three years at the Board. The work undertaken by Cranfield College had established the value of reduced journey times but we researched with them further how passengers viewed punctuality in comparison with the planned journey time. The conclusion from the research and surveys conducted indicated a value between two and three times greater than the same number of minutes of planned time which had enabled us to put a rough value - or rather, cost - to the delays and their cause. This now gave us estimated figures that could be postulated to justify investment to remove those causes of delay.

This approach came into its own when the 1987 East Coast timetable began to fall apart and I was asked by John Prideaux, InterCity Director, and John Nelson, ER General Manager, to assess whether the plan or its implementation was at fault. The conclusion I came to was that acceleration in the schedules had removed unnecessary 'recovery time', but the completion of the electrification work early the previous year meant that the ECML timetable had luxuriated in surplus recovery time for several months and that a miscellany of lost time for operating and engineering reasons had been hidden – only to be revealed as this time was stripped out. We identified some 25 reasons for regular lost time and began the task of analysing each and counting the cost of correcting them, to establish priorities we could plan and budget for.

This led to a request for me to be the main speaker at the German Railways Operating Conference in Bamberg in 1988, when I was asked to address their Board Member and senior colleagues for three 45 minute sessions on the system I had developed on the

West Coast Main Line in 1986 and refined for the ECML study. An interesting aside is that I prepared three 45 minute presentations in English and had them professionally translated for me to deliver in German. On my first run through rehearsal I found each of my talks took a full 70 minutes to say the same thing in German and I had to be ruthless in using the blue pencil. The end result was satisfying, however, and DB adopted my 'punctuality budget' system for its whole EuroCity and InterCity timetable two weeks later. I dined out for years 'on telling the German Railways how to run their trains on time'! Despite my success there and on the East Coast, I never did succeed in persuading my successor on the West Coast to adopt the system also!

I guessed that there was a balance between the continental obsession with quality at any cost (or the cost of this not even quantified) and the British culture of paring everything to the bone under the pressure of successive governments. I decided that I'd have to look at other industries for guidance and spent a more useful time exchanging ideas with British Airways and the oil industry and being introduced to the concept of TQM (Total Quality Management) the philosophy of which was the value of spending more time in planning to get it right first time, to avoid the greater cost of correcting error. My attention was drawn to the TQM philosophy as outlined by the American management guru, Phil Crosby, and I discussed this at length with David Rayner who'd replaced David Kirby as Board Member with special oversight of the production functions. He suggested that I write a paper to the Board outlining the philosophy and proposing some pilot studies.

The proposal was approved and I was delegated to contact a number of consultancy companies with experience in quality management, including Phil Crosby, Brooks International, and Cooper Lybrand. I then spent time looking for Business Sector backing to identify suitable opportunities for trials. One pilot project set up involved looking at track renewal standards in the Grantham - Stoke Summit - Peterborough high speed section on the East Coast Main Line, to test whether higher standards (and costs) at implementation would result in lower maintenance costs and fewer infrastructure failures in the long run. The problem with this pilot was that it would take several years before its success could be proven and there were no conclusive results before I was overtaken by greater priorities. Another pilot project embraced by the Scottish Region Provincial Services management was to look at the diagrams for train crews at Yoker depot and work with the staff there to involve them in quality improvement discussions and proposals.

Of greater impact in the short term was the study we set up at the InterCity maintenance depot at Willesden where electric locomotives of class 86 and 87 were serviced and maintained. Brooks were represented by a larger than life affable and very competent American, John Herter - I can still feel his iron handshake now - who quickly got to grips with the way that the depot planned its maintenance to keep the functional costs low but which ignored the wider impact on the business. By replanning the maintenance to fit the slack times when the locos were not required, at a higher cost in shift work by the maintenance staff, the Brooks team was able to demonstrate the saving of four a/c mainline electric locomotives, a huge payback for this investment in TQM processes. They also came up with quality assurance recommendations which would improve the reliability of these locomotives giving a further locomotive as surplus and available for other duties. This was impressive and drew the attention at Board level in several departments.

There then developed pressures to adopt TQM philosophies in a number of departments and these divided themselves quickly into two quite different schools of thought. The Chief Mechanical & Electrical Engineer and the Chief Signal & Telecommunications Engineer both decided to adopt the British Standards approach, known as Quality System B.S.5750, which later became International Standard I.S. 9000. This involved a rigorous review of procedures in the installation and maintenance activities and written detailed instructions to be followed and audited to ensure compliance. An alternative approach was championed by the Chief Personnel Manager who saw training in quality thinking, philosophy and methodologies as key to TQM. The Board decided to back both approaches and while the engineering functions got on with implementing B.S. 5750, the Personnel function employed consultants to work with me to run a series of courses for the top 500 managers of BR, called inevitably 'Leadership 500'. This was a much broader education of senior management into the values of quality - essential after the previous thirty years of indoctrination of management into cost-cutting to meet government budget cuts and targets. Ultimately 800 senior managers went through this course and a similar course at an appropriate level was developed for the middle rung of managers and senior supervision.

I began to notice a new direction, especially in the InterCity business where growth was taking place and the cost-cutting priority of previous years was being replaced by a more positive approach and a willingness to invest in quality. My contribution was being recognised - in 1987 I was one of the select few who were sent on a course of short high level seminars at Templeton College, Oxford, attended by such lecturer luminaries as Denis Healey covering our exposure to business and politics. Then in 1989 there was the 25th World Congress of Railways in Moscow with Sir Robert Reid leading a team of eight BR officers, where I was to be scheduled to make a presentation on the application of TQM to the rail industry and to highlight in particular the ascribing of value to train quality aspects such as train reliability and punctuality.

One lighter moment during the conference occurred when we discovered that it was Deputy Chairman John Welsby's birthday. The BR team decided to celebrate with a special meal in our hotel (the giant 6,000 bedded 'Rossiya') and we had a spread consisting mainly of sturgeon, caviar, tomatoes and cucumber - about the only food which they seemed to have a supply of - accompanied by bottles of champagne. The bill for the 14 of us (conference participants plus partners) came to just over 200 roubles (the official exchange rate was £1 = 1 Rouble) but the waiter asked if we had dollars. We rustled up 49 between us which the waiter accepted in lieu of roubles with great delight. Apparently the system was for the waiter to purchase our food from the kitchen, then obtain what he could from the customers. As roubles had virtually no purchasing power and he could use hard currency to buy luxury goods in the Moscow diplomats' and officials' shop that only accepted dollars and sterling, he was well content with his 'bargain' - as were we. In due course, I went and made my presentation, but something else had happened in December 1988, which had shifted my career yet again….

SNCF 4-phase electric 40110 which the author rode from the
Belgian border to Paris, July 1986

Author in the driving cab of the TGV 27 on 07.00 Paris –
Marseilles, July 1986

The switchback route seen from the TGV cab

On arrival back at Paris Gare de Lyon, 12 noon, July 1986.

Naming of HST 43118 *Charles Wesley* by Crewe driver and Methodist Lay Preacher, Peter Stuffins and the 1988 President of the Methodist Church, Rev Bill Davies, May 1988

The three presenters of the BBC 'Songs of Praise' recorded in May 1988 and broadcast in August – Cliff Michelmore, Sally Magnussen and Roger Royal.

The two 'Wesley' specials about to depart from St Pancras with over 1,000 guests from the American Methodist Church, May 1988

Andrew McTavish, Ian Brown and John Welsby with some of the
BR team's partners at the Moscow World Congress of Railways,
1989

John Welsby's impromptu birthday dinner at the Rossya Hotel,
Moscow

Chapter 13: 1988 - 1989
Clapham Junction

In December 1988 BR suffered the tragic multiple train crash at Clapham Junction. I was asked by David Rayner, the Board Member to whom I now reported, to use the techniques I had developed for reliability management to evaluate BR's safety management systems and compare with best practice in British industry. He asked me also to chair a team of operators and engineers collating the evidence to brief BR's legal team at the Judicial Inquiry ordered by the government on the accident, following a similar public outcry after the Kings Cross underground station fire the previous year. As well as chairing this team which included experts from the S&T function and from the Southern Region, I was asked to look at safety management systems used by other industries and to assess the robustness of BR systems in comparison.

   I had been developing risk assessment methodology as part of my reliability management armour and from the evidence given to me by other members of the team I constructed a comprehensive Fault Tree starting with the top events which were essential ingredients of the accident - the error by an S&T technician when decommissioning wires in the old signalling system, the movement or disturbance of the offending wire during subsequent renewal work a couple of weeks later, the absence of supervision or auditing to pick up the error, the absence of personnel or functional standards to ensure the fitness and competence of the technician to undertake the work and the inability or absence of action by others who may have noted something unusual about the signal at fault that morning. I then traced the underlying causes for each of these top events and eventually drew a tree that had ultimately 50 roots deep and hidden. These ran through the long hours the technician worked and his fitness, his lack of training other than learning bad practices from others 'on the job', the absence of the required safety audit because of a hurriedly introduced reorganisation, the way in which the engineering work at Clapham had been planned between trains to minimise disruption to passengers - the list went on and on. If any one of those fifty root causes had been identified earlier and action taken to correct them, one of the ingredients to a top event would have interrupted that line and the accident might have been prevented.

I established that BR's safety management was heavily dependent on a prescriptive rules culture, particularly in the Operations function, and the adherence to technical standards in the engineering functions. In both cases this meant learning, often by rote, information necessary to be retained in the memory and correctly applied. Elsewhere I have written about the way in which British education had changed from the 1950s' heavy dependency on prescriptive learning and moved towards experiential learning and problem solving. I had discovered, as written in a previous chapter about the Dorridge accident, that this prescriptive rules learning in the 1980s was not effective when confronted with a different culture. Basically BR's systems - like those of other traditional industries such as coal mining, ship building and heavy engineering - were reactive. An accident occurred, it was thoroughly investigated and as a result new rules or technical standards were introduced to cover that particular fault or failure in future. As a result rules and standards had become complex and often difficult to understand or interpret and were all too often used after the event to blame rather than prevent.

I then talked to a number of safety specialists in British Airways, one of the oil companies and at the Ministry of Defence as well as a safety management consultant, David Shillito, and identified some of the ingredients in proactive systems such as risk assessment and understanding human error and instituting control measures to minimise risk. It was clear to me that BR, like the other traditional industries - and railways abroad as I discovered later - were not abreast of these proactive systems developed by the high tech industries in the 1970s and early 80s and it was likely that we would receive criticism at the Inquiry as a result. I shared my findings with David Rayner and Roger Henderson, the QC representing the company, and we agreed that whatever the outcome of the Inquiry, BR would review its safety systems and would make that commitment publicly during the Inquiry proceedings. Because basically the proactive systems were the TQM application to safety, David Rayner asked me to stay on after the Inquiry was over and apply my TQM experience that I had gathered over the previous two years to apply to safety management in the future.

I chaired the meetings of the small working group pulling the evidence together at the Paddington headquarters office of the Board's Operations function beside platform 1 at that station. One day, attending one of our frequent get-togethers, I nearly had an accident that both almost terminated my career and forced me to think about safety in its widest application - to staff and the public as well as trains and their passengers. Contractors were undertaking renovation work on the outside of this office block which was some four storeys high and ran from the taxi rank at the departure side of the station to the Bishop's Bridge Road at the West end of the station. They had scaffolding the entire length of the building. I was walking one morning down the taxi road as the entrance door was off that side and happened to look up just in time to see the top rung of scaffolding begin to bend over like the crest of a huge wave and the whole scaffolding the length of the wall began to come away and curl over and came crashing down.

I fled back between parked cars arranged in a herringbone fashion against the retaining wall of Eastbourne Terrace above and the poles slammed down either side of me crashing through the roofs of the parked cars. When the dust settled, I emerged shaking and made my way to Maurice Holmes' office where I duly made my entry into the accident book and despite protestation, was accompanied home and told to take it easy and rest for fear of delayed shock. I'm not sure about the 'delayed' bit - I was pretty shaken at the time. Apparently the investigation identified that an inexperienced member of the contractor's staff had started untying the scaffolding at the bottom and had weakened the entire structure. I only know that someone subsequently wrote in the last column of the accident book the cause as 'overenthusiastic dismantling'!

Around the same time I suffered a more embarrassing accident that involved a caustic response from whoever would see the entry in the same accident book. I have since early childhood had a phobia of butterflies and moths. One day I opened the cupboard to pull out a file and a Small Tortoiseshell butterfly flew out into my face. I turned instinctively to rush out of the door, and in my moment of panic, I slammed into the half open door and hit my nose and cheekbone rather badly on the door's edge, luckily not breaking any bones. We deliberated at length what to write in the accident book as the cause and eventually I reluctantly permitted them to write 'victim chased by a butterfly' with 'lepidoptoraphobia' added in brackets!

When we had completed our investigations into the Clapham accident and written up our conclusions, we briefed the legal team who would be representing British Rail at the Judicial Inquiry and the key management witnesses including the senior managers who would be giving evidence - senior Signal &Telecommunications management, Gordon Pettitt, General Manager of the Southern Region, Chris Green, Managing Director of Network SouthEast and the Chairman, Sir Robert Reid, as well as Board Member David Rayner. Roger Henderson, our QC, had been heavily critical of London Underground management at the Inquiry on the Kings Cross fire the previous year. In fact he had only agreed to represent BR if we revealed everything to him as the London Underground team had suffered embarrassing revelations dragged out of them throughout the Inquiry. He said that he would make an opening statement that British Rail accepted complete responsibility and had committed themselves to learning the lessons and implementing the recommendations including an undertaking to review its safety management systems by an organisation of high repute. We therefore received banner headlines in the press on the first day of the Inquiry but after that, relatively low media attention compared with the Kings Cross fire as there was very little new evidence coming available - all had been put on the table on the first day.

It had been decided that I should give evidence on my findings on safety management systems and state what BR had been developing under TQM, especially the application by BR of BS 5750. One of the things I had uncovered was that the Signal & Telecommunications Department had committed itself to implementing this standards system before the accident and the very first standard to be written up, which was in progress the day of the crash, was of all things about the correct procedures to follow when wiring and decommissioning wiring, the very aspect of major concern to the Inquiry. I duly spent most of the day in the witness box at the Methodist Central Hall Westminster where the Inquiry was held and I'm told that it was the only day on which no press bothered to appear - they'd seen the draft of my evidence and concluded that nothing of substance or interest to them would emerge - in fact I was BR's secret weapon to bore the media away!

We ploughed through BS 5750, what it was, what the S&T organisation was doing to implement it and whether it would have prevented this accident had it been in place earlier. Whilst it's good practice to have such standards properly considered and recorded, I'm unconvinced that this - of itself - will be the definitive saviour of safety. It can too easily become a 'tick-box' process and a means of covering one's backside without changing reality. It must at least be combined with the 'softer' side of systems as instanced in the Leadership 500 course and the addressing of safety culture. Anyway, the Inquiry duly took it on board and it took up another day of an Inquiry which was running out of time. In hindsight, the Inquiry management spent too much time calling witnesses about the detailed clerical audit and safety check systems and never really got to the crucial issues of the safety culture, the loss of status and influence of the production functions in the new business sector world and the impact of reorganisations that were hurried and not fully thought through. However, British Rail's management had learned this despite the Inquiry failing to identify these as crucial, and BR's senior management ensured that these issues were part of the remit in the review of its safety management systems, which were to be undertaken by Du Pont, one of the most reputable (and expensive) safety consultancy companies in the business.

When the Inquiry was over and before the report was produced, David Rayner immediately contracted a very senior consultant from Du Pont to carry out a pilot review of BR's safety management. I was appointed as the Project Manager for the five month assignment and worked closely throughout with Bob Webber, a 'wise old owl', whose approach and considered ways I came to appreciate and value very quickly. He was not the sort of American I had expected. He was a man of few words, but every one of them was weighed carefully. He recounted to me the early history of his company and their preoccupation with the safety of their staff – they had started in the 1830s with explosives as their main product and the early employees were family members!

We were assigned to the West Coast Main Line for our studies, convenient for me, but also providing the full mix of activities necessary to ensure we covered all aspects of safety. I drew up a series of meetings with staff to Bob's requirements and accompanied him on all his visits, introducing him to staff, taking due notes of any key issues emerging. He made me very much a part of his assignment using me to fill in about my roles in the Operations function and the TQM work. His approach was usually very informal - he would, after introductions, just ask staff how safe they were, how did they know, how did they compare with others, what were the hazards they faced, the risks they took. He was so informal and conversational that the men and women he spoke to were very open. No-one appeared to hold back. I liked the man immensely and had great respect for him.

He also insisted on meeting members of the Board and asked them very similar basic questions. I shall never forget the interview we had with Sir Robert Reid. I actually thought we might get thrown out of his office. Bob Webber just asked the Chairman how he judged safety - what information he used for its management. There was a long pause and eventually the Chairman asked his secretary to find the latest Railway Inspectorate report, which was produced annually, later to come under the Health & Safety Inspectorate. The latest report could not be found and one about two years old was produced. Bob then asked, all innocently, 'I suppose, Chairman, you use information of similar vintage to manage your financial performance.' I saw the Chairman's knuckles tighten and go white, his face went bright red and I awaited the explosion. It didn't come. Sir Robert realised the point that Bob Webber was making and thenceforth all Board meetings had safety on their agenda - a subject that had previously been considered by top management as the responsibility of the operators and engineers. The point was well made and despite the fact that I was party to it, I could never have made such a remark to the Chairman and got away with it. That was part of the value of having a guy we were paying £2,000 a day in 1989! He could and did say things that the Board may not have wished to hear.

When he produced his final report - a simple document with ten recommendations - a bit like the 'Ten Commandments' - he felt able to say to the Board that 'you say one thing and do the opposite'. He meant that we'd produced rule books and standards but that if these stood in the way of getting things done, instead of challenging the rules and changing them if justified, we'd long condoned rule 'shortcuts' as long as nothing happened - ie we'd left staff at ground level to take the risks and receive the blame if things went wrong. This was typified by an incident I observed at Bletchley during shunting operations we were watching. A shunter was riding on the steps of an 08 shunting diesel and hopped off while it was still moving. Bob watched to see what the supervisor who was standing by us would say. He said and did nothing. Bob then asked him if such a movement was allowed. The supervisor then said 'no' and chased off after the shunter to tell him not to do it again' (at least while being observed by management - my interpretation). Bob Webber called the supervisor back and said he'd not intended that. He wasn't saying it was wrong but wanted to know if the supervisor thought it was. Bob said that if the shunter had safety boots, the siding ground was even and the steps on the loco were suitable and safe for riding on, the lighting was good etc., then perhaps it was safe but what did the rule say? Bob was strongly of the view that there should be more delegation to local staff to develop in conjunction with management realistic safe methods of working and sign off for them as long as the working was local and did not require people like main line train crews to have to face different rules in every location.

Du Pont had a long history of excellent staff safety and it took some time for Bob Webber to enhance the normal Du Pont response to incorporate train, passenger and public safety as well as workers. He wanted to institute managers watching staff working on a regular basis and ensure safe methods, not just the environmental conditions but safe methodology of working. He wanted staff and management to be trained in this. I arranged for a group of General Managers and Functional Chiefs to meet us one evening in Willesden freight yard and Bob briefed them to carry out a typical Du Pont style inspection called 'STOP'. There was a certain amount of cynicism until we went out in the yard and actually watched the conditions under which the staff were working. The underfoot conditions were deplorable and we saw staff flying around trying to get trains away thinking we were watching their performance in despatching trains to time rather than their safety working methods. The point was driven home when Cyril Bleasdale stood on a metal plate covering mechanism of a point handlever and the metal subsided and squirted a stream of filthy water over several participants. The freight manager was persuaded to spend a relatively small amount of money cleaning up the yard after that.

The one thing that I never got Bob Webber to accept totally was the concept of risk management. He was much more for setting proper realistic rules, training people in them fully, getting staff involvement and commitment and then ensuring 100% compliance without exception backed by strict discipline. Bob and I used to have a friendly difference of opinion at the pedestrian crossing outside Euston House. He would wait for the little 'green man' to appear before he would set foot on the road. I would look at the oncoming traffic in both directions, assess the risk and if nothing was coming I would 'jay walk' ignoring the sign on the traffic light. Bob's huge palm would suddenly rest on my shoulder with an admonitory pursing of the lips. However, it was Bob Webber, not me, that actually got knocked over by a cyclist who ignored the traffic lights, a fact that I knew was a common hazard at that location. Luckily he was not injured although a little shaken. I tried to persuade Bob to take risk assessment more seriously, but I think he was more on the side of requiring the police force to prosecute cyclists who disobeyed the highway code and cycled through red lights!

At the end of the five months' pilot studies the Du Pont report was received and endorsed by the Board despite some harsh things it said about them. I was charged then with developing an implementation plan for the whole of BR and Du Pont was retained for a further year on a part time basis to assist me. One of the key recommendations had been to pull together all the different strands of safety management throughout BR - train safety with operators and engineers, staff safety with Personnel, public safety all over the place - and recommend the setting up of one Safety Directorate to be an advisory service to all managers, pulling together the development of safety policy and strategy, the administration of rules and standards and safety audit to ensure compliance. I was appointed to the role of Head of Safety Policy to implement the Du Pont recommendations, develop an annual safety plan, devise a means of justifying and prioritising safety investment and developing research into safety management methodology. David Rayner moved Maurice Holmes to be the first Director of Safety from the important role of Director of Operations, thus signifying in one action the importance now attached to safety management.

Chapter 14: 1990 - 1996
Safety management

After approval by the BR Board of the Du Pont report and recommendations, one of the first moves was to gain its acceptance by Regional and Business management and the railway trade unions. I made a number of presentations to various BR management teams and attended a Board conference with the trade union senior officials of the NUR, ASLEF and the TSSA at the Grove, Watford. The trade union officials were broadly supportive of the proposals, although on the issue of staff safety, were inclined to take the attitude that 'we've been telling you this for years'. Whilst there was some truth in this, in my view the trade unions were just as culpable for the issue of staff safety being contentious and subject to dispute and argument, because all too often safety was used as a lever – often without justification – to achieve other trade union objectives.

One of the problems was that staff safety representatives were part of the formal trade union/management consultation and negotiation machinery so that safety was discussed in the same forum and with the same people as other non safety issues. By eating some humble pie and admitting that management had not been as forthcoming on staff safety matters as it should have been in the past, we got the very useful concession that staff safety representatives should be independent of the trade union/management negotiating machinery and Local Departmental Committees and therefore have one objective only – the safety of the staff they represented. Management could then feel more confident that meeting staff requests for improved safety would not be the 'thin end of the wedge' for other non-safety related demands.

There were some hard words for management to accept in Bob Webber's presentation which I found myself delivering to a number of audiences, but to be fair, most recognised the truth of what he was saying. We set in motion a number of the 'STOP' training sessions for managers who would then commit themselves to undertaking monthly inspections in their areas looking not only at safe and unsafe conditions – that was relatively easy – but also at the safety or otherwise of staff working methods, harder to spot and even harder for some managers to intervene after years of condoning less safe practices that got the job done.

As well as the Du Pont proposals which homed in particularly on staff safety, although this would create a safety aware culture that should also benefit passenger and public safety, David Rayner and I were keen to use the technique of risk assessment, which we felt the Du Pont approach ignored, to identify the risks to general railway safety. The report by the chairman of the Clapham Junction inquiry, Anthony Hidden QC, and the Fennell report on the Kings Cross fire had, between them, come up with over 200 recommendations relevant to the railway industry and BR operators and engineers were already holding more than 100 schemes of their own devising to address safety.

One of the experts I had received advice from during my investigations on safety management systems was Tony Taig, then with the Atomic Energy Authority, later to be advisor on railways to the Select Committee on Transport. He advocated undertaking comprehensive identification of risks from all BR's activities to passengers, staff and the general public. With data from the annual Railway Inspectorate reports and the functional reporting of incidents many of which could be considered as precursors to accidents involving injury or fatality, there was no shortage of data to undertake such an exercise. We undertook this together in 1990 and with the help of a couple of consultants from Cooper Lybrand, Patrick McHugh and Andrew Wells, we were able to link the judicial report recommendations and other BR schemes with the risks that they were designed to reduce or eliminate. We then assessed the benefits likely from implementation of the recommendation or project in terms of reduced number of annual fatalities, serious injuries and minor injuries and linked these with the investment and running costs involved, thus producing a cost-benefit analysis for every project.

The prime benefit of this was to put some order of priority into the large number of potential actions most of which required additional resources and funding. The projects ranged from around £64,000 per life saved (we used a formula agreed with the Railway Inspectorate and the Department of Transport to convert major and minor injuries to 'equivalent' lives) to almost infinity, as some schemes – especially those stemming from the Fennell

Inquiry – were addressing risks that had been eliminated or nearly so by other higher value projects. The government, in the wake of the public concern over the two disasters, had ring-fenced £200 million a year for a maximum of three years for BR to make a step improvement in safety, but costs of all the schemes BR had identified to address the risks from the joint work with AEA and Cooper Lybrand amounted to more than £300 million a year. The Board therefore set up a Safety Panel chaired by Maurice Holmes, Director of Safety, with a senior member of one of the Businesses to scrutinise every proposal put forward, test the assumptions made, the realism of the benefits claimed and the accuracy of the costs.

We therefore finished up with a list of some 300+ schemes in some sort of priority order. The question now was where to draw the line. How much should BR spend to save a 'theoretical' life? Should we use the government money available to determine the boundary? Was there any objective work elsewhere on this? What cost criteria, for instance, did the Ministry of Transport use for investing in road safety highway schemes? I drew a graph of the schemes in ascending order of cost benefit and it was interesting to see that the vast majority of schemes fell in the area up to around £1 to 2 million per equivalent life or over £10 million. Only about five schemes fell in the £2-£10 million range. Most of the 'best' schemes seemed to be arising from either 'soft' schemes like training or improved supervision, or environmental schemes involving correcting unsafe ground conditions or removing lineside clutter and redundant materials.

Many of the major investment projects such as Automatic Train Protection came in the third quartile with a value of around £14million cost for every equivalent life potentially saved and some of the recommendations from the Kings Cross fire inquiry were over £100 million per life saved or even impossible to quantify because we could identify no add-on value at all. The most important recommendation to address risk of fire was the banning of smoking at underground and other 'enclosed' stations such as Birmingham New Street - frankly this halved the fire risks we had identified. By the time we reached recommendation number 118 from the Fennell report, there was no risk left to be controlled as earlier and higher priority schemes had eliminated the risk from everything we could think of! The problem was that these judicial inquiries would put forward any recommendation that addressed risk without any prioritisation or consideration that some projects addressed the same hazard.

The usual 'pareto' principle applied. 20% of the cost would eliminate 80% of the risk - well it was not quite as clear cut as that but the third of projects that cost over £10 million per life saved only addressed around 10% of the risk, much less if you left out ATP. The Ministry of Transport used a figure of around £200,000 per life saved as their criteria for highway safety engineering schemes. We undertook later some research on public attitude to transport risk and found that in certain circumstances travellers were willing to pay more - or expected the transport company to pay more. Road vehicle drivers assumed they had control of their own risks - a dubious assumption - and were prepared to accept more risk than when they placed their lives completely in the hands of another - plane or train. Whether the risk-taker benefits from the activity causing the risk is another element - clearly travellers derive benefit from their 'hazardous' journey whereas a farmer living next door to a nuclear plant does not appear to directly benefit and is therefore much more inclined to be risk averse. Some types of fatality are more dreaded than others - fire or drowning, for example - and a more contentious issue is whether catastrophic events are to be weighted more heavily than a 'routine' accident. Is killing 100 people in one incident worse than killing 100 people one at a time over a year? Logic says one thing, but the media plays a big part here and the 35 people killed in the Clapham accident apparently warranted far more attention than the 35 people killed in road accidents over a 3 day period in the same month. We developed much of our thinking in close consultation with Professor David Ball and his team at the University of East Anglia.

As a result we identified that the 'value of life' we would use to determine investment in safety would be much higher than that used for the same Ministry for avoiding road accidents. From comparisons in other countries and by extrapolating data from other industries, it would seem that a realistic value for investment justification would be around £1 million per equivalent life saved. This linked well with our risk assessed cost benefit studies which showed a marked dropping off of projects valued at over £1.5 million, so we chose this figure as our guideline. In fact we said that any project costing less than £1 million per life saved would be implemented and anything between £1 and £2 million would be subject to more detailed consideration before a decision was taken. Anything over £2 million would not be in the budget unless an exceptional case was made for it.

There was one further guideline that we had to take into account - what is known as the 'ALARP' principle ('As Low As Reasonably Practicable'). Guidelines issued by the Health & Safety Executive and used in some industries set individual risk rates, above which the risk was said to be 'intolerable'. At the other extreme, some risks were so unlikely that the risk was purported to be 'acceptable'. In between these risk levels it was the duty of management to reduce the risks 'ALARP'. In the railway industry the maximum individual risk for a staff member was deemed to be 1 chance per 10,000 of a fatality per year, and the 'acceptable' risk, 1 in 100,000. For passengers and members of the public the risk levels were an order of magnitude tougher - worse than 1 in 100,000 would be intolerable, 1 in a million (roughly your chance of being struck by lightning) 'acceptable'. Nearly all BR's risks fell in the ALARP region where we would use the cost formula to denote what was reasonable. Only with a couple of staff activities did we identify intolerable risk and here we either had to reduce the risk to ALARP whatever the cost, or get out of the activity. The two 'intolerable' activities were track installation and maintenance where moving trains were killing up to 15 of our staff annually in the 1980s - the risk was assessed as 1 in 1,650 or 1 fatality per 40 staff over a career length, the second most dangerous activity in the UK next to North Sea fishing. The other was train shunting where a much smaller group of staff were being killed crawling under moving wagons or being caught between buffers and crushed during coupling or uncoupling.

The Board deemed the first fatality rate completely unacceptable and two very senior managers (Graham Eccles and William Hill) were given a two year task of improving the safety of these staff to acceptable levels. They devised a threefold strategy - firstly by staff briefing and training, to make men working on the track much more safety conscious; secondly, to introduce stricter rules; and finally to invest in technical means of warning and protecting men on the track. It was of great interest and some surprise that the first element was so successful that within a couple of years no staff were killed on the track and this performance was sustained for 2-3 years until privatisation and a myriad number of contractors took over track work and we had to inculcate a safety culture all over again. With the shunting activity, the answer was easier. The activity had almost finished - parcels and wagonload freight traffic involving significant remarshalling of rail vehicles had gone. Passenger trains were now virtually all fixed formation trains, many 'multiple units' only capable of being parted or joined in factory/depot conditions.

The major contentious item was the one project that was very costly but did address a major risk - Automatic Train Protection (ATP) which would minimise the risk from trains passing signals at danger (SPADs). It was estimated that this would save around four lives a year (including the formula for injuries - serious = 0.1 fatality; minor = 0.005). Over a 30 year project lifespan at a cost of £1 billion, this gave, as previously indicated, a value of £14 million for every life potentially saved. Even if we used a variety of assumptions to test this, we could get no better value than £9 million. As BR had given a commitment at the 'Hidden' Inquiry to introduce ATP, it was installed on the Western Region mainline only as a pilot (and even there failed to stop the Southall collision between an ATP fitted HST and a freight crossing the main line). BR was asked by the Ministry to test this project cost benefit at a seminar with academics and other industries and as BR's methodology was considered robust, the proposal to fit ATP to all trains was replaced by a simpler system TPWS - Train Protection Warning System - although even that costs about £5-6 million per life saved, well outside our criteria. However, because of the prevalence of SPADs (900 a year of which 100 were potentially dangerous) it was agreed that this was an exceptional case and warranted that degree of expenditure.

It is interesting, however, to consider the different criteria used by different government departments and industry authorities to set safety standards. The money we suggested would be spent on ATP and save at most an average of 4 lives a year would, if spent on road safety save 400 lives, or if spent in the NHS on preventative treatment, probably 4,000 lives - or if spent by the Department for International Development on simple health care such as diarrhoea medicines, would save at least 45,000 children's lives in Sub-Saharan Africa or the Indian sub-continent.

One reason for the decision to fund the 'Train Protection Warning System' (TPWS) despite the high cost for every potential life saved was because of research work we had been carrying out in the Safety Directorate on human error or 'human factors' as it is known by professionals. We linked with Professor James Reason (an appropriate name) at Manchester University who had advised British Airways and had been a member of the team commissioned by the government to look at the Hinkley Point nuclear power station plans from a safety viewpoint. He worked closely with a number of European researchers, including Jens Rasmussen, a Dane who had done a lot of work on the potential for human error in the nuclear industry. Professor Reason had evidence for the potential risk of error with certain types of decision under normal or stressed conditions. The evidence suggested that the human brain made around 3 errors per million decisions when undertaking routine work in normal conditions - such as drivers observing and obeying signals. We assessed that a driver over a 40 year career might have had to obey around 2 million red signals, therefore it would not be surprising if he (or she) had at least two or three SPADs in a driving career which was not considered acceptable because of the potential heavy consequences of a train collision. Some form of support technically for a driver was therefore essential, and TPWS would substantially reduce, if not eliminate, the risk.

There was one other safety issue which came to the fore in our list of priorities revealed by the risk assessment and cost benefit analysis. People had been falling from trains from time to time - about twenty a year on average - and traditionally railway management had tended to give these low priority, assuming them to be drunks or people messing around with doors. However there were around this time one or two cases where this was obviously not the case - a young girl fell to her death from a train crossing a viaduct and then there were five fatalities in three months from trains on the West Coast Main Line between Nuneaton and Lichfield - it became known in the media as the 'Tamworth Triangle'. The maintenance department continued to argue that it was not faulty doors, but there were many tests which revealed that some doors could get caught with the lock not engaging properly, and one of our Board members made the succinct remark that he was unaware we had the death penalty yet in the UK for being drunk. I was asked to look at the case for fitting locks to all doors of mainline stock using our new ALARP criteria and found that there was a good investment case based on a forecast of around £300,000 to save a life annually. There was a speedy decision to equip all InterCity rolling stock with a guard operated door secondary locking system.

A few months later I was spending a day at the Grove lecturing to a group of senior Indian railway officers who were undertaking an eight week management course in the UK. I quoted this example of the way we were using cost benefit analysis for safety investment and received the rather incredulous query from one officer who wanted to confirm that he had heard aright when I mentioned twenty deaths a year. He revealed himself to be the manager of the Bombay suburban service and said they had twenty fatalities a day from falls from trains or passengers knocked over while trespassing. Having travelled on the service from Bombay Churchgate station to Bombay Central in the rush hour, I well understood his point. However, I later compared the individual risk to a passenger on UK railways with one on Indian Railways and found the risk was almost identical despite a number of horrific train crashes reported each year in India. The reason was that the sheer number of passengers meant that the risk to any one individual was spread much wider. As an example, I was told that the number of commuters travelling into the three major Bombay stations of Churchgate, Central and Victoria Terminus was around 6 million a day - compared with Waterloo's 170,000!

By this time the safety organisation had matured into three main groupings - the Safety Policy unit, which I headed, looking at BR's safety management systems, measuring annual performance and setting objectives through an annual Safety Plan, using our research into risk assessment and human factors; the Safety Standards unit which had an overview of operational rules and engineering standards; and the Safety Audit unit that conducted periodic reviews of safety in the field to ensure standards were being maintained. Mike Siebert had been brought in from outside the industry to set up and run the Audit function and he took over the Directorate after Maurice Holmes retired, although I reported directly to David Rayner, Board Member, for the research and innovative work the Policy Unit was progressing.

The other main activity of the Policy Unit in which I was personally heavily involved was in the training of senior management in BR's new safety management systems. We devised a 3 day residential course in which I was assisted by consultants, initially from the Safety Science unit of Birmingham (Aston) University. The course was unique for senior BR managers in that there was a one hour written examination at the end of the course which managers were required to pass. This at least meant it was taken very seriously for a couple of people were taken out of their jobs when it was found that they were unable to meet the standard even when offered extra tuition. In the initial pilot course, we deliberately brought together people from different functions and one, who was an architect, kept moaning that he failed to see the relevance for his job. It was only at the end of the course that we discovered he was the architect responsible for the terrazzo tiling floor at Waterloo station which - in wet weather - had been the cause of more slips and falls of passengers there than any other reason for injury. Even two of the high level Business Sector Managing Directors managed to fail the exam at first go - I suspect it was 30 years since they had last taken an exam and one of them admitted not reading the questions properly, a classic schoolboy mistake. We were kind and arranged for both to attend Aston for a special day's personal tuition from the Professor there - and we did it on a Bank Holiday so that there were no questions asked by their staff as to where they were! We also gave the Executive and Non-Executive Board Members a 48 hour course, although we refrained from examining them on it - we chickened out on that!

The work we were doing on British Rail was becoming well known among railway circles. This led to enquiries from railway systems worldwide on safety management – especially from Commonwealth countries whose railways had been built by the British. The first international safety conference we attended was in Japan in 1990 which inspired annual seminars thereafter. The Japanese do these things in style – vast conference hall, 500 attendees, lavish gifts. After the conference David Rayner and I were invited to visit the JR driver training school to see their simulators and both of us were introduced to the controls of a cut down EMU to drive to a half hour realistic video unfurling on a wide screen in front of us. This was part of a safety briefing all Japanese drivers received which included testing in an emergency situation. All we knew was that we would be faced with some emergency during our 30 minute drive to which we would have to react. After a few minutes, as I was passing through a station at 60mph, a person threw themselves off the platform in front of me committing suicide. I braked fiercely – not that I could avoid him – and went through the emergency procedures when the train came to a stand. It was so realistic that I found that I was trembling with the shock! David then took over and a quarter of an hour later he had collided with a JCB on an ungated farm crossing.

As a result of the work we had initiated post Clapham, I found myself making presentations at international safety conferences and attending an annual seminar for safety specialists, which we initiated with the Japanese and New Zealanders. I was asked over the following three to four years to provide advice from BR to the railways of Australia, New Zealand, South Africa, Canada and Hong Kong and I set up and attended quarterly meetings in Europe with my opposite numbers from Germany, France, Switzerland, Holland and Belgium, which we hosted in turn, discussing the learning from any serious incidents we'd had and research that might be of mutual benefit. I found that we and the Dutch had an immediate rapport and were developing similar lines of research - especially on human factors - which we shared. The French and German Safety Managers were somewhat envious of the high level status of safety in the BR management team and were still constrained in what they could achieve by being a relatively lowly unit within their Operations function. After a bad train accident at Rüsselsheim near Frankfurt, I was asked to share my views on the accident with DB management and there was hope that this might be the catalyst for a review of the German approach to rail safety as the Clapham accident had been for ours, but it was not to be.

In 1990 I attended a 1,300 delegate World Congress of Safety Science in Cologne and in 1993 I was invited to address the Second World Congress in Budapest on the pioneering work we had been doing to transform BR's reactive safety management system to a proactive one. The work we'd done on cost benefit analysis and human factors caused great interest and led directly to some of the consultancy work I undertook in later years. In one of the main presentations a distinguished Indian scientist presented research he'd been undertaking on developing a similar prioritisation system for evaluating hazardous work and when asked to give examples of the results of the application of his sophisticated mathematical technique he quoted the top industrial risk in India was 'women carrying hods of bricks all day' and the second highest was 'children under ten carrying water in buckets for more than a mile'. So much for sophistication! This shook the assembly and I related it to my experience of visiting India in 1989 and 1992, more of which in the last chapter on the 'Railway Children'.

From the mid 1990s I was invited as only one of two industry managers (the other was from Shell in the Hague) to share experience with safety science academics from Europe and the USA. We met annually at the Werner Reimer Institute, a conference centre in beautiful grounds in the spa town of Bad Homburg, a few miles north of Frankfurt-am-Main. My job and that of Kurt Visser, the Shell Manager, was to provide case histories from our industries which would be discussed in the light of the theories and research they were presenting and to challenge the practicality and usability of their ideas. Each year the papers presented by the academics were edited into a book by one of the conference professors, either Bernhardt Wilpert from Berlin or Andrew Hale from Delft, and published - mainly as a text book for students - by the Pergamon Press. I contributed a number of chapters over the years on the application of safety science methodologies and philosophies to the UK railway industry and impact of state regulatory authorities and the Inquiry process.

I also attended a number of meetings with the Union Internationale de Chemins de Fer (UIC) in Paris to exchange safety data with other railways so that we could identify railways that had particularly good safety records in specific activities and from which one might learn. Equally, the knowledge of where one was weak compared with other railways could point to lessons that could be identified in order to improve. This was only partially successful as nearly every railway collected different data over different periods of time making true comparison difficult. For example, we even found it hard to define a fatality from a railway event, with at least three different definitions of the time span in which a fatality could be ascribed to a railway related event - only immediate deaths counted, or within 30 days or within a year.

I wrote a paper giving some examples of comparisons of safety - individual risk - from a number of industries, with data obtained mainly from Aston University and then collated some data from railways and put it in the context of societal safety. However, attempts to standardise data between European railways failed as not only was it difficult to get railways to change their data requirements but in many cases the form in which it was produced was required by the state regulatory authorities. A similar attempt at our annual international railway safety seminars failed also - the conference in Hong Kong in 1994 made a big attempt to do this and again papers were written which I thought might have been the first steps in the process, but they were not followed up as organisations changed, for instance, the BR Safety Directorate moved to Railtrack and key people in other railway administrations who were interested changed jobs or retired.

The most success we had was in our quarterly European exchanges, when we would look at specific accident causes or research in sufficient depth to understand comparisons. We shared data on SPADs and BR and NS (the Dutch railways) exchanged a lot of our research and information. We were able to do many helpful comparisons of staff safety and I particularly remember - because it was such a surprise - the poor record of the Swiss Railways on track staff safety. The results we'd achieved with Du Pont's input caused their management to hire the same company to advise them on this issue. We all identified that we were particularly vulnerable when the normal routine protection systems were disturbed for some reason - usually planned or emergency engineering maintenance work. During our briefing to each other on incidents that had caused injury or death we noted in a couple of sessions that over 80% of what we were recounting was associated with disruption of traffic during engineering line possessions. As technology was increasingly providing protection against human error, so when that protection was removed the likelihood of human error was much increased as staff had less practice in working with reliance on knowledge and experience. This was a subject which much exercised the academics at Bad Homburg with a lot of discussion on how to train staff to cope with emergencies when normally their routine was to watch an automatic system perform.

Further sharing of information was encouraged and networking between safety professionals in different industries became common. As well as with my colleagues in other railways, I met regularly with the Safety Directors of British Airways and Shell UK and also at the Parliamentary Advisory Committee on Transport Safety (PACTS) at the House of Commons. There were sub-committees which met regularly to brief parliamentarians on shipping, air, road vehicle design and highways and I helped set up a rail sub-committee chaired by Professor Andrew Evans of London University, a chair funded by London Transport. Each quarter we would meet altogether with the Transport Secretary of State or one of the opposition party spokesmen on transport which was where such issues as the different standards of risk laid down by different departments and regulatory authorities were aired.

In the late 1980s Margaret Thatcher had instructed the Treasury to pull together the different standards used and try to find some common ground - apparently her specific words were 'How many bangs do I get for my bucks?' (A Reaganism?) The Treasury laboured and when the Prime Minister became entangled later with other issues such as the Poll Tax, she forgot about her request and the Treasury never completed their study which they were finding 'too difficult'. By the time PACTS debated the issue the only party spokesman that took any interest was the Liberal Democrat - perhaps he'd had his ear bent by Lord Bill Bradshaw, ex General Manager of BR's Western Region. He accepted that the different standards were a major obstacle to rational decision-making on societal safety, but saw the entrenched position of many civil servants defending their own departmental practices as a major stumbling block to progress, and were unlikely to change unless a strong political will came from their Ministers.

One of the key findings of our own investigation into Clapham had been the role played by organisational change and, in particular, a hurried implementation without all the checks required for safety assurance taking place. As a direct result, the Safety Directorate devised a 'Safety Validation' process that every organisational change proposed had to go through. This involved identification of all the posts associated with safety and tracing where their responsibilities moved to in the new organisation. Was the activity still of vital importance for safety reasons and was it adequately covered? Were the posts filled with qualified people? Was additional training required? If so, had it been done before the reorganisation was implemented? This became a critical part of the privatisation safety assurance process.

One safety issue which was extremely hard to tackle was that of suicides on the railway. There were around 250 - 300 suicides a year, by far the largest number of fatalities on the railway from any cause. Not only was this of great distress to the victims' families, but it affected the train drivers involved and the track staff that were forced to deal with the consequences. I remember when Regional Operating Manager on the London Midland Region travelling in the cab of a diesel with a 28 year old driver on a train diverted from Nuneaton to London via the Midland Main Line, because of a line blockage south of Rugby. As we approached Wigston Junction to gain access to the Midland, just south of Leicester, this driver suddenly told me that he'd suffered three suicides in front of his train at this spot in the previous few months. I was horrified, but the guy seemed calm and I guess he was suppressing the experience. Apparently the suicides had escaped from the Rampton Hospital nearby. With the subsequent policy of getting people suffering from mental health problems back into the community where possible, such concentration of incidents is now no longer common.

This of course means that an instance of suicide might happen anywhere and the systems we set up with the management of Mental Health hospitals to advise us when a patient had gone missing so that we could warn station and signalling staff to be on the lookout at the 'black spots' ceased to be of so much help. In the early 1990s I had set up a special initiative to discuss with the Samaritans and other counselling organisations and see if we could control any of this situation or whether it was something the railways could do absolutely nothing about. Aidan Nelson, then at York, and the Community Affairs Officer there, Sue McKinstry, were interested and got involved – in fact when I retired Aidan was my successor and continued work in this area.

We identified that railway suicides had a distinct difference from the national average 'stereotype'. They were mainly male and 50% had had recent psychiatric help for mental health problems. One clear message was that a railway suicide meant it – it was not a cry for help. Another issue was that, despite my experience with the Nuneaton driver, such incidents were traumatic for drivers and caused lost time through subsequent sickness and shock. We established that this was worse if a driver had made eye contact with the victim immediately before the person was hit by the train.

The consultations also identified the underground drivers' problems from suicides jumping in front of trains as they emerged from the tunnel at the platform end. Drivers of LT trains were advised to switch on their cab lights when entering stations as it was suggested that seeing the driver, another human being, caused a would-be suicide to hesitate for a crucial few seconds and station staff alerted before the next train entered the station. I hesitate to say that we made a significant inroad to the problem, but we gained insights which we briefed to people who managed staff who were most likely to be affected and the managers of hospitals dealing with those at most risk were alert to our concerns and encouraged to contact us when possible.

Having undertaken the comprehensive risk assessment of all BR activities in 1991, I was now under pressure to disaggregate that to identify the key hazards to be addressed on specific routes or at particular locations. This was prompted initially by concern over the growing practice of replacing double junction leads by single leads with the potential for collisions if the signals protecting the junction were overrun. This concern grew when just such a collision occurred at Newton near Glasgow and operators began to challenge the business intention of cutting costs at Ely by installation of such single leads at the 4-way junction to the north of the station. Consultants A.D.Little undertook a specific risk assessment with us, but many began to ask whether a computer model could not be developed to inform such decisions on a routine basis.

David Rayner and I therefore commissioned a project to develop a 'Risk Model' that could be used by businesses, operators and engineers. We started with a consultancy organisation with great confidence, but the first problem we identified was the sheer number of 'top events' that we could specify and the myriad combinations of circumstances of geography, route layout and weather conditions that could be relevant and without which the model would only be a broad indicator with management interpretation to play too large a part. I seem to remember that we had amalgamated over 800 such nodal risk points which were beyond the computer's capacity for pursuing all the options that were conceivable. The team then suggested using heuristics instead of the standard computer logic programming which would have the drawback of not being able to prove all the assumptions built into the model to assure that these were reasonable. However, the team were optimistic and began to load data into the model. We decided to demonstrate the model to interested engineers, operators and business managers when I had been assured that there was sufficient data in the system to show what it could do.

I made the mistake of not seeing the demonstration in advance and pressing the consultants to show some examples knowing that our audience would be wanting to see something concrete and not just abstract theory. As soon as the model began to spew out results on the first suggested download, I knew we were in trouble. The risk figures produced were highlighting 98% of the hazards on a particular route were from so called 'bridge-bashing' – lorries or double-deck buses colliding with rail underbridges – a clear nonsense. We were able subsequently to identify the reasons for this absurdity but only because the area of error was so obviously with the data assumptions about this hazard which to date had never caused a serious train accident although the potential was there. Apart from losing the confidence of our audience, we realised that without a logical trail of data and decision-making processes open to inspection, we would be powerless to investigate results that were dubious but less obvious, and the project was aborted. We were too ambitious on this occasion, but I understand a 'Risk Model' has now been subsequently produced and used.

British Rail's Safety Directorate was transferred 'en bloc' to the newly formed Railtrack in 1994 and it is pertinent to understand just how much BR had achieved in the five years since the Clapham accident. A totally new proactive safety management system had been embraced and accepted throughout the organisation. BR's experts on this were being sought throughout the world to advise on the application of such systems to other railways. And most important of all, BR's safety performance had dramatically improved through 1989 to 1994. There had been no major train accident involving significant loss of life since Clapham. Staff safety had dramatically improved, with a couple of years having no fatalities compared with the previous decade's average of twenty deaths a year. Twenty passenger deaths from train falls every year had been virtually eliminated. There were many people out there in the community who owed their lives to what we had all achieved although neither we nor they knew who they were.

The transfer of the Safety Directorate under Mike Siebert to Railtrack took place in March 1994 virtually without noticeable effect. Railtrack would be government owned for a further two years and we continued life as usual. The most obvious change was in our designations. I had become Controller, Safety Policy, instead of Head of Safety Policy although my duties and responsibilities were exactly the same. It unfortunately made no difference to my salary! I had a small but very able team of a dozen people with Roger Taylor leading the small unit to develop and implement our annual Railway Safety Plan with all the necessary negotiations with businesses, operators, engineers and the railway regulatory authorities. Julian Marshall led the Risk Management unit and, having been our lead with the UEA studies on societal risk, was now researching the potential application of the Safety Case methodology as used by the off-shore oil industry since 'Piper Alpha'. Sarah Tozer was my expert on human factors liaising closely with Professor Reason and other academics and with Hilary Wharf and her colleague, Adam Sedgwick, who were undertaking many studies on the issues of fatigue and human error, especially looking when SPADs were mostly likely to occur within the shift, where data they were uncovering was producing some surprising results.

There was one new major task in which the whole Department became heavily involved – that of ensuring the new privatised railway companies went through a vigorous validation process before they were allowed to take on their new responsibilities independent of BR. They were required to do this by preparing a wide-ranging and comprehensive 'Safety Case' which was then scrutinised by a team from within the Safety Directorate and further subject to questioning by the whole Safety Directorate top team and key engineering and operations managers. A Safety Case sets out the safety policy of the company and catalogues in detail how this will be delivered in practice through its commitment to standards, through issues such as managerial experience and competence, training, personnel policies, staff communications, understanding of safety management techniques and methodologies, data collection plans and use of past safety performance information to comprehend the risks its organisation will need to control.

The Safety Director appointed three senior managers – Phil Dunkley, Stan Judd and Jim Ward – to chair the Safety Case validation process on a full time basis and other managers were seconded on the days of the interviews with a new Train Operating Company's management team to probe the areas in the documentation submitted for apparent ambiguous or contentious points. I was frequently present to seek clarity and commitment to the company's safety policies and culture and looked for signs that the whole team understood and showed a personal resolve that safety would be treated at top level with the same priority as production or financial performance. I looked with interest at who took the lead on such fundamental questions and worried if the Managing Director looked to his safety specialist to answer and even more if a safety consultant hired in was the spokesperson, even if the written and spoken words were perfect. I would much rather gauge the personal interest and commitment of the MD and his senior managers, even if the words were not from the text book.

As the day approached when Railtrack would become fully privatised and no longer government owned, I began to discuss the implications with David Rayner, especially the future likely policy towards some of the ground breaking research and seeking of new initiatives to which we had been committed. There was the strong possibility that a privatised company would see its safety responsibility as meeting the set standards of good practice within the law rather than pioneering new thinking, which might be considered to be more the role of the regulator or consultants when a particular problem needed addressing. I had been privileged for some six years to be allowed a very free rein to drive the railway industry's safety performance forwards within the priorities that I had been party to setting. However, the signs were that this freedom would be more constrained as shareholders might not see being among the world leading railways on safety as their priority - as long as they were protected from their company being found negligent of complying with its accepted Safety Case.

I had founded the Railway Children charity some nine months previously and David Rayner pointed out that, with just two years to go to retirement, I might find it more fulfilling to spend the time developing the charity, especially in the light of the financial incentives that Railtrack were offering for early retirement to many senior experienced managers in an effort to reduce their costs and increase their profit potential. I think in hindsight that they let too many engineering, operating and safety managers with experience go, and several of us subsequently found ourselves hired back as consultants, often at fees greatly exceeding what we were paid as employees. I therefore decided to take early retirement and was immediately approached by a small new safety management consultancy and offered a part time Principal Consultant's role. With my own financial future assured through pension and 'golden handshake' arrangements, I saw the opportunity to build the charity's funds in its initial growth from the consultancy fees I could earn and committed myself to a minimum of 60 days a year to International Risk Management Services (IRMS) and their Managing Director, Andrew Smith.

Three months before my retirement my career was crowned by receiving the OBE in the 1996 New Year Honours list for my services to the railway industry and I saw this as a recognition from colleagues in the industry of all that my teams had been doing to turn around the industry's safety performance in conjunction with dedicated managers and staff all over the system. I was well looked after by the company on the day I received the honour from the Queen herself and was able to celebrate with my family – Pat, my three children and my father – at lunch in the Savoy Hotel. My only regret was that my mother had died some seven years previously, as this might have vindicated her efforts to appease my two year old interest in trains when she would wheel me in the pushchair all the way to Esher Common where I insisted I could see 'proper' trains!

David Rayner, a JR Safety Manager and the author on a depot visit at the end of the International Railway Safety Conference in Tokyo, 3.11.90

A JR supervisor conducts a safety briefing with a driver before he takes up duty, Tokyo Safety Conference, 3.11.90

From the cab of a JR electric locomotive – note the driver wearing white gloves to enable station supervisors and signallers to see the driver's hand acknowledgement of safety rules en route, 3.11.90

The academic safety science research seminar in discussion at Bad Homburg, May 1994

The author receives the OBE from the Queen, March 1996

The author at the Savoy Hotel reception with Pat, his wife, father and two of his children, Catherine and Chris.

Chapter 15 : 1992 - 2001
International railway safety consultant

The first time came as a surprise. It was the summer of 1989 and I'd just finished acting as the main liaison with BR's legal team at the Clapham Junction Judicial Inquiry. I was approached by the BR international consultancy organisation, Transmark, to ask if I would be prepared to spend three weeks in Western Australia advising the Freight Manager of Westrail, Martin Baggott, based in Perth, on quality management. All my work on TQM in the UK had been applied to the passenger businesses, but I didn't see why the same principles shouldn't work for freight traffic also and the thought of a funded trip to Australia was a big temptation, so I accepted.

The main freight activities of Westrail were between Perth and Kalgoorlie where trains for the transcontinental route across the Nullarbor Plain were marshalled. I spent sometime with Martin gathering data about the causes of unpunctuality and complaints and then assessed and prioritised the investment necessary to make serious improvements – in many ways a similar exercise to the study I'd done for John Nelson and John Prideaux on the ECML. It was spring in Australia and I shall never forget the profusion of wild flowers I saw on that trip, including some very exotic ones in and around Perth and Freemantle. The Transmark consultant in Australia wanted me to return home via Sydney and meet some of the railway people there, but there was an internal air strike going on and that brought home to me just how remote Perth was from any other city. The only way I could reach Sydney was via a 17 hour flight to Singapore and back to New South Wales, so we agreed that visit would have to be postponed. I spent a couple of days sightseeing in Singapore and then 48 hours in Bombay visiting the girl, whose education my own family sponsored through 'Save the Children'. This visit had enormous repercussions to be recounted later in chapter 16.

On my return I became Project Manager for the Du Pont Safety Management Review, Brian Burdsall succeeding me as BR's Quality Manager. This led to an intensive three years' work as Head of Safety Policy before another overseas opportunity arose.

In March 1992 my presence was requested in South Africa. The nationalised transport industries of South Africa were being privatised starting with the national airline, and plans were being discussed for Spoornet, the state railway company. The South African Spoornet top managers were engaging with government on the legislation required for safety of the railways and seemed to think that something like the operating rulebook could be enshrined in law.

However, before signing off they arranged a conference and invited three safety specialists from different regulatory regimes – a senior manager from the Federal Railroad Authority (FRA) of the United States, an Italian from the European Union of Railways (UIC) and Alan Cooksey, Deputy Chief Inspector of the UK Railway Inspectorate. For some reason I cannot now remember, Alan was not available and I was asked to go in his place instead. Each of us described our systems to the Spoornet and South African Ministry of Transport officials. I remember the American advising the South Africans to avoid the FRA approach at all costs – it was far too prescriptive although probably essential for the USA, which had over 600 independent railroads, many of them comparatively small. The Italian reeled off the lists of standards that were being laboriously developed by the UIC and my description of the UK Safety Case regime, which had just been agreed as the means of validating the new privatised train operating companies, aroused most interest.

The conference was taking place in a small game park about 40 miles from Johannesburg – it was novel to wake up and see the middle part of a giraffe's neck passing the window – and about midway through the proceedings the result of the referendum about negotiations to end Apartheid was announced, with over 68% of the 2.8 million white voters supporting President de Klerk's proposals. The railway managers were relieved at the outcome – they feared revolution had the vote been for Apartheid's retention – but now realised that probably within months they might have an ANC Minister of Transport who could demand to see investment in the suburban railways into the townships. The Chairman of Spoornet asked me how I would apply a Safety Case to the Soweto suburban railway and I merely stated that he would need to identify the highest risks first from accident and incident data collected. I asked him what he thought his greatest risks were.

'Oh, that's easy,' came the reply, 'we have on average five murders a week on the suburban service.' He went on to tell me that they locked a driver in at either end of the EMUs as it was too dangerous to walk up the platform at the Soweto terminus. He also told me that the average life expectancy of a travelling ticket collector on that service was six weeks – although I found that difficult to comprehend. I'm not sure if he meant literally 'life expectancy' or whether no-one was prepared to do the job for more than six weeks. On any criteria no other railway management I knew would contemplate running a service at such a high risk. When the conference was over, celebrated by a traditional Zulu dinner and dancers from a local native village, I suddenly found that the last planned days of my visit were to be spent with my American and Italian colleagues as guests of Spoornet on the Blue Train all the way to Cape Town with 36 hours sightseeing there on the Table Mountain and at the Cape of Good Hope before returning home.

A couple of months later in May 1992 I was asked by an Australian consultant, David Hyland, to undertake some work to underpin investment priorities for Sydney's City Rail network. In previous years I had engaged David to help me develop prioritisation of investment cases for the infrastructure departments of BR as part of my reliability remit. He now wanted something similar for City Rail – the management was looking to see if modernisation of the system or its replacement by road was the best option. I spent a couple of weeks undertaking this work with David – including a Sunday sailing in David's yacht under the Harbour Bridge and in front of the Sydney Opera House – and when it had been successfully concluded I was invited to visit Bill Casley, whom I'd met previously on one of the annual railway safety conferences when he was the Executive Director of the New South Wales Transport Safety Bureau, and was now heading the Australian national rail regulatory authority in Canberra.

I went by train from Sydney to Canberra, not a particularly fast or popular journey, and when I'd finished there I found myself invited to fly to Melbourne to spend an evening meeting the Victoria State railway team led by Ian Dobbs who had been a very young manager I'd appointed – with some reluctance from my Operating colleagues – to the post of Area Manager Watford. They were all very keen to hear of the changes BR had made in safety management since Clapham and, in particular, about risk management and the prioritisation of investment by the use of cost-benefit analysis.

In 1994 I was asked by David Churchill, formerly a BR Manager, now Head of the transport safety regulatory body of Canada in Ottawa, to spend time with him and his department applying some of the methodology of safety management that I'd helped to implement on BR. I was asked to go to Montreal to meet both managers and trade union officials of VIA Rail and was invited to travel there in the cab of a massive diesel electric locomotive on a 'huge' load of four 'tilt' coaches with a few desultory passengers. The trip was mainly memorable for the number of open crossings over which we screamed with horn blaring, and the number of times the driver and inspector pointed out otter dams being built in streams and wetlands beside the track which – unless dismantled - would flood and damage the permanent way.

Earlier, in 1992 David Rayner and I had visited Wellington in New Zealand as part of the programme of annual safety seminars we'd set up after the Tokyo safety conference in 1989. We'd developed a high regard for the privatised Tranzrail's safety management system which their Safety Director, Ray Ryan, had devised with help from an academic, Professor David Elms, from Christchurch University.

It was with some concern, therefore, that we learned that Tranzrail (TZ) was being prosecuted in the Crown Court over the severe injury to a six year old boy who'd fallen several years before from the coach end veranda of the 'Coastal Express' running between Picton and Christchurch in the South Island. Apparently the transport regulatory authority had failed to make any case against Tranzrail within the allowed timescale, and such was the public and media concern that the Crown Prosecutor had charged Tranzrail with 'unlawful killing', a very serious charge, even though the accident had occurred before privatisation. Tranzrail asked BR to send someone to review their safety systems and give evidence in court for the defence as an expert witness and David asked me to go. I spent the month of December 1995 in Wellington being briefed by Tranzrail's QC and Ray Ryan, with John Mitchell, a senior BR mechanical engineer who'd been asked to examine Tranzrail's engineering standards and practices as the accident had occurred through the failure of a metal handrail which had come adrift as the boy passed through the veranda and fallen from the train as it lurched.

I went painstakingly through all the safety documentation in the legal office with Ray and began to write my evidence of what I found. I paid particular attention to TZ's accident information system for the company admitted that an unauthorised local depot modification to the handrails in 1981 had led to the failure – apparently the coaches were so old (1936 vintage) that standard replacements were unavailable and the depot people in Christchurch had improvised without Headquarter's authority. If previous similar accidents or failures had been reported and nothing done, either the communication and information system had a weakness or management at the time had been negligent. I found that Ray Ryan and his colleagues had introduced a very robust safety information system in the late 1980s and had painstakingly briefed it in throughout the system. In fact we discovered that there had been one or two incidents without causing any injury and local people had grumbled – but as so often is the case – no-one had reported it to their management.

The other major area I took an interest in was the vigour of their safety audit system, the extent to which management checked that the systems they had introduced were being implemented in practice. Again I found a robust system, well documented in both its processes and visits and findings carefully logged. At the end of the month I completed some forty pages of evidence that I was prepared to give indicating not only the strengths of these particular procedures but also that in my opinion TZ's safety management systems were well ahead of the majority of national rail organisations at that time. I then relaxed by enjoying an evening of carol singing on the beach in the warm evening sunshine and went home for Christmas.

The case was to be heard in Wellington's Crown Court in February 1996 and I duly went out and listened for the first fortnight to the prosecution case. The police had searched the TZ offices for relevant evidence and had taken copies of everything they thought useful in the case and the prosecution had hired an expert witness also, another safety consultant from the UK of whom I'd heard, but had had no dealings. My role during this time was to advise the defence QC on points made by the prosecution relevant to my area of knowledge and I was astonished to hear the expert they'd hired claim that TZ had no safety information or audit systems. During cross-examination, our QC handed the witness a copy of TZ's safety audit system and asked him what he thought it was.

The man was most embarrassed and had been let down badly by the police who'd failed – in their ignorance – to find and select the relevant paperwork for the case. A series of witnesses claimed that they knew about the handrail design defect but had to admit under cross-examination that they were unaware whether management had been advised. When the prosecution case had been completed and John Mitchell went into the witness box, he'd only begun to read his evidence when, at the end of the day the judge called the lawyers to his chambers and asked if the defence wanted to submit that – after hearing the prosecution case rebutted so strongly – there was no case to answer. We had a long debate that evening trying to tease out any potential drawbacks from taking up the judge's suggestion and concluded we were being given a very strong hint by the judge that he felt the prosecution had failed to make their case. We therefore made our submission in the morning and after an hour's deliberation, the court resumed to hear the judge dismiss the case through lack of evidence.

There is no doubt that the New Zealand regulatory authority could have made a successful prosecution using health & safety legislation even though the accident happened under a previous management and the defect causing the accident had occurred some 15 years previously. However, there was no way that the serious accusation of 'unlawful killing' could have been upheld. Even so, it had been a great strain for Ray Ryan and others most closely involved. I was now faced with complex return flight arrangements and important assignments planned in India en route meeting people about the start up of some of the recently founded Railway Children charity projects in India. I therefore decided to let the arrangements stand and hired a car and spent nearly two weeks exploring the South Island 'on holiday' – my wife and son had joined me in 1992 at the safety conference and we'd had a 'taster' then of the beauties of the South Island as well as special train trips to the North Island volcanoes and Rotorua.

Fourteen years later I encountered an amazing coincidence. I was standing on the platform at Crewe waiting for a London train and there had been a major disruption. I saw an elderly couple on the platform looking bemused and offered to help. They turned out to be tourists from New Zealand and we got chatting – my 1995/6 visits came up in conversation – and then, extraordinarily, the man turned out to have been the schoolmaster of the young boy who'd fallen from the 'Coastal Express'! What's more, they'd kept in touch with him and were able to tell me that despite his severe injuries, including blindness, the boy was now a university student doing well and nearing graduation. I was able to feed this back to Ray Ryan and John Mitchell to round off the experience.

By the time I'd returned from New Zealand I'd only a month to go until retirement after a 36 year career on the railways. I was given a farewell send-off by my colleagues in the Royal Society of Medicine atrium in Wimpole Street (a further coincidence was an invitation to become a Fellow of the RSM some ten years later as a Chairman of a charity involved with the health care of children) and then started to order my life – as I thought – 33% to the safety consultancy work with International Risk Management Services (IRMS), 33% to the development of the charity and 33% to home and the family.

Even before I started work with IRMS, however, I was asked by Transmark to join a former colleague from Safety Audit, Ben Keen, to train Mexican Railways management staff in safety management. Although we stayed in a five star hotel in Mexico City we were both queasy – I seemed to make a habit of only ever succumbing to upset stomachs overseas in five star premises having been sick in the Bombay Gymkana Club and among the gold taps of the washroom of the Calcutta Club. Between us we somehow managed to complete the training well enough to be asked back a second time. The Mexican Railways were very concerned about the extent of their claims from customers whose freight had been destroyed by a number of derailments and were keen to become more proactive. I took advantage of the visit to spend a day at the end of our assignment travelling the 70 miles south by road to Puebla where Railway Children had partnered its second overseas charity, 'Juconi'. The street children used the bus terminus to change from buses from the rural and indigenous land in the south to the shuttle service using the dual carriageway to the capital and our charity funded staff to work with the bus companies to bring children found there to a half-way home in Puebla for rehabilitation and return to their families where possible. I had turned up, however, on the very day that the Duchess of Gloucester was making a visit to the charity with Embassy officials and for convenience I was made a member of the Duchess's party for the tour.

Another brief interlude was a visit to Pakistan in October 1996. Cyril Bleasdale was Director of the Institute of Transport & Logistics that year and he invited me to their annual international conference in Rawalpindi to give a presentation during a two day seminar on the application of a modern safety management system to the issue of environmental management. It was relatively easy to transfer the concept using risk management to identify the hazards and potential consequences and cost-benefit analysis to prioritise possible control measures. During the conference the Institute's AGM was chaired by its President, the Princess Royal, who conducted the meeting in a brisk and business-like fashion, and then the delegates were treated, with their partners, to a couple of spectacular sight-seeing excursions.

Firstly, we were guests of the Pakistan section on a trip on the Khyber Pass railway from Peshawar to Landi Khotal, climbing past the tribal villages that seemed still to dwell in an era of 2,000 years ago, in an ancient train, topped and tailed by two venerable 2-8-0 freight locomotives built by Armstrong Whitworth in Manchester around the time of the first World War. We were accompanied by Pakistani Army riflemen standing at every door, and three or four perched on what seemed to be a garden bench balanced on the buffer beam of the leading locomotive.

We endured no more than a few stray stones thrown by young boys; in fact the majority of children ran to the trackside to wave to us, as the trip of a train to the Khyber Pass was a rarity those days. Then the train wove between the bare mountains reversing and twisting through many tunnels until the border post with Afghanistan was reached and we could look over the gun emplacements to the valley of the Pass. The next day we were due to be guests of PIA, the Pakistan national airline, for a quick flight around the Karakoram range including encircling the second highest mountain, K2, but unfortunately the cloud cover made it dangerous so we set off in a group of jeeps on a hair-raising climb to 14,000 feet in the snow covered mountains and spent a somewhat chilly night in a lodge at 12,000 feet.

After my retirement from the government owned Railtrack a few days before privatisation, I undertook my first consultancy assignment for IRMS, which involved flying to Hong Kong as they had won a contract to undertake a full scale risk assessment of the five main divisions of the Kowloon Canton Rail Corporation (KCRC) whose railway ran from Kowloon to the Chinese border at Guanzhou. The corporation ran EMU suburban services, a tram system, freight train and road terminal activities and an administrative organisation. They also ran a couple of through trains to mainland China each day. The exercise was similar to that carried out by BR in 1990-1, although on a smaller scale. Most of their activities were well inside the 'ALARP' boundaries although the tram unit had suffered staff injuries in tram/lorry collisions and we recommended strengthening of the shell encompassing the tram cab. The main Division where we had many significant recommendations to make concerned the road vehicle and freight depot activities where we had identified a number of hazards, which needed addressing. One outcome from this was an invitation to present a paper to the Asia Rail Conference, which led in turn to a request several years later to lead a major safety review of the Hong Kong Mass Transit Railway.

In the meantime, IRMS had bid for a contract advertised by the Irish Government to undertake a full review of Iarnrod Eireann's safety performance. The company had lacked investment and was suffering a number of accidents, especially severe and costly freight derailments, which were causing the railway company to demand funding from government to invest to avoid these. The government was unsure how genuine this protest was and wanted it independently assessed. If proven realistic – which it was – the state had then to decide to invest heavily in the system or cut the service back to the Dublin commuter trains (the 'Dart'), and the mainline to Cork and Athlone only. Four consultancy companies were shortlisted and were instructed to make presentations to the Irish government railway inspectorate in Dublin. Unfortunately I was in Madurai in southern India at the time and I was summoned to the phone in the middle of the night from my chalet accommodation in the grounds of a Methodist university to see if I could attend on a specific date only a few days away. Although I would be back in the UK by then, it clashed with the AGM of the Railway Children in London, which I was required to chair. The

Irish government personnel were good enough to transfer our presentation to 4pm to allow my company to charter a light aircraft to pick me up from London City Airport immediately at the conclusion of the AGM. It was all down to split second timing, whisked by taxi to the airport, light aircraft propellers already turning, with a car waiting for me at Dublin. I felt a bit like 007 until, just after take-off, I realised that in my haste I'd omitted a toilet stop and flew over the Irish Sea with my legs crossed as there were no facilities in the tiny plane! I'm pleased to say that we got the contract.

My role was to review the IE's safety culture and performance overall and I had a number of interviews with the organisation's senior managers as well as sampling activities on the ground. I discovered that broadly the culture was very similar to BR pre 1989 and many of the steps we had taken on BR were relevant to Ireland also. Of particular interest to the Irish Rail managers was the recommendation to conduct regular safety briefings with staff in small groups and these were put in hand before I returned a few months later to see how they were getting on. We had discussed staff safety with the trade unions and were doing fine until one of our number talked about the problem of literacy among the track workers and we found headlines in an Irish daily newspaper accusing all its track staff of being unable to read! I found ready allies among the managers including Ted Corcoran, the Safety Director, and I'm pleased to say that the Irish government decided to invest in its rail network before the current financial crisis hit the Irish economy especially badly.

IRMS was also commissioned by Network Rail when it took over from the failed Railtrack to conduct due diligence on its safety regime in six key areas. I was asked in particular to look at signallers' competence standards and training, route crime, and Network Rail's revised track safety system, the latter in particular being controversial and subject at the time to much internal criticism. There is no doubt that in the early stages the revised methods of working were causing problems but I concluded that we were being ask to evaluate the new methods too soon before they'd had a chance to become ingrained in the network. I worked closely with Sue McKinstry (now Sue Nelson) and Aidan on the route crime programme and followed up on our earlier work on trespass and suicide in which both had taken a proactive and enthusiastic interest.

In addition to work with IRMS, Network Rail asked a number of retired Operators and Engineers to form a panel of experts willing to chair internal Network Rail Accident Inquiries, only some of which would be followed by formal Railway Inspectorate investigations. In the first four years after my retirement I chaired a number of these Inquiries, the most high profile of which was the train collision at Watford Junction when one member of the public was killed when the first coach of the down EMU commuter train overturned. The primary cause was obvious – a SPAD by the driver of the train from London – but the root causes were more complex and went back to the design of the junction layout and the number of permanent line speed restrictions approaching the junction which might have confused or distracted the driver. I soon became the panel member most frequently asked to chair Inquiries caused by SPADs – incidents involving a London Underground train at Harrow & Wealdstone, and other incidents at London Bridge, West Byfleet, Bearley Junction and Bickley Junction. All were clearly SPADs but in all cases there were other factors increasing the likelihood of error by the driver – in particular a sequence of delays caused by seeing a string of single or double aspect yellow signals, which caused the driver to forget or misread the key signals he needed to obey. I also had a couple of level crossing accidents, one on the Newquay branch when road traffic signs misled a lorry driver and we found ourselves in dispute with the highway authority over recommendations to prevent a recurrence.

One accident inquiry I was not available to chair was the Southall collision in 1997 between an HST from Swansea and a stone hopper train which was crossing from Down Relief line to the sidings on the Down side of the main line at Hayes. The HST was fitted with Automatic Train Protection (ATP), which on this occasion was not operative, and I was asked as an expert witness to examine the revised policy on train regulation promulgated by Railtrack as there were many who questioned why the stone train had been given the priority over the junction, stopping the HST in full flight. The issue was whether the policy had increased risk, whether it was a case of wrong regulation by the signaller - or both. The Railtrack policy on train regulation had moved away from the

BR priorities which was the historic practice of giving priority in headcode order – ie class 1 express passenger trains had priority over class 2 local passenger trains, over class 3 express freights and so on. The infrastructure controller was now trying to give a better balance between the different business companies and the priority was now to regulate for the least delay to all trains rather than just the class 1s. I examined the train registers on the day of the collision and discovered that for a potential two minute delay to the HST in order to clear the freight from the Down Relief line, not only was the freight not delayed but two further local trains behind it to Oxford and Reading would also have avoided delay. Had the freight not taken that opportunity to cross, there was no further opportunity for several minutes as there would be another express on the Down Main, then another on the Up. I expressed the view that the policy was defensible and that on this occasion the signaller's train regulation would indeed have minimised the delay to all the trains concerned. The issue was clearly the driver's SPAD at a location at which he did not expect to be cautioned and the various reasons for the train ATP not being operative and why the train was allowed to run in that state.

In 2000 I was asked to lead a small team to review the safety of the Hong Kong Mass Transit Railway Corporation (MTRC). It was the practice of this corporation to hold an independent safety review every three years and I was following one undertaken in 1997 by a team led by Gordon Pettitt. I was supported by David Sedgwick of Risk Solutions, engineer Bert Hope, formerly Signal Engineer of BR's Scottish Region and James Catmur from the safety consultancy firm, A.D.Little. We spent two weeks looking at the network on which the citizens of Hong Kong relied and judged them against their mission statement – to be the best and safest system in the world. The company had to be efficient – a five minute delay warranted a paragraph in the local media and a twenty minute stoppage would cause a headline article!

We were given full co-operation, and a demonstration of the importance the top management gave to safety, being invited to the regular management meeting on the subject chaired by the Chairman of the company who was no figurehead on this. Data collection was all computerised and it was hard to identify areas for improvement except by taking the company at their word re wanting the very highest standards and therefore we judged every aspect of their plan and execution against the best practices in each activity that we were collectively aware of worldwide. Our study was to include also the new airport railway, which was about to be opened. Our report finally included seventy recommendations, which was a shock to our hosts and in particular there were a couple of instances of poor signal maintenance that our Signal Engineer expressed in his usual blunt manner that both shook the MTRC engineer responsible and caused him considerable embarrassment. We learned that there are cultural ways of being able to criticise the Chinese and direct blunt speech or written statements do not figure in that culture. The European members of the MTRC team understood us and accepted our premise that we indeed did rank them among the best systems in the world, but the Chinese engineers took a lot of diplomatic convincing.

In the year 2000 IRMS was sold to the consultancy company EQE as a limited cash flow always meant continuing problems as we had to take on new consultants to manage an ever increasing workload. Although one of the main reasons of the acquisition by EQE was to tap into the expertise of the small IRMS team, in fact many of the staff were not happy in the new situation and some left quickly for other companies. By 2002 many had graduated back to MHA, the company which had been closely associated with IRMS, which itself was taken over by Lloyd's Register, with Andrew Smith, previously the MD of IRMS becoming Lloyd's Development Manager in the USA.

One former IRMS consultant who had joined DNV, asked me to assist him with a review requested by the Network Rail Safety Directorate of which I was once a part – now Rail Safety & Standards Board (RSSB). The policy of ALARP was under pressure in the political climate after privatisation and further high profile and disastrous accidents at Hatfield and Potters Bar, and RSSB had commissioned a study on societal risk and how it should be incorporated in safety decision-making. This was exactly the subject I had researched with Julian Marshall and Dr David Ball at the University of East Anglia back in 1993-4, but in the organisation's convulsions of 1994, 1996 and 2000, all traces of that work had been lost and the company's corporate memory was lacking as so many experienced managers had been prematurely released in 1996 and subsequently. It seemed a bit profligate of Network Rail to have to pay again for work previously commissioned and little new was unearthed in this study. However, a new attitude was prevailing in the Railway Inspectorate, now under the UK Health & Safety Inspectorate, and it seemed that a more prescriptive approach was being adopted causing costs to rise considerably because of political rather than logical pressures. There is no doubt that safety on Britain's railways has improved enormously in the last twenty years, despite the much publicised 'blip' in the first couple of years of the privatised Railtrack, but in recent times safety regulatory requirements have been held partly responsible for the escalating costs of the infrastructure that the privatised railway industry has to bear.

A Spoornet diesel locomotive and Officers' Saloon takes the conference visitors to a Johannesburg freight yard and the Soweto suburban railway, March 1992

The South African Railways management team and the three visiting safety advisors before departure for Capetown on the 'Blue Train' at Johannesburg, March 1992

David Hyland

Ray Ryan and his wife, Janet

The Tranzrail special train in the North Island carrying members
of the International Safety Conference, 1992

Cyril Bleasdale surrounded by members of the Institute of Transport conference on the buffer beam of the Khyber Pass special, during a halt for the two locomotives to take on water half way to Landi Khotal, October 1996

Chapter 16: 1995 – 2013
The Railway Children

I have mentioned the Railway Children charity a couple of times. After my first consultancy trip to Australia in 1989, under the guise of Transmark, to look at the application of quality management to Westrail's freight business, I returned via Bombay. My family had sponsored the education of a girl and her younger brothers in that city through 'Save the Children' and I asked if it would be possible to visit her and her family as I passed through. Arrangements were duly made and I arrived at Bombay International Airport at midnight and must have been the last person off the Jumbo jet as I found myself at the end of a two hour immigration queue in a stifling sultry building without (then) air conditioning. After a novice's frantic and panicky attempts at finding my way to a taxi and my hotel on Marine Drive in the south of the city, I got to bed around 3am, feeling nauseous – I had unwisely taken my antimalaria tablets on an empty stomach. I tossed and turned and at 7 o'clock I could stick it no longer and got up. Unable to face breakfast, I dressed, took a few deep breaths on the promenade facing the Arabian Sea and debated with myself what to do next, as I was not due to meet the girl and her family at the 'Save the Children' agency in Colaba, on the Eastern coast side of the city until 10 o'clock.

I decided therefore to fill in the time by walking across the city to my destination, the flat of a couple who belonged to the Theosophical Order of Service and acted as Save's agents in managing over 700 sponsorship grants. After half an hour or so, I was lost until I stumbled across Churchgate railway station. I entered the crowded concourse to scrutinise my street map and as I was doing so, I was accosted by a small girl, probably around six or seven years of age, begging. I had no small change, so I waved her away, when to my shock, she brought out a plaited whip from behind her back and started lashing herself across her naked shoulders. I stood there stupefied, like a dummy, when she repeated her actions. I was feeling fragile anyway and emotionally I couldn't cope. I fled the scene and when I'd pulled myself together, I thought, 'I can't leave her like that', and I went back.

I've no idea what I thought I was going to do and in the event I couldn't find her again on the chaotic concourse.

As I went on my way, my mind was racing to explain what I'd just witnessed and I soon realised that this girl was the exploited victim of some unscrupulous adult who was using her to extort cash from gullible tourists like me in return for a meal or so a day. I am still haunted by the eyes of that girl and when the truth of the situation dawned on me, I got sufficiently angry to search for organisations, which would protect such vulnerable children. To cut a long story short, on my return to the UK I got involved initially with Amnesty International's national 'Working Group for Children' and a few months later, became their representative on a newly formed UK Consortium for Street Children, a group of a dozen or so British non-government organizations (NGOs) working for street children internationally.

A few weeks later, the then Prime Minister, John Major, offered the Consortium a launch and reception at No.10 Downing Street and I got involved in the discussion on how to use the occasion.

When the debate turned to the causes of children coming to the street, I doodled a simple risk assessment of being a street child on the back of an envelope as I listened – a Fault Tree highlighting root causes and an Event Tree which explored consequences. The Fault Tree highlighted three key immediate causes: children coming from destitute families searching for earning opportunities; children running from abusive situations, physical and sexual; and children abandoned or neglected for a variety of reasons. Rarely was poverty a root cause on its own. It was usually coupled with the experience of violence or abuse and often went back to the root causes that were behind families in trouble – armed conflict, health breakdown such as the AIDS pandemic, natural catastrophes such as earthquakes, hurricanes and floods causing family disruption, economic collapse and loss of employment opportunities. All these put immense strains onto families and created the scenarios in which some children suffered traumatic experiences with which they were unable to cope. When children opted for escape to the street they were then met with the urgent needs of finding food, shelter and friends and I explored the actions they took to satisfy those basic needs, often with consequences that made them further rejected by society.

I asked each of my colleagues round the Consortium table what their NGO's intervention strategy was, and to my surprise found a glaring gap. Whilst large international NGOs like 'UNICEF' and 'Save the Children' did little work directly with 'detached' street children, their partners worked in both urban slum and rural situations on preventative measures – education and health care in particular. 'Amnesty' was working on extreme consequences when the behaviour and life style of the children made them victims of violence and abuse, especially from the police and other agents of 'normal' society. I had identified that the first few days – or indeed hours – after a child has turned to the street and travelled to some city are a key risk time in that child's life. As BR's Head of Safety Policy, I had been introduced by the BT Police to two Salvation Army Officers who patrolled the large London railway termini in the 1980s and early '90s, looking for runaway children at risk. They told me that they had picked up 3,600 under 16 year olds in the ten years of their mammoth self-imposed task – an average of one every evening. They also said that a young teenager alone there had on average ten to twenty minutes before they'd be targeted by a pimp, paedophile or drug dealer. In the last few years such children are not so obvious as the introduction of stricter barrier control, CCTV cameras and extra police presence has caused the children to avoid London and go where they are less easily discovered.

Anyway, as a result of my discussions at the Consortium, I explored the opportunities to intervene with these children to offer support before they were abused, exploited or corrupted, and came to the conclusion that the transport terminals of the world – railway stations in Asia and Eastern Europe, bus stations in Africa and Latin America – were obvious places to make a first contact. I therefore persuaded some of my railway colleagues to raise money to work in partnership with local organisations that would go out onto the platforms and offer help to the children as soon as possible, backed by drop-in centres where the children could obtain immediate food and health care while longer term options were explored with them. On May 31st 1995 this came to fruition and the 'Railway Children' charity was launched on the concourse of Waterloo station 'under the clock'.

Had this experience come 'out of the blue'? It may depend on whether you believe in 'guidance' or 'fate' or just luck or coincidence. I had been an orthodox or traditional Christian for as long as I could remember. My parents were staunch members of the Methodist Church – as were both sets of grandparents – and much of my early life had been spent in East Molesey Methodist Church where my paternal grandparents were Sunday School teachers and my father was Circuit Steward and Treasurer. By the time I was 18, I was a Sunday School teacher myself and Secretary of the Woking Church Youth Club. I was attracted to the radical thinking of Bishop John Robinson of Woolwich in the 1960s and rejected the literal or fundamentalist Christian viewpoint. In the 1970s and early 80s I found my liberal views often at odds with the increasing number of 'charismatic' Christians in my church, now in High Wycombe and felt myself to be drifting from the church, when I read a fascinating and very radical little book called 'Mr God, this is Anna speaking' which prompted me to stop engaging in theological argument and get on with life working to the humanitarian and compassionate demands of the person of Jesus as recorded in the Gospels.

Because of the number of responsible positions I held within the church, especially in youth work, I had been afraid to speak out about my doubts and reservations, fearing to undermine what I was doing. I'd been reading the book I've just mentioned on the platform at Maidenhead while waiting for my train one morning and just got to the bit where the six year old precocious Anna talks to her mentor about the importance of 'not being afraid' of life when my train drew in, not the expected DMU, but a long distance commuter train headed by a class 50 diesel, named of all things 'Dreadnought'! Seven years later, still convinced in my mind that I needed to get more involved in something, but not quite sure what, I'm confronted by that girl on Churchgate station. If challenged for my 'Christian' story, I'll admit to being 'converted' by two six year olds and a railway engine! And I'm sure it led, in that very roundabout way, to the moment on Waterloo station concourse when I'd at last 'stuck my head above the parapet' and taken the risk of failure or being considered naïve or eccentric.

I'd been encouraged to discuss my ideas with Geoff Myers, a BR Board Member, who was then also on the Board of 'Save the Children'. He suggested I link with a group of railway staff in Yorkshire who were raising money for children in Romania, but after a couple of meetings I found my vision and theirs did not coincide. Others tried to put me off, describing the difficulty of what I was taking on, especially that I was seeking help for slum and vulnerable children on another continent, but I kept talking with the encouragement of others at the Consortium for Street Children who acknowledged the gap in intervention that I'd identified and reassured me that this need was very real. David Rayner continued to support me and once the die was cast, Bob Horton, Chairman of Railtrack, and John Welsby, Chairman of British Rail, promised to help me launch the charity.

I'd seen photos of street children in Bombay reproduced in the Observer newspaper and got permission to use some from the book's author, photographer Dario Mitidieri and his publisher, Dewi Lewis of Stockport. They went a stage further and generously offered me their photographic exhibition, which supported the launch and stayed on the concourse where I spent the week talking to people about the issue and the photos and the fledgling charity.

After the launch itself, which was centred round speeches by Bob Horton, Tony Roche (John Welsby was detained at a meeting at the Ministry of Transport) and Dario Mitidieri, and I'd explained to around 150 people gathered there the objectives of the charity, I was approached by Christian Wolmar, then Transport Correspondent of the Independent. He expressed interest and offered help. He is still a trustee of the charity 18 years later. In addition to funds collected at the launch and exhibition and resulting from the media coverage, Christian went to Romania and got a two page article printed in the Independent about the street children on Bucharest's main railway station. Christopher Campbell, the non-executive Vice Chairman of Railtrack got me a grant from a trust fund he knew well, and within a few weeks I had enough money for the Railway Children's first project.

I'd talked at length to Consortium members about the opportunities to contact running and abandoned children at stations and Nic Fenton, then Director of 'ChildHope', suggested I support him in funding one of two projects that he had identified in Bucharest and Sofia stations in Eastern Europe. Two young men in London Transport's Planning Department then undertook a sponsored 3,500 mile cycle ride across Europe to Istanbul and we were off, partnering a local Romanian NGO that 'ChildHope' vouched for, called 'ASIS' who would provide a home and care for

50 boys aged between 10 and 14 found living in the sewers under Bucharest station.

By November 1996, I'd registered the charity with the Charity Commission and got permission to use the name 'Railway Children' – the only other organisation with this name was a playgroup in Kent whose premises backed on to a railway line and whose organiser was happy for us to share the name. I'd had the help of a number of railway people who'd formed a Committee to advise me and several of these stayed on to act as our first Board of trustees – my friend and 'best man', Stan Judd, Christian Wolmar, Gordon Pettitt, Terry Worrall among them. For the first year until I retired I'd been given permission by my boss, David Rayner, to use my BR office facilities to get the charity off the ground and from March 1996 I'd run the charity from my home, until I had a number of local volunteers and needed an office nearby. The former BR health insurance company, 'Health Shield' had an office in Crewe and offered me a small room in their building, which I gratefully accepted.

Although I'd taken advice from colleagues at the Consortium about potential partners in Eastern Europe, Latin America and India, a number of my colleagues in the railway industry were concerned about the situation in the UK and felt we should not ignore the problems on our own doorstep. We therefore decided that at least 20% of any income we received should be devoted as far as possible to partnering organisations that would offer early assistance to runaway children in our own country. At first I was introduced to a group interested in developing the crypt of St Pancras parish church on the Euston Road for a drop-in and emergency shelter for such children and youth, but on inspection the huge cost of such restoration became obvious and way beyond the resources and capability of a new non-government organisation.

The British Transport Police then introduced me to Diana Lamplugh, founder of the Suzy Lamplugh Trust in memory and as a positive response to the disappearance and presumed murder of her estate agent daughter. She had become aware of the dangers to homeless and runaway young people from predatory individuals – it was shortly after the conviction of Fred and Rosemary West who preyed upon homeless young people at their Gloucester home. She was concerned that many young people with a variety of problems did not know where to turn for help and was developing a new phone helpline service in conjunction with a number of interested NGOs and I became part of that founding committee. In due course we registered the charity as 'Get Connected' independent of the Suzy Lamplugh Trust and I helped it find its initial office accommodation in the Kings Cross East Side offices thanks to my contacts with Railtrack station management. I also became its Chairman for around three years when no-one else volunteered to take on the role, until our Chief Executive, Justin Irwin, developed a strong partnership with the Carphone Warehouse and their founder and Chairman, Charles Dunstone, took over the role and threw the resources of his company behind the project in a very powerful and successful partnership.

Early fundraising initiatives for Railway Children included a reception for potential donors at the LT Transport Museum in Covent Garden; a very generous contract with Britt Allcroft, then owner of the 'Thomas the Tank Engine' franchise, to provide anecdotes of my days as a 'Fat Controller' for a 'Thomas and Friends' video and to review scripts to check that the company was not subject to a barrage of criticism from pedantic rail 'gricers' because the railway detail was inaccurate; and a Channel 5 TV telethon called 'Give 5' based on our first Indian projects which raised the most reaction and response from the few who viewed the week's five charities featured, but was overshadowed by the death of Princess Diana at the beginning of the week. In May 1998 we partnered Centrepoint to mount our first Railway Ball at the National Rail Museum - which raised £30,000 for Railway Children and the donation of the nameplate 'Lady Diana Spencer' from a Class 47 diesel, which we eventually auctioned for £10,500. Virgin Trains ran an HST from Euston to York via Birmingham for the event and arranged for a naming ceremony before departure when Sally Thomsett – Phyllis in the 1970s film, 'The Railway Children' – named power car 43098 after the charity, unveiling an impressive nameplate, which included the charity's phone number. After we'd learned how to run such an event Railtrack provided £20,000 risk capital up front for us to work with a banqueting company, Conference Line, to organise a dinner and ball at a London hotel in 2000, which raised £110,000. This was the forerunner of what is now an annual event at the Grosvenor House Hotel in Park Lane and by 2012 had raised over £3 million.

By 1997, through contacts at the Consortium for Street Children, I had arranged partnerships with projects in Mumbai, Ahmedabad and Calcutta and I felt bold enough to apply to the National Lottery for a grant to develop our work to six other partners in India. I was pleasantly surprised and not a little astonished to receive £225,000, spread over three years at the first time of asking and our India work took off. At that stage I was reliant on making personal visits to India to interview applicants for funding and supervise the work and ensure that we were complying with our objective of making early intervention. Two years into the grant, the Lottery Fund's International Grants Officer visited one of the partners in Tamil Nadu, and whilst confirming that the children were safe and well looked after, recommended that we used the greater experience of some of our other partners to network, identify and spread best practice. This led to a major discussion among trustees at which we accepted the Lottery Board's suggestion and decided to invest sufficient resource to become a development agency with add-on value instead of just a grant making organisation.

We moved office to Breeden House in Crewe in 1998 and appointed our first two part time staff – Administrator Julia Worthington and Fundraiser Katie Mason. With office backing in the UK, I was able to spend more time abroad with our partners and went with Stan Judd to India early the next year for a pretty intensive tour of duty. By this time we'd linked with a remarkable charismatic Catholic nurse from Cork, Edith Wilkins, whom we'd first met as the Urban Director of CINI Asha's street children programme in Calcutta. Through 'Save the Children' we'd worked with one of her projects supporting the children of sex workers at Sealdah station and Rambagan red light district. She'd introduced us to another local NGO, 'SEED' in Howrah, who'd found thirty young girls aged between 4 and 13 who'd been living rough on Howrah's crowded and chaotic platforms, all of them the victims of sexual abuse or rape.

'SEED' had hired two social workers as 'Aunties' for these girls and a local school allowed us to use one of their classrooms and kitchen overnight as an emergency night shelter. During the opening ceremony, while a number of local dignitaries made long speeches in Bengali, a small girl of seven crawled from the ranks of bored looking children on the front bench and plonked herself on my lap and promptly fell asleep. I learned that this was 'Babli' as she was known, who survived by fetching and carrying water for the local slum community eight hours a day, seven days a week, 52 weeks a year for the princely sum of one rupee a day on which she had had to survive (remember the example given in the previous chapter of the risk to children carrying water quoted by an Indian safety scientist at the Budapest Safety Science Conference?). Ten years later I received an e-mail from Babli 'thanking me for giving her a childhood back'. This is more than reward enough.

It was during this visit that Stan and I visited a slum community at one of the Calcutta suburban stations, Tollygunge, where our partner had set up an informal school. The night after our visit, someone upset a stove and the flames spread throughout the entire community destroying all the makeshift homes and killing one of the children we'd seen the previous day. I abandoned my proposed meeting with the local railway manager (Stan Judd took this on board) while I went to see how I could help. Typically no fire engines or ambulances turned up to an illegal settlement and Edith galvanised us and a couple of her visitors from Cork to act as the emergency medical team to treat dozens of people with burns who waited patiently in a long queue to have their wounds examined and treated. The trouble was that we had no medical supplies so we all pooled whatever cash we had and a volunteer doctor and I walked a mile to the nearest chemist's shop and bought as much relevant first aid equipment and ointments as we could afford (and carry) and the chemist had in stock. The only building left standing after the fire was the straw and bamboo school we had built which the community had managed to save as their priority and we set up our 'surgery' there. One of Edith's volunteers was also a nurse, so the doctor examined each patient and diagnosed what treatment was appropriate, Edith and her friend bathed and bandaged and I acted as a medical auxiliary cutting bandages, finding plasters, looking for the right medicine and antiseptic bottles and pain relieving tablets, trying to respond to and interpret the cacophony of Bengali, Hindi and Irish voices. After four hours in the heat and dirt squatting on the charred earth we came to the last patient in the queue. No-one complained or screamed. A few children whimpered when the antiseptic ointment stung their open burns. Just as we were finishing, a local politician turned up with a TV crew to try to take the credit for what we were doing. The crowd sent him packing and two children took Edith gently by the arm and escorted her and us reverently through the still smouldering wreckage. It still chokes me up to think of it.

During the same visit I started to try to influence the Indian railway authorities to co-operate with our efforts to help the street children on their stations. I had met the General Manager of the Central Railway, Mr Balakesari, at VT station in Bombay previously and he had since been promoted to Member, Staff, of the Indian Railways Board and Ministry – his responsibilities included control of one branch of the railway police – the Railway Protection Force (RPF). As a retired senior manager of British Rail, I could use my former contacts to gain access as BR used to run senior management courses for Indian railway officers and I had been involved to deliver safety management training as mentioned in a previous chapter. I was concerned to push for two main areas of support – the allocation of space on key stations which partners could use for emergency shelter and the co-operation of the railway police to work with our partners to rescue rather than beat up or throw the children off the stations. This was a gradual process – slowly some of our partners had built good relationships with the local Divisional Railway Managers or District Officers of the RPF, but these were personal and I wanted it systematised to withstand the changes of personnel every two years or so.

In the same period I'd acquired other responsibilities. I'd become a trustee of the Methodist Relief and Development Fund which collected about £1 million a year from churches for its humanitarian work overseas and I was asked to make a monitoring visit to a project in the foothill of the Himalayas while I was in India for Railway Children purposes. Deforestation of the 8,000 feet slopes above the Nainital valley area was threatening to bring major problems destroying the local ways of life, causing landslides and flash floods and I visited a programme of tree planting and environmental education in the little schools in the tribal village areas. At the end of a several days visit, I was taken to a viewpoint to see the high Himalayas – unfortunately there had been a thunderstorm the night before and everything was covered in a thick mist. One of the local volunteers told me anyway that she'd been there for two months and hadn't seen the Himalayas yet through the haze. It seemed pretty hopeless but as we stared the mist dramatically lifted and the range emerged in front of my eyes, the huge bulk of Nanga Parbat right opposite. Then after drinking it in for twenty awe inspiring minutes, as I turned to go, the mist dropped down again and the mountains disappeared...

I was also busy at 'Amnesty International'. I was still a member of the Children's Human Rights Committee and we had persuaded the UK Section's AGM to mount a UK campaign for Children's Rights, specifically for children caught up in conflict situations including child soldiers, street children and girls subject to female genital mutilation (fgm). Half way through preparation for the campaign, the Amnesty staff curtailed our ambitions on the basis that they had insufficient resources to support us and restricted our initiative to campaigning for the end of forced child recruitment into government and rebel armies in Sub-Saharan Africa. The Chairman and Secretary of the network resigned in protest and I had to choose whether to stay or go as well. I concluded that half a loaf was better than none and I'd stay to fight another day. As a result I found myself Chairman of the AIUK network by default and eventually – as my committee had virtually disappeared through resignations and ill health – I was appointed as (volunteer) Children's Rights Advisor to Amnesty International UK to input children's rights concerns into country and theme campaigns and to communicate cases for action to the network of supporters by internet. Eventually as Amnesty overhauled its website, and I obtained new volunteer support – young members who were more internet-literate than me – our network grew to over 8,000 members willing to act on Amnesty cases involving human rights abuse and violations of children and young people.

Meanwhile Railway Children was beginning to grow beyond my capability to manage it on a voluntary basis. We advertised for a Chief Executive and in 2001 appointed Terina Keene, who had been Financial Director of 'Climb', an NGO supporting children suffering from rare metabolic diseases and their families. Terina had interrupted her employment, spending two years in the USA as her husband was working in Houston, and was looking for employment on her return. In fact she'd been appointed to a good job in IT, but opted to come to us even though we could not afford such a high salary as her other offer. A year later during a visit to India I realised I needed help there also and with the assistance of a former UNICEF officer based in Mumbai, Gopal Dutia, who later became a Railway Children trustee, I appointed two Indian

Programme Officers – Mrinalini Rao for the West and North and Mohan Rao (no relation) for the East and South of India.

Support in the UK, especially in the railway industry, was growing very fast. In June 2000 I was invited to address the ASLEF annual conference in Southport by Mick Rix, their General Secretary. In August EWS invited me to name an electric locomotive, 90031, 'The Railway Children Partnership', at the Old Oak Common Open Day, the Railway Ball had a separate Ball Committee drawn from companies associated with the railway industry, and Select Service Partners (SSP) – the food shop franchise holders at main stations – took us as their key partner setting up collecting boxes at all their outlets which by 2010 raised a significant sum every month for the charity. Then HSBC Rail, one of the three rolling stock leasing companies, offered Railway Children a number of redundant nameplates from diesel and electric locomotives and the auction, held at the London Zoo auditorium and run free for us by Ian Wright's Sheffield Railwayana company, raised as much as £80,000, to everyone's surprise. Further events for the railway industry followed and especially popular was the '3 Peaks by Train' challenge which was suggested by Robin Gisby of Network Rail and costs born by his company, Virgin Trains and EWS initially with many other rail connected companies getting involved and fifty teams of four participants.

The growth of income to nearing £1 million early in the new century encouraged us to widen our horizons and the Board allowed pilot study projects in Latin America – partnering 'Casa Alianza' in Guatemala as well as our continuing programme with 'Juconi' in Mexico. We also had had a couple of projects in Russia partnering two relatively small UK based Christian charities – 'Love Russia' which supported state run emergency shelters in Moscow and 'ARC' which funded a project for street children in far off Chita in Siberia on the Trans Siberian Railway. There children sheltered from minus 40 degree temperatures among the heating pipes under the station and other public buildings and ARC funded with us a charity called 'Helping Hands' run by the local Pentecostal Church of Russia. The Russian Orthodox Church had reacted negatively to this initiative, which they saw as competition, but surprisingly the state authorities rejected their complaint with the advice that when that church was prepared to undertake such humanitarian work, their complaint would be given more credence!

More recently we explored with 'Love Russia' the situation on Moscow's railway stations, hearing the railway police say that over 500 children a month were migrating through the six key stations, especially Kurski station where trains were arriving from Kursk, the south east Urals and the former USSR central Asian republics. We needed a Russian based NGO partner to make progress on these stations and formed a partnership with 'NAN' (No to Alcohol and Narcotics) led by Oleg Zykov, a former member of Putin's Human Rights Commission representing youth issues. The action research undertaken went well identifying the issues and raising the possibility of training state appointed social workers by NAN as outreach to the children there instead of the railway police, but I regret to say that the recommendations got bogged down in the State's bureaucracy between Ministries and Putin's scepticism and increased scrutiny of foreign funded NGOs and any further development is in abeyance until NAN indicates that a positive way ahead has been sanctioned.

In 2002 Railway Children received a £600,000 grant from Comic Relief to be spread over five years and two years later the BBC filming for Sport Relief of partnered projects in India fronted by comedian Patrick Kielty raised the public awareness of Railway Children. The impact of the BBC film for Comic Relief and the effectiveness of what they saw our partners undertaking caused Comic Relief to talk further to us and encouraged us to seek a larger grant – a full £1 million over 4 years which we applied for in 2004. That year we were selected by the Independent on Sunday as their Christmas Appeal and successfully sought weekly introductions to the appeal from David Dimbleby, Richard Branson, Jon Snow, Jenny Agutter and Mark Tully when we were overtaken – as in the 1997 telethon – by a much bigger event, the Boxing Day South Asian tsunami and the devastation it caused. Three of our Indian partners mounted emergency projects on the Tamil Nadu Coast and the Andaman Islands and we obtained a further £200,000 grant from Comic Relief to support this work.

In January 2002 I was invited by the Director of the Delhi located Indian Railway Museum to a conference in Ghum just a few miles from Darjeeling to join the railway authorities and UNESCO to discuss the development of the Darjeeling Himalayan

Railway in the light of it being named a UNESCO World Heritage site. UNESCO was keen to ensure that the local population benefited from any investment and development and I was asked to contribute ideas on how local school and slum children might participate and gain commitment to the project. I tried to involve one of our partners in New Jalpaiguri and Siliguri at the bottom of the railway, but the major issues concerned the investment necessary from Indian Railways and the fact that the railway was subject every year to significant disruption and damage during the monsoon season. I used the opportunity to see some of Edith Wilkins' work in the area, although we did not now partner her NGO, and saw the desperate situation of the drug and HIV affected slum dwellers at the Truck Stand in Siliguri. I later learned that she had focused in particular on protecting and rehabilitating trafficked and sexually abused girls in Darjeeling, a role that must have put her at risk from those whose activities she was challenging.

The work in India continued to grow. We conducted situational analyses at some of India's largest stations and identified that somewhere between 100,000 and 120,000 new children were arriving on the stations there every year, with 20 or 30 a day at stations like Howrah, New Delhi or Mumbai CST (the former Victoria Terminus). Of those on the station at any one time, one would find new arrivals; youths who'd been present for years and had their gangs, territory, income generating activities (legal and illegal); children of street living families around the station, usually scavenging or begging; and children from the slums in the suburbs who travelled in daily looking for opportunities to augment their family's income. We also identified that most children in these big stations in mega cities were migrating from the northern states of Bihar, Uttar Pradesh and Rajasthan and our second Comic Relief grant in consequence was designed to start new partnerships in cities like Lucknow, Samastipur, Patna and large towns like Malda and Asansol on the line from Calcutta to New Jalpaiguri and North Bengal. In this way we would be contacting children earlier and closer to the community they'd left and efforts to reintegrate them with their families and communities again would be more likely to succeed. By the mid decade we had an outreach presence at 45 stations in 14 states working through more than 20 Indian partners. In 2011 after joint working by the station staff, the railway police and our local partner organisation, Lucknow station was actually officially designated a 'Child Friendly Station'. In 2012 plans were completed for Sealdah station in Calcutta to receive the same accolade.

In June 2005 the charity celebrated its 10th anniversary with a reception on the terrace of the House of Commons facilitated for us by Nantwich MP and Chair of the Select Committee on Railways, Gwyneth Dunwoody. Moreover she had twisted the arm of the Minister of Railways, Derek Twigg, to attend and make a welcoming speech to a good crowd of supporters and other NGO partners and colleagues including two former Chairmen of British Rail, Sir Bob Reid and John Welsby. Gwyneth had been a big supporter of the charity – in fact she agreed with me on one occasion despite her steadfast opposition to the privatisation of the railways, that the privatised industry's ability and willingness to support the charity was the one and only advantage she could see as the nationalised industry could not have used taxpayers' money to donate to a charity. Her view was that that the breaking up of the industry into myriad competing companies was a rotten way of running a national railway system but 'jolly good for supporting a relevant charity'!

We'd also moved twice from our early days in the Crewe Health Shield office and Breeden House, first to Scope House, the Crewe Borough Council's office for developing businesses, then, when we outgrew that, to our current office at the Commons in the centre of Sandbach, about four miles from Crewe. Our income had now grown to well over £2 million a year and needed the support of a dozen programme officers, fundraisers, accountants and administrators, although we managed to keep our admin costs below 5% and our fundraising costs to under 20% establishing a ratio of at least £4 raised for every £1 spent raising it. Our India staff had grown too to support the much larger activities and number of partners with our first Programme Officer becoming the India Programme Director with a modest office in Andheri in northern Mumbai.

The pilot projects we'd carried out in East Africa – in Kenya, Tanzania and Zimbabwe – were now established by the Board as the next overseas area for development as we considered that our India model and experience was more relevant there than in Eastern Europe or Latin America. As a result of this decision our

East Africa Programme Officer, Pete Kent set up and registered the charity in Tanzania and recruited staff in Nairobi and Mwanza to develop our work in East Africa. There are partner projects in Kenya and Tanzania and in the latter country we are working with the Consortium for Street Children to assist the Tanzanian government develop a 'National Plan for Street Children'.

The work in the UK did not go unnoticed – on the contrary, it was becoming of great significance. We had carried out a joint project with the 'Children's Society' to research the needs of Roma children living in the UK and particularly many who were found begging and hanging around London Undergrounds trains and stations. We were impressed with one of their key experts on child runaways, Andy McCullough, and we appointed him as Railway Children's UK Policy & Strategy Officer to develop our UK work and increase our influence with government on this issue. He quickly helped us develop partnerships with nine NGOs in England and Scotland and formed the Coalition of UK Runaways, a group of 35 UK NGOs, mostly working at grass roots level, in order to get the voices of these organisations on the needs of runaways and children living on UK streets to government. He supported Helen Southworth, MP for Warrington South, to set up a new All Party Parliamentary Group (APPG) on English Runaways and encouraged us to recruit an experienced researcher – Emilie Smeaton of the Children's Society and York University – to undertake an in-depth qualitative research into the lives of 103 'detached' children – children who under the age of 16 had spent more than a month living on Britain's streets. The report 'Off the Radar' detailing their stories with recommendations for government, communities and NGOs was published in November 2009.

Partly as a result of this work and a commendation from the Consortium for Street Children, the insurance giant, Aviva, decided to partner Railway Children in campaigning and providing services for UK runaways and children at risk of taking to the street, developing with us a support to schools who identify children showing signs of vulnerability; delivery of materials and school presentations warning children about the dangers of running away and help they can turn to; and tackling government on the desperate shortage of short term emergency refuge accommodation for the most at risk children – in 2010 Railway

Children funded the remaining five such bed places in the UK in Sheffield and Glasgow.

Looking back over the last fifteen years it is interesting to consider the factors, which have contributed to the growth and success of the charity. Clearly identifying the real need and the lack of focus from other voluntary organisations on early intervention for the increasing number of street children was vital. Having a niche market of donors from a relevant industry – rail – was also crucial, allowing awareness of the charity to build quickly with the support and push from senior managers in the industry several of whom became trustees. 50% of the estimated £20 million raised since the founding of the charity has come from individuals, companies and events within the UK railway industry. Networking with other street children charities through the Consortium for Street Children was important too, as it meant we had experienced personnel to share ideas with and test our concepts, learning fast as we went. I believe too that the managerial experience we were able to bring to bear on the development of the charity was vital. Many charities have developed expertise in fundraising but often fall short of professionalism in other aspects of their activities. We identified our vision and stuck to it, staying focused. We put as much effort into refining our objectives, ensuring what we did was effective, paying attention to the quality and motivation of our staff.

We selected a Chief Executive who shared our vision and supported her as the charity grew rapidly with top management training at Ashridge – expensive but a valuable investment. We used risk assessment techniques to identify our role and normal business practices in setting up the robust procedures, financial and management accounting systems, most of which we'd learned during our apprenticeship for this in the management of British Rail. We were the first UK charity to use the 'Balanced Scorecard' technique for identifying and defining strategic objectives and measures of effectiveness, receiving free advice and support in its implementation by the Harvard originated Palladium consultancy company. We said we were a learning organisation and meant it, prepared to accept that things don't always work but learning from setbacks and the experiences of others. As a result we are trusted by donors such as Comic Relief and are introduced to such corporate partners as Aviva, whom we had to convince of our effectiveness against strong competition from better known and larger organisations.

For the future, I hope to see the charity become supported by railwaymen and women and their companies the world over and all railways safeguarding and caring for the abandoned and destitute children found on their own platforms. Having reached my 70th birthday five years ago, I decided it was time to hand over the reins to another Chair. I therefore retired at the end of 2010 and our trustees selected a successor, Haydn Abbott, former Managing Director of the Angel Trains rolling stock leasing company and sponsor for many years of elements in the annual Railway Ball. But I still take an interest as volunteer, speaker, adviser and Ambassador, as I want to hand on a growing organisation that can make a real positive difference to some of the most vulnerable children in the world. The charity is invited to attend a number of Heritage Railway Gala Days and railway industry events to have stands to raise awareness of the charity and the cause and raise funds.

Very recently we were invited to have a stand at the 2013 Network Rail Plant Exhibition at Long Marston and Tom O'Connor, owner of Rail Media, generously purchased 150 copies of 'The Other Railway Children' book I'd written to describe in greater detail the foundation and development of the charity, and donated these to the companies mounting stands at the exhibition. In the afternoon I was invited to attend a demonstration at the site, which turned out to be a train naming, and when a Network Rail Manager, Steve Featherstone, started speaking to the audience about the 'Railway Children' and called me forward to unveil the nameplate, I expected to uncover the fifth locomotive named after the charity. However, I got a shock when I found the Colas Freight Rail liveried 66850 was named 'David Maidment OBE'. It's a great honour of course and gave me the opportunity to thank the thousands of railway people who had supported Railway Children since its beginning in 1995. However, the best reward will be when thousands, or even hundreds of thousands of children like Babli can say to all of us at the charity, 'Thank you for giving me my childhood back.'

Prime Minister John Major with the author at the launch of the
Consortium for Street Children, 1993

The author at the launch on Waterloo concourse with Dario
Mitidieri's photographic exhibition, 31.5.95

The author with Railtrack Chairman, Bob Horton, at the launch
of Railway Children, 31.5.95

Government Minister Paul Boateng names a West Coast Virgin Train 'Get Connected' with the charity's founder, Diana Lamplugh, Euston station 1997

Sally Thomsett names HST 43098 'Railway Children' at Euston station, May 1998

The first Railway Children Ball reception at the National Railway Museum York, May 1998

The nameplate presented to Railway Children by EWS Chairman, Ed Burkhardt, at the Ball, held by the first volunteers to help the charity – all from local churches in Nantwich, Methodists Les and Betty Williams and John Walkington on the left, Anglicans Coral and Brian Carton and Mike Gear on the right, May 1998

Gordon Pettitt and Chris Jago, Railway Children trustees and leaders of the Ball Committee with the author at the Railway Ball at the Grosvenor House Hotel, November 2001

A fundraising effort in Cornwall, being celebrated at Bodmin's Heritage Railway with actress Jenny Agutter, who has supported Railway children on a number of occasions.

The naming of 90031 at Old Oak Common Open Day, 2000, by Sally Thomsett and Clare Thomas, who took the identical role of 'Phyllis' in the Carlton TV remake of the famous film, 5.8.2000.

Another HST, 43082 of East Midlands Trains, is named 'Railway Children' at the Neville Hill Open Day in 2009 – the author with East Midland Trains Managing Director, Tim Shoveller

Robin Gisby of Network Rail with the Railway Children team ready to embark on the first 'Three Peaks by Rail Challenge', 16.9.2004

The author is presented with a replica nameplate of Colas Freight Rail locomotive 66850 by Steven Featherstone of Network Rail and Steven Haynes, Managing Director of the Colas Rail Services Division, 25.7.2013

Chapter 17
Making sense of it all

I look back now and realise that I'm drawn to view the key events, successes and failures in my life in the same way that I was taught to analyse German poetry and drama back in Professor Wilkinson's flat with my college friend, Gordon, fifty five years ago. For that discipline taught me to recognise patterns and critical events or turning points in the literary epics. It strengthened my ability to see trends and patterns in many things in life, so what do I see now if I put the chapters I've written here under the microscope? My friend, Stan, read through the manuscript which finished at the end of chapter 16 and commented, 'What about the coda? You just seem to stop. It seems to me that so many parts of your story were preparations for the most significant parts of your career – your part in the development of a proactive safety culture for the railway industry and the founding and development of 'Railway Children.'

This set me thinking. Suppose I treat the draft text of this book as one of the works to analyse as I was taught to do so many years ago – what are the key events, the critical points which shaped and prepared my future?

Of course, the first critical decision was to join the railway in the first place, despite the absence of any family connection with the industry. That decision must have found its root in the vivid memory I still have as a six year old on the 26th December 1944 when I travelled with my family back from unofficial evacuation, and I stood with my father on Bristol Temple Meads station watching a pair of locomotives pulling our train into the crowded platform and stared at one of them, 4087 *Cardigan Castle,* long enough for it to leave an indelible mark on my brain. And then a couple of years later, when my father exasperatedly asked a bored boy, 'Why don't you collect engine numbers like other boys?'

My years of schooling built on that foundation in what seems now a logical way, until that afternoon three weeks into my second year at college in October 1958, when Gordon pleaded with me to leave my barren lectures on nineteenth century drama and join him exploring the unknown world of poetry and patterns and the study of language itself and the link between 'form' and 'content'. This was the critical moment when I realised that education was not just about learning facts and vocational skills but was about creativity and imagination and that – in the university environment – this was more highly prized than conventional learning. I remember in gatherings of safety science academics and experts at conferences and seminars in later years, when everyone introduced themselves reeling off their relevant academic and industrial experience, I could stop the show by throwing in the comment that my chief academic qualification was the ability to analyse twelfth century German epic poetry! This led to fascinating conversations and a realisation of just what a different and beneficial sort of education this had been.

I was lucky that my railway management training was as wide and deep as it was. I know that many people thought it too long and subsequently it was considerably curtailed, but I believe it gave the time to understand and reflect and build up the contacts and supports that were so useful later in my career. But the next critical action that is pinpointed in the title of this book was the chance choice of the operating job at Aberbeeg – the outcome of the fateful toss of the coin that was in fact no choice by me, but one that in effect was chosen for me. As I've stated earlier, I'm sure this post shaped my career, for it led me directly down the path of train operations, and although I strayed from that path for a time, I returned to it quite naturally at the key times in my career.

After seven years of a welter of experience in train operations in South Wales, I had a brief two year interlude at the Board Headquarters at Marylebone leading a team in an abortive attempt to retain a profitable parcels business. At the time I felt great disappointment that our efforts were wasted when the Mail Order companies left the business suddenly in the lurch when they opted to control their own transport with road haulage. But so often, I've discovered, you learn most through failure, which causes you to reflect and reassess. Despite the unsatisfactory outcome, the experience taught me new skills, gave me an insight into policy making at a different level and stretched my analytical ability, preparing me not only for my role in Management and Consultancy Services over the following eight years, but equipping me to become a rather different sort of Chief Operating Manager than was traditional.

Eight years in an advisory but influential role as an 'internal railway consultant' broadened not only my knowledge but enabled me to step back and reflect on what was happening instead of being caught up and reacting to the hurly burly of the executive roles of running a railway. I was fortunate in having a strong team of extrovert managers on the London Midland Region which meant that I could take the time to think about some of the issues facing the department during a time of great change and transition, with the organisational changes - the closure of the Divisional level and introduction of business sector management. Two of my key concerns during my four years at the helm of operations on the West Coast and Midland Main Lines were train punctuality and reliability, and safety. Both these themes were to become central to my subsequent career. During 1984 my Region suffered a number of train accidents, worrying me and unearthing evidence of operating as well as engineering failures. At a critical meeting of my Area Managers in 1985, we reflected on these and I began to realise that the railway tradition of relying on the strict discipline of working to prescriptive rules was breaking down in the latter part of the twentieth century. I wrote at the time for one of the conferences I attended a paper contrasting the way children were taught to learn in schools with the rote learning we still seemed to expect railwaymen to master. I was already beginning to think that the railway safety culture had serious weaknesses, a theme that the Clapham accident forced me to address.

And Malcolm Southgate's order to review train punctuality with my engineering peers and my preference for looking at and analysing trends rather than dealing with specific incidents led to the model that later became a punctuality budgeting system, a cost benefit study. I used this type of analysis in my review of East Coast train punctuality when commissioned by John Nelson and John Prideaux and later 'sold' it to the German Federal Railway operating hierarchy. This interest in reliability and punctuality modelling on the WCML led directly, I understand, to David Kirby sending for me and asking me to be BR's first overall 'Reliability Manager'. The rather pointed joke he made – 'As operating manager of the West Coast Main Line, you know more about failure than anyone else', - actually struck home to me the fact that I was learning fast about the causes of failures and errors (with, of course, the purpose of putting things right). This stood me in great stead when I was asked to be part of the investigation and review of BR's safety management systems after the Clapham Junction accident in 1988. Here the encounter with Professor Reason of Manchester University was crucial and he imparted his knowledge of the causes of error to me in a very profound but easily understood way. This and the knowledge of risk management I'd acquired in the Reliability post were crucial in helping me to play a part with David Rayner, Bob Webber of Du Pont and many others in initiating the change in BR's reactive safety management system to one much more geared to proactive prevention, and then in subsequent years sharing that learning with many other railways in the world.

And lastly, after the encounter with the small street child on an Indian railway station, all this experience seemed to equip me to start the Railway Children charity. I'd learned business systems and techniques – Total Quality Management, Risk Assessment – that I applied to identify one of the key issues for street children. There was a gap – early intervention – revealed that other charities had not clearly recognised. I had the contacts within the railway industry to support me and rally round with substantial help. I realised that had I met that street child ten years earlier, it's likely that I would not have reacted the same way, or had the experience to identify the problem properly or get the large amount of support that I was later able to generate from the whole industry.

They always said that BR's management planning in the 1970s was one of the leading examples of good practice in the country. I obviously benefitted from that process, whether by accident or design, I'm still unsure. Anyway, I can't help but feel, as Stan suggested to me, that each step of my career prepared me for the next post or sometimes for activities way into the future. And now I feel the urge to write about it, partly because I just love writing, partly because it's a useful and pleasurable way of raising funds for the Railway Children and partly because many people have told me that some of these events and changes were important and they should not be forgotten. When I wrote my history of the Railway Children charity, it was in response to what Rosemary Day, Vice-Chair of the charity, called my 'brain dump' – something she said I had to do, before the origins of the charity were lost to the corporate memory. Some patterns are complete in themselves but many are ongoing, like on wallpaper, forever repeating or developing. My bit may be nearly complete but others will continue the patterns as railways become even more important in today's environment and the issues of street children become just as important to address as the consequences of doing nothing will build bigger problems for future generations.

Now I have to market and sell what I have written. I was never any good at that. I lost the toss and got the wrong job to develop those skills. But perhaps they were never my gifts anyway…

THE END

Glossary of Railway Terms & Other Acronyms

ACE	Atlantic Coast Express
AEA	Atomic Energy Authority
AGA	Assistant Goods Agent
AGM	Assistant General Manager
ALARP	'As Low As Reasonably Practicable'
APT	Advanced Passenger Train
ASLEF	Associated Society of Locomotive Engineers & Firemen (trade union)
ASM	Assistant Stationmaster
ATP	Automatic Train Protection
AYM	Assistant Yardmaster
BRB	British Railways Board
Brute	British Rail Universal Trolley Equipment (for holding/moving parcels)
BTP	British Transport Police
C&D	Collected & Delivered (Parcels)
CP1	Contingency Plan 1
CPA	Critical Path Analysis
DB	German National Railway - Federal Republic
DHR	Darjeeling Himalayan Railway
ECML	East Coast Main Line
ECS	Empty Coaching Stock
EWS	English Welsh & Scottish Railway (privatised railfreight company)
HST	High Speed Train
ICS	Internal Consultancy Services
IRMS	International Risk Management Services
KCRC	Kowloon Canton Rail Corporation
LDC	Local Departmental Committee (elected local trade union representatives)
LMR	London Midland Region
MRDF	Methodist Relief & Development Fund
MTRC	Mass Transit Rail Corporation (Hong Kong)
NAN	'No to Alcohol & Narcotics' (Russian NGO)

NGO	Non-Government Organisation (charity)
NRM	National Railway Museum (at York)
NS	Dutch Railways
NUR	National Union of Railwaymen (now merged to become the RMT)
O&M	Organisation & Methods
PACTS	Parliamentary Advisory Committee on Transport Safety
Red Star	BR station to station parcels transport service
ROM	Regional Operating Manager
RPF	Railway Protection Force (India)
RSM	Royal Society of Medicine
RSSB	Rail Safety & Standards Board
SE&CR	South Eastern & Chatham Railway
SNCF	French National Railway
SPAD	Signal passed at danger
S&T	Signals & Telecommunications Dept.
TGV	French High Speed Train
TPWS	Train Protection Warning System
TQM	Total Quality Management
TSSA	Transport & Salaried Staff Association (trade union)
TZ	Tranzrail, New Zealand
UEA	University of East Anglia
UIC	Union Internationale de Chemins de Fer (International Union of Railways)
VT	Victoria Terminus Bombay (now Mumbai CST – Chhatrapati Shivaji Terminus)
WCML	West Coast Main Line
WR	Western Region of British Railways

Locomotive Classes & Rolling Stock

Steam Locomotives

Castle   Western Region 4 cylinder 4-6-0, built from 1923

'City of Truro'   Western Region preserved inside cylinder 4-4-0 credited with the first 100mph reached in the UK (in 1904)

D   Southern Region inside cylinder SE & CR 4-4-0, built 1901

D15   Southern Region 4-4-0, designed by Drummond, built 1912

Hall   Western Region 2 cylinder 4-6-0 for mixed traffic duties, built 1929

'Ironside'   Southern Region 0-4-0 Saddle Tank, built 1890 by Hawthorn Leslie

King   Western Region 4 cylinder larger 4-6-0, built 1927

King Arthur   Southern Region 2 cylinder 4-6-0, built 1925

L11   Southern Region Drummond 2 cylinder 4-4-0, built 1903

Lord Nelson   Southern Region 4 cylinder 4-6-0, built 1926

Merchant Navy   Southern Region Pacific 4-6-2, built 1941, rebuilt 1956

'Paddlebox'   Southern Region class T14, rebuild of Drummond 4 cylinder 4-6-0, built 1911 and modified by Maunsell in 1930

Pannier Tank   Western Region 0-6-0 tank locomotive designed for shunting and local freight trips, built over the period from 1929 to nationalisation

Schools   Southern Region class 'V' 3 cylinder 4-4-0, built 1930

West Country   Smaller version of Merchant Navy pacific, built 1946

Diesel Engines
- **08** Diesel Shunting loco
- **14** Paxman engined 0-6-0 diesel for trip working, built 1963
- **35** Hymek Beyer Peacock 1,700 hp diesel hydraulic locos built 1962
- **37** English Electric 1,750 hp diesel electric, standard loco for Welsh Valley coal traffic from 1963
- **42** WR 2,200 hp diesel hydraulic 'Warship' class, built 1958, based on German V200
- **43** High Speed Train Power unit, built from 1975
- **47** Brush type 4 2,750 ho diesel electric, built from 1962
- **52** 'Western' diesel hydraulic 2,700 hp locos, built 1961
- **66** General Motors 3,300 hp diesel electric locomotive, received in bulk by EWS in 1998
- **DMU** Diesel Multiple Unit

Electric Engines
- **81-85** Electric locos built for West Coast Mainline electrification, 1959
- **86** Electric locos for WCML, built 1965 and subdivided to 86/0 – 86/6
- **87** Electric locos built for WCML Crewe – Glasgow extension, 1974
- **90** Electric locos built for WCML, 1986
- **EMU** Electric Multiple Unit

Rolling Stock
- **Mark 1** BR standard passenger coaches built throughout 1950s.

Index

Abbott, Haydn, page 241
Aberbeeg Stationmaster, pages 65-87, 252
    Acting Shedmaster, pages 74-75
    Dieselisation, pages 69, 75-76
    Earth Slip at Cwm (Ebbw Vale branch), pages 74, 83
    Hanbury Hotel, pages 65, 68, 77
    Llanhilleth track rationalisation, pages 70-71, 79-80
A D Little, pages 197, 217
Agutter, Jenny, pages 236, 247
Allen, Cecil J, page 4
Amnesty International UK's Children's Rights Network, pages 226, 234
Aston University, pages 190, 193-194
'Babli', SEED, Calcutta, pages 231-232
Baggott, Martin, page 206
Balakesari, K, page 234
Ball, Dr David, pages 186, 218
Barnes, Albert, page 123
Bassett, Phil, pages 136-137
Bath, Alec, page 148
Baynton-Hughes T.C. pages 51, 111
Beard, Gordon, pages 120, 129
Bleasdale, Cyril, pages 134, 138, 152, 165, 181, 213, 223
Bowles, George, pages 31, 43
Breakwell, Bob, page 149
Brennan, Jack, pages 45-46, 51, 70-71
Bridgend Area Manager, pages 88-105
    Chapel preacher, page 98
    Collision at Bridgend station, pages 91-92
    Learning to drive, pages 89-90
    Southerndown, pages 93-94, 103
    Train runaways, pages 95-96, 104-105
Brown, Bob, pages 151-152
Burrage, Ken, pages 135, 151-152
Butt, John, pages 138, 157

Campbell, Christopher, page 228
Cardiff Divisional Office, pages 49-52, 107-114
    Divisional Terminals Supt, pages 107-108
    South Wales Freight Strategy Scheme, pages 110-113
    Train Planning & Control, pages 108-110
Casley, Bill, page 208
Catmur, James, page 217
Charterhouse Railway Society, pages 5-6
Churchill, David, page 209
Claesson, Professor Åke, page 165
Clapham Junction train accident 1988, pages 176-182
    Clapham Fault Tree, pages 176-177
    Du Pont Safety Management review & recommendations, pages 179-182
    Judicial Inquiry, pages 178-179
    Personal safety incidents, pages 177-178
    Rules culture, page 176
    Safety Managements Systems – traditional BR comparison with high tech industries, page 176
Colas Rail Locomotive 66850 'David Maidment OBE', pages 241, 250
Consortium for Street Children, pages 225-226, 230
Corcoran, Ted, page 215
Corfield, Charlie, page 71
Craig, Hylton, page 125
Craik, John, page 124
Crewe Remodelling, pages 148-150
Crowe, John, pages 45, 49
Day, Rosemary, page 254
Dobbs, Ian, page 208
Dunwoody, Gwyneth MP, pages 149, 238
Dutia, Gopal, page 234
Eccles, Graham, page 187
Elms, Professor David, page 209
Englert, Alan, pages 118-119, 123
Evans, Professor Andrew, page 195

Featherstone, Steve, pages 241, 250
Fenton, Nic, page 228
Ferrand, Michael, pages 125, 128
Fielden, Gordon, pages 8, 251
Fiennes, Gerard, pages 61-62, 97
Forrester, Stafford Road Fireman, pages 23, 29
Fortt, Richard, pages 119, 124
Gerstenberg, Dr., page 7
Gibbs, William (Billy), pages 19-20
Gillingham (Dorset) Stationmaster, pages 58-64
Gisby, Robin, pages 235-250
Goldstone, Geoff, pages 119, 124
Grand, Keith, page 24
Greaves, Tom, page 122
Green, Chris, page 120
Griffiths, Bert (Stafford Road Driver), pages 23, 29
Henderson, Roger QC, pages 176, 178
Herter, John, page 167
Hidden, Anthony QC, page 184
Hill, William, page 187
Hilton, Bob, pages 51-52, 65-67, 107-108
Hodge, John, pages 51, 111
Holmes, Maurice, pages 161, 182, 185, 190
Hope, Bert, page 217
Horton, Bob, pages 228, 243
HSBC Rail, page 235
Hyland, David, pages 208, 221
Ibbotson, Lance, pages 43, 47, 50-51, 97-98
Internal Consultancy Services BRB, pages 123-128
    Challenge of the Eighties Productivity Deal, pages 126-128
Discretionary Cost Analysis, page 128
International Railway Safety Consultancy, pages 206-223
    Canada, Ottawa & Montreal 1994, page 209
    DNV, Societal Risk Project, Network Rail, 2002, pages 219-220

    Institute of Transport & Logistics, Environmental Risk Management, Pakistan 1996, pages 213, 223
    IRMS KCRC Hong Kong 1996. page 214
    IRMS Irish Government, 1996, pages 214-215
    IRMS Network Rail Due Diligence Check, pages 215-216
    Mexican Railways, Mexico City 1996, pages 212-213
    MTRC (Hong Kong) Safety Review 2000, pages 217-218
    Network Rail Internal Inquiry Panel Chairman, page 216
    Railtrack Review of Train Regulation Policy (Southall accident), pages 216-217
    Spoornet, South Africa, 1992, pages 207-208, 220
    Sydney City Rail, Canberra & Melbourne 1992, pages 208-209
    Tranzrail, New Zealand (Expert Witness Court Case) 1995/6, pages 209-212, 221
    Westrail TQM project, Australia 1989, page 207

Jago, Chris, page 246
Jenkins, Hugh, page 129
Jones, Islwyn, pages 65-67
Judd, Stanley, pages 55-56, 65-76, 87, 120, 200, 229, 231-232, 252
Keen, Ben, page 212
Keene, Terina, pages 234, 250
Kent, Pete, pages 238-239, 250
Kielty, Patrick, page 236
Kirby, David, pages 152, 162
Lamplugh, Diana, pages 229, 244
Latham, Bill, pages 102, 115
Llewellyn, William, page 6
Lloyd, Leslie, pages 111, 122, 128
London Division Passenger Train Office, pages 24-25
London Division Freight Train Office, page 25
Major, John, pages 226, 242

Management Services, Western Region, pages 119-123
Manning, Sidney, pages 119, 124
Marshall, Julian, pages 199, 218
Mason, Katie, pages 231, 250
McCullough, Andy, page 239
McKeever, David, page 143
Meadows, Rodney, pages 17-18
Middle Management Course, Derby, pages 93, 102
Millard, Charles, page 129
Mitchell, John, pages 209, 211-212
Mitidieri, Dario, pages 228, 242
MRDF India project, Nainital, pages 233-234
Myers, Geoff, pages 124, 227
Nelson, Aidan, & Sue (nee McKinstry), pages 196, 215
O'Brien, Jim, pages 119, 122, 124, 130
O'Connor, Tom, Rail Media, page 241
Old Oak Common, pages 17-23, 26-28, 33-43
Orbell, Gerry, pages 110-111
Oxford commuting, page 33
Parcels Planning Assistant, BRB, pages 115-118, 252
Parker, Sir Peter, page 126
Parrott, Joe, page 21
Parsons, Terry, page 69
Paterson, Frank, page 128
Pettitt, Gordon, pages 178, 218, 229, 246
Power, Douglas, pages 144, 150-151
Princess Royal, Chair of Inst of Transport & Logistics, page 213
Price, George, page 22
Railway Children, pages 200-201, 224-250, 254
    ASIS, Railway Children's first project in Bucharest, pages 228-229
    Aviva partnership, pages 239-240
    Comic Relief grants, page 236
    Encounter with small girl beggar, Bombay Churchgate, pages 224-225

    Fire at Tollygunge, Calcutta, pages 232-233
    Fundraising for the first projects, 1996-8, page 230
    Get Connected UK project, pages 229-230, 244
    Growth of work in India, page 237
    Independent on Sunday Christmas Appeal 2004, page 236
    Indian Railways & Railway Protection Force, page 234
    Juconi, Puebla, Mexico, pages 212-213
    Launch of Railway Children, pages 226, 242-243
    Lottery grant for India, page 231
    Network Rail Plant Exhibition at Long Marston, Railway Children books and locomotive naming, pages 241, 250
    Pilot projects in East Africa, pages 238-239
    'Off the Radar' research on UK runaway children, pages 239-240
    Old Oak Common Open Day & naming 90031, pages 235, 248
    Railway Ball, pages 230, 244-246
    Railway Children Trustees 1996, page 229
    Reasons for success, pages 240-241
    Russian projects, pages 235-236
    Salvation Army Officers on London stations, page 226
    Save the Children sponsorship, Bombay, page 224
    SEED, Calcutta, pages 231-232
    UK projects, page 239
    UNESCO/Indian Railways Conference at Ghum on the DHR, 2002, pages 236-237

Rao, Mrinalini, page 235

Rao, Mohan, page 235

Rayner, David, pages 166, 175-176, 178-179, 184, 190-192, 197, 200, 202, 228-229, 254

Reason, Professor James, pages 146, 189, 254

Rees, Philip, pages 122-123, 142

Reid, Sir Robert, pages 128, 178, 180

Regional Operating Manager, Crewe, pages 130-161, 253

    APT test runs, pages 134-135, 154
    Bedford – St Pancras electrification, pages 136, 155
    CEGB Nuclear Flask Test, pages 135-136, 154-155
    Conversion of 86/0, 86/3 to 86/4, pages 133-134
    Crewe remodelling, pages 148-150
    Dorridge accident, pages 145-147
    Eccles accident, pages 147-148
    Great Cockcrow Miniature Railway, page 138
    Linslade Tunnel train accident, pages 132-133, 153
    Operating Conference, BRB, pages 148-149, 161
    Punctuality modelling, WCML, pages 150-152
    Reorganisations, pages 142-145
    Royal Train Officer, pages 138-142, 158-160
    Safety concerns, pages 145-148
    Steam Specials safety audit, pages 136-138, 156-157
    Track speed tests, page 133
    Wembley accident, page 147
Reliability Management, pages 161-174, 253
    25th World Congress of Railways, pages 168, 174
    BS 5750/IS 9000, pages 167, 178-179
    French & German Railway reliability policies, pages 162-164, 169-170
    German Railways Operating Conference, Bamberg, pages 165-166
    Leadership 500, pages 167-168
    Methodist 250th Anniversary special trains and 'BBC songs of Praise', pages 164-165, 171-173
    Punctuality Modelling and Budgeting, pages 165-166, 253
    Review of East Coast Main Line Punctuality, page 165
    Swedish Railways Quality Conference, Malmö, 1986, page 165
    Total Quality Management policy & pilot schemes, pages 166-167, 253-254
Retirement from BR, page 212
Rix, Mick, page 235

Robinson, John, Bishop of Woolwich, page 227
Roche, Tony, page 228
Rose, Cliff, pages 92, 110, 126
Ross, Les, pages 131, 153
Ryan, Ray, pages 209-212, 221
Safety Management, pages 183-205, 253-254
    ALARP principle, pages 187, 189-190
    ATP Cost Benefit Study, pages 185, 188
    Comprehensive BR risk assessment, pages 184-185
    Cooper Lybrand Project, pages 184-185
    Du Pont 'STOP' safety inspections, pages 181, 183-184
    Exchange of safety experience and research with British industries, pages 194-195
    Exchange of safety experience and research with European railways, pages 193-194
    Fennell Inquiry, pages 184-185
    Human Factors & Errors, pages 189, 194
    Intolerable risk – staff safety, pages 187-188
    PACTS meetings and research, pages 194-195
    Passenger falls from trains, pages 189-190
    Privatisation, pages 199-200
    Risk modelling, pages 197-198
    Safety Cases, pages 199-200, 207-208
    Safety Cost Benefit Analysis, pages 184-187
    Safety Management Training, page 191
    Safety Performance achievements, 1989–1994, page 198
    Safety Policy Unit, pages 190-191, 199
    Safety Validation, pages 195, 199-200
    Suicides, pages 196-197
    Trade Union consultations about safety management, page 183
    Value of life, pages 184-187
Safety Management Conferences, pages 191-194
    Bad Homburg Safety Science Academic conferences, pages 193-194, 203
    Cologne 1990 & Budapest 1993, pages 192-193

Hong Kong 1994, pages 193-194
Tokyo 1990, pages 191-192, 202-203
UIC seminars on rail safety, pages 193-194
Sargeant, Charlie, pages 69-70, 74
Sedgwick, David, page 217
Sedgwick Wharf, page 199
Select Service Partners, page 236
Shepherd, Jack, pages 66-70
Shillito, David, page 176
Shingleton, Ken, pages 97-98, 120
Siebert, Mike, pages 190, 199
Sims, Ray, pages 21-22, 34
Shoveller, Tim, page 249
Smeaton, Emilie, page 239
Smith, Andrew, pages 201, 218
Soane, Leslie, page 127
Southgate, Malcolm, pages 138, 150-152, 253
Stokes, Richard, pages 138, 143
Taig, Tony, page 184
Taylor, Roger, page 198
Thatcher, Margaret, page 195
Thomas, Old Oak Common Fireman, page 42
Thomsett, Sally, pages 230, 244, 248
Tidy, George, page 124
Tozer, Sarah, page 199
Traffic Apprenticeship Scheme, pages 17, 31-63
    Cardiff Divisional Office, pages 49-54
    Control Graphs project, pages 49-51, 54
    Cumberland Lodge, page 55
    Fishguard Harbour, pages 51-52
    Footplate training, Old Oak Common, pages 33-43
    High Speed Track Test, Paddington – Wolverhampton, pages 39-40
    Maidenhead Station, pages 31-32
    Pontardawe Stationmaster, pages 48-49
    Slough Goods, page 32

South Lambeth Goods, pages 32-33
　　　Supernumery Posts, pages 57-64
　　　　　ASM Plymouth North Road, page 57
　　　　　AYM, Taunton, page 57
　　　　　AGA, Exeter St David's, page 58
　　　　　Stationmaster Gillingham (Dorset), pages 58-64
　　　Swansea District Office, pages 45-49
　　　Western Region HQ, Paddington, pages 55-57
　　　Work Study Training, London & Laira, page 49
TSSA, page 31
Underhill, Charles, page 121
University College London (German Language &
　　Literature Course), pages 7-9
Urquhart, James, pages 123, 128
Visser, Kurt, page 193
Walmsley, Fred, page 130
Ward, Old Oak Common Driver, page 42
Warr, Eric, pages 88, 90-91, 95
Webber, Bob, pages 179-182, 254
Weighall, Sidney, page 126
Welsby, John, pages 168, 174
Wickens, Dr Alan, page 150
Wilkins, Edith, pages 231-233, 237
Wilkinson, Prof. Elizabeth, pages 8, 251
Woking Staff College, pages 119-122, 129
　　Swiss Railways visit, pages 120-122
Wolmar, Christian, pages 228-229
Wood, Alistair, page 137
Woodruff, Grant, page 46
Worthington, Julia, page 231
Young, Brian, page 89
Zykov, Oleg, page 236

Other books by David Maidment:

For a fuller account of the founding and development of the Railway Children charity, David published 'The Other Railway Children' in 2012, paperback available direct from the author (£8 incl p&p) or from Amazon in paperback or Kindle format.

'**The Child Madonna**', a religious historical novel of the childhood of the Virgin Mary seen through the eyes of a children's rights specialist, researching the likely fate of a young woman having a child out of wedlock in 1st century Judea, published 2009 Melrose Books hardback, paperback & Kindle PublishNation 2012, hardback available direct from the author , (£10 incl p&p) or from Amazon in paperback or Kindle format.

'**The Missing Madonna**', second of a Madonna trilogy, covering the Herodian 'Massacre of the Innocents' and the Holy Family's flight to Egypt as near destitute refugees, published paperback and Kindle PublishNation 2012, paperback available direct from the author (£10 incl p&p) or from Amazon in paperback or Kindle format

'**Lives on the Line**' a novel of drama and conflict set in the authentic backcloth of Old Oak Common locomotive depot in the early 1960s as steam changes to diesel traction, published paperback Max Books, 2013, available direct from the author (£10 incl p&p).

'**Nobody ever listened to me**', a book of essays, case histories and quotations from street children collated by the author from material offered by member organisations of the Consortium for Street Children, published paperback and Kindle, PublishNation, 2012, paperback available direct from the author £7 incl p&p)

Further details about these books can be found on the author's website.

All profits and royalties from these books will be donated to Railway Children.

David Maidment
32 The Broadway, Nantwich, Cheshire CW5 6JH
Maidmentrail@aol.com
www.davidmaidment.com
www.railwaychildren.org.uk

The Other Railway Children

David Maidment

The Child Madonna

David Maidment

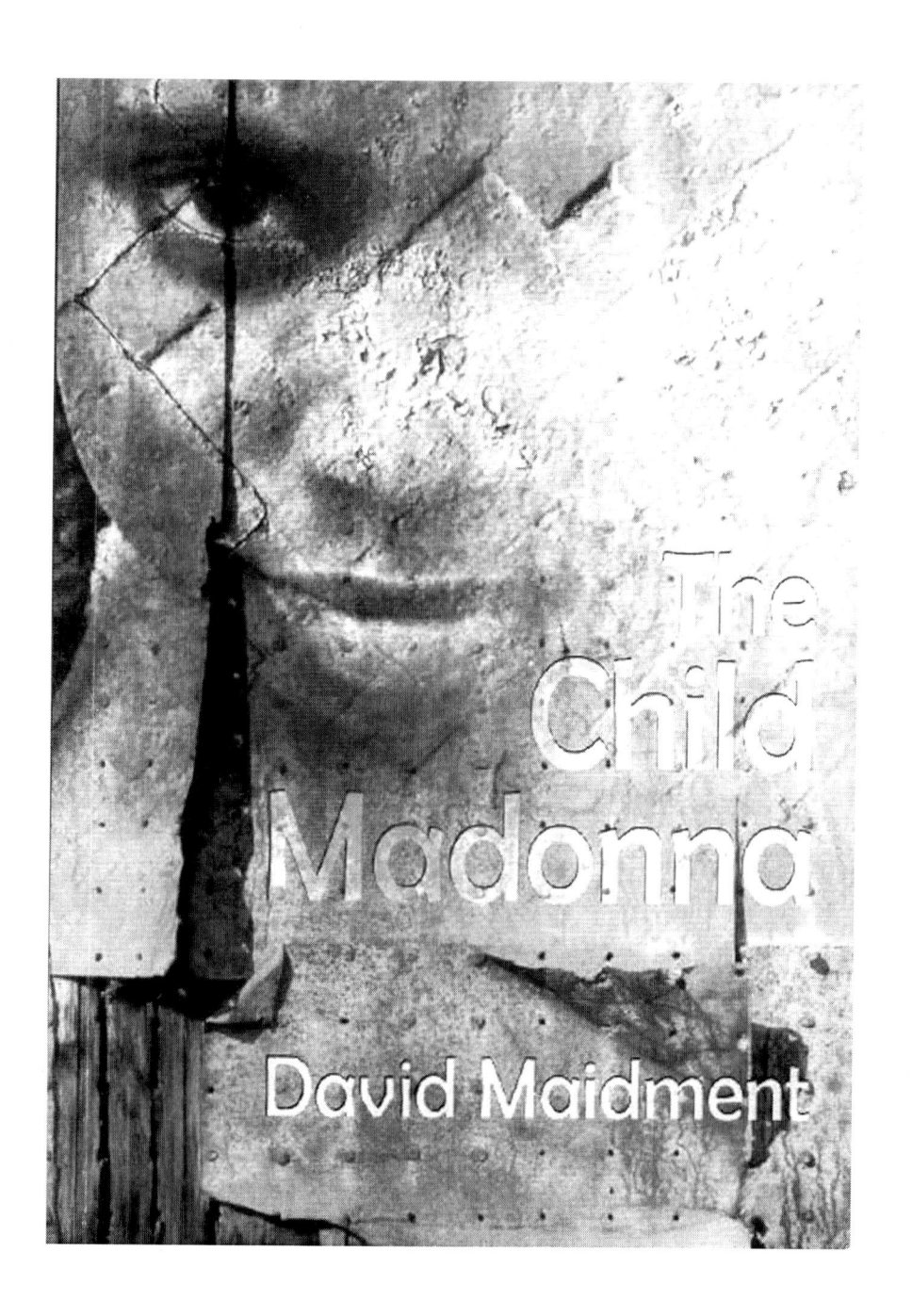

The Missing Madonna

by David Maidment

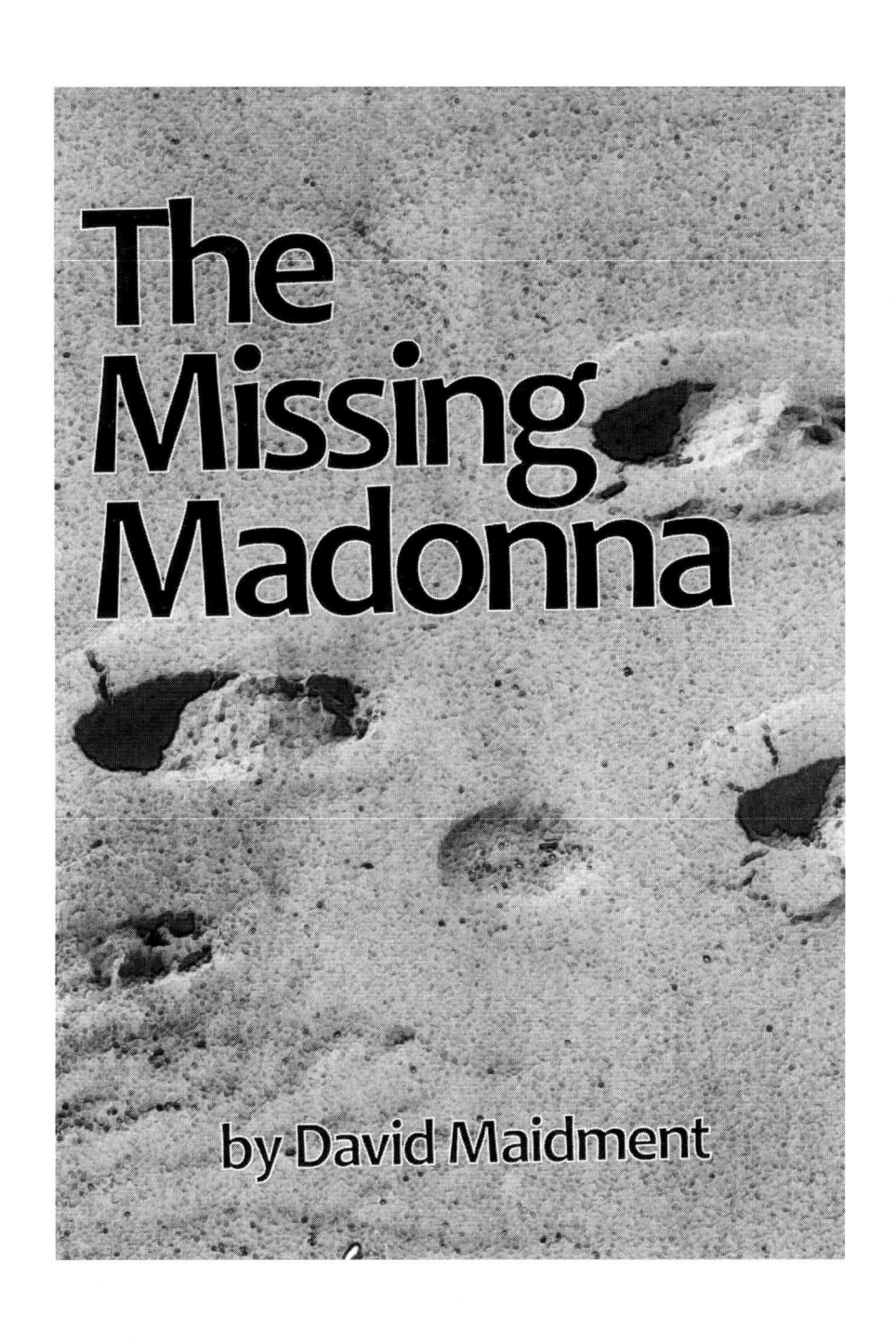

LIVES ON THE LINE
by David Maidment

A novel of drama and conflict set in a large steam locomotive depot in the 1960's

NOBODY EVER LISTENED TO ME

by

David Maidment